WHEN FORMER U.S. AUGHT IN THE EXPLOSION OF AN ALIEN DEVICE, SHE WAS TRANSFORMED INTO ONE OF THE WORLD'S MOST POWERFUL SUPER-BEINGS. NOW, SHE'S AN **AVENGER** AND EARTH'S MIGHTIEST HERO.

BUT BEFORE ALL THAT, CAROL DANVERS WAS JUST A GIRL FROM NEW ENGLAND.
THIS IS HER STORY.

THE LIFE OF CAPTAIN MARVEL

WRITER **MARGARET STOHL**
PENCILER (PRESENT DAY) **CARLOS PACHECO**
INKER (PRESENT DAY) **RAFAEL FONTERIZ**
COLORIST (PRESENT DAY) **MARCIO MENYZ** WITH **FEDERICO BLEE** (#5)
ARTIST (FLASHBACKS, #1-3 & #5) **MARGUERITE SAUVAGE**
ARTISTS (FLASHBACKS, #4) **ERICA D'URSO** & **MARCIO MENYZ**
LETTERER **VC'S CLAYTON COWLES**
KREE "KLEANER" DESIGN **JOSHUA JAMES SHAW**

COVER ART **JULIAN TOTINO TEDESCO**

EDITOR **SARAH BRUNSTAD**
CONSULTING EDITOR **SANA AMANAT**
EXECUTIVE EDITOR **TOM BREVOORT**

SPECIAL THANKS TO **AXEL ALONSO** & **STEPHEN WACKER**

THE LIFE OF CAPTAIN MARVEL. Contains material originally published in magazine form as THE LIFE OF CAPTAIN MARVEL #1-5. First printing 2018. ISBN 978-1-302-91253-6. Published by MARVEL WORLDWIDE, INC., a subsidiary of MARVEL ENTERTAINMENT, LLC. OFFICE OF PUBLICATION: 135 West 50th Street, New York, NY 10020. **Printed in Canada.** DAN BUCKLEY, President, Marvel Entertainment; JOHN NEE, Publisher; JOE QUESADA, Chief Creative Officer; TOM BREVOORT, SVP of Publishing; DAVID BOGART, SVP of Business Affairs & Operations, Publishing & Partnership; DAVID GABRIEL, SVP of Sales & Marketing, Publishing; JEFF YOUNGQUIST, VP of Production & Special Projects; DAN CARR, Executive Director of Publishing Technology; ALEX MORALES, Director of Publishing Operations; DAN EDINGTON, Managing Editor; SUSAN CRESPI, Production Manager; STAN LEE, Chairman Emeritus. For information regarding advertising in Marvel Comics or on Marvel.com, please contact Vit DeBellis, Custom Solutions & Integrated Advertising Manager, at vdebellis@marvel.com. For Marvel subscription inquiries, please call 888-511-5480. **Manufactured between 11/23/2018 and 12/17/2018 by SOLISCO PRINTERS, SCOTT, QC, CANADA.**

10 9 8 7 6 5 4 3 2 1

PART 1: TRAPPED

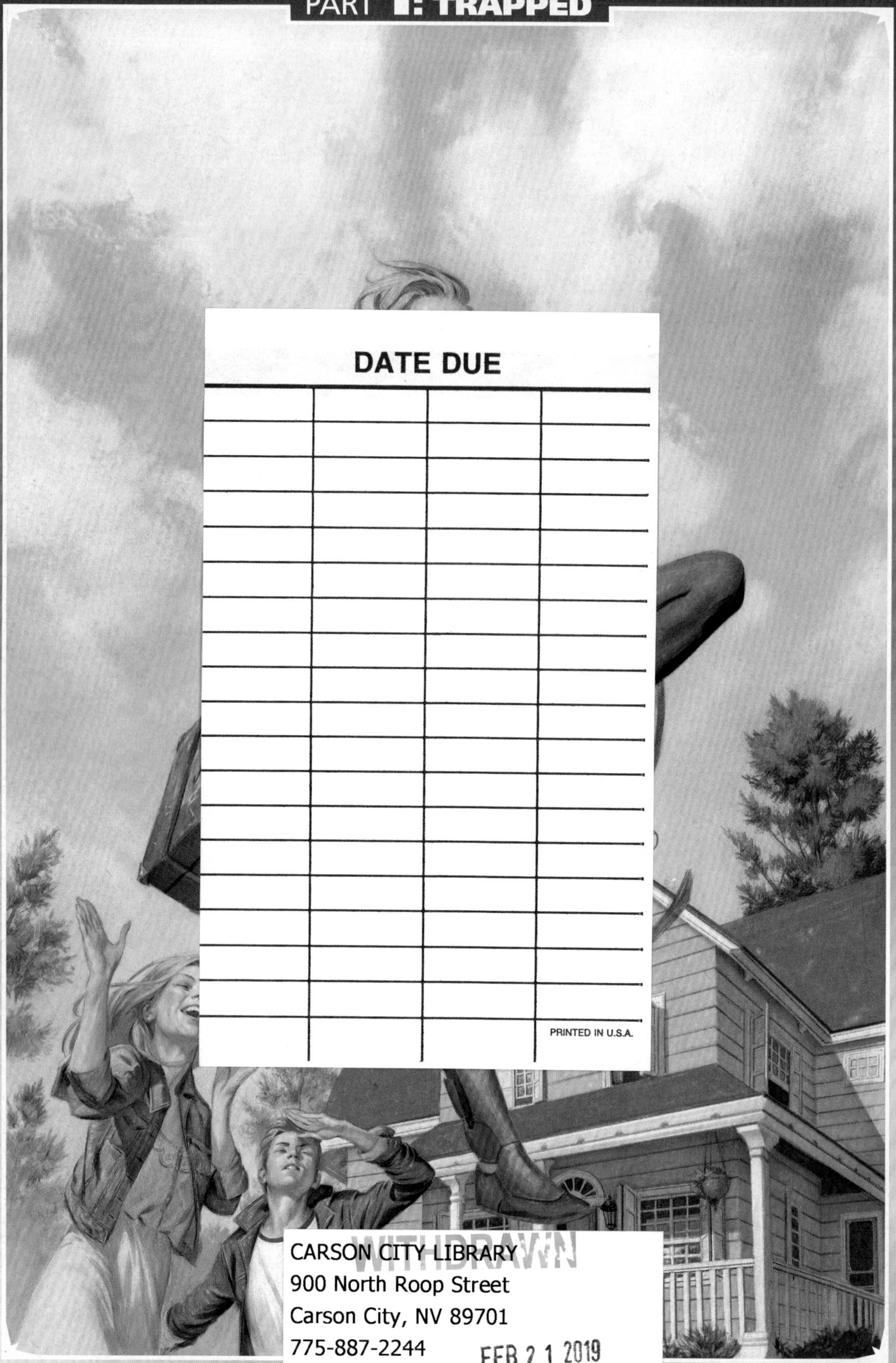

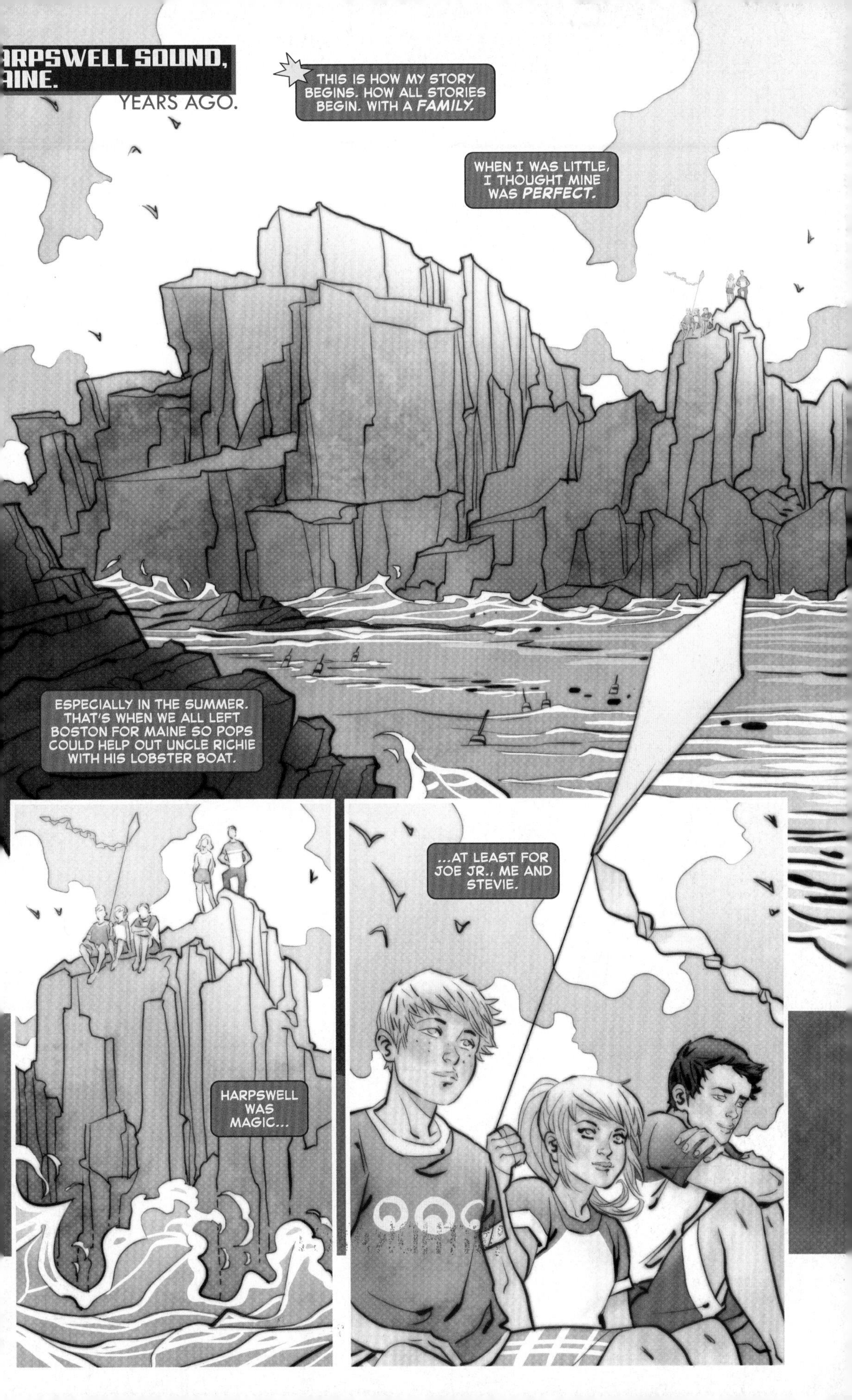

ARPSWELL SOUND,
AINE.
YEARS AGO.
THIS IS HOW MY STORY BEGINS. HOW ALL STORIES BEGIN. WITH A FAMILY.
WHEN I WAS LITTLE, I THOUGHT MINE WAS PERFECT.
ESPECIALLY IN THE SUMMER. THAT'S WHEN WE ALL LEFT BOSTON FOR MAINE SO POPS COULD HELP OUT UNCLE RICHIE WITH HIS LOBSTER BOAT.
HARPSWELL WAS MAGIC...
...AT LEAST FOR JOE JR., ME AND STEVIE.

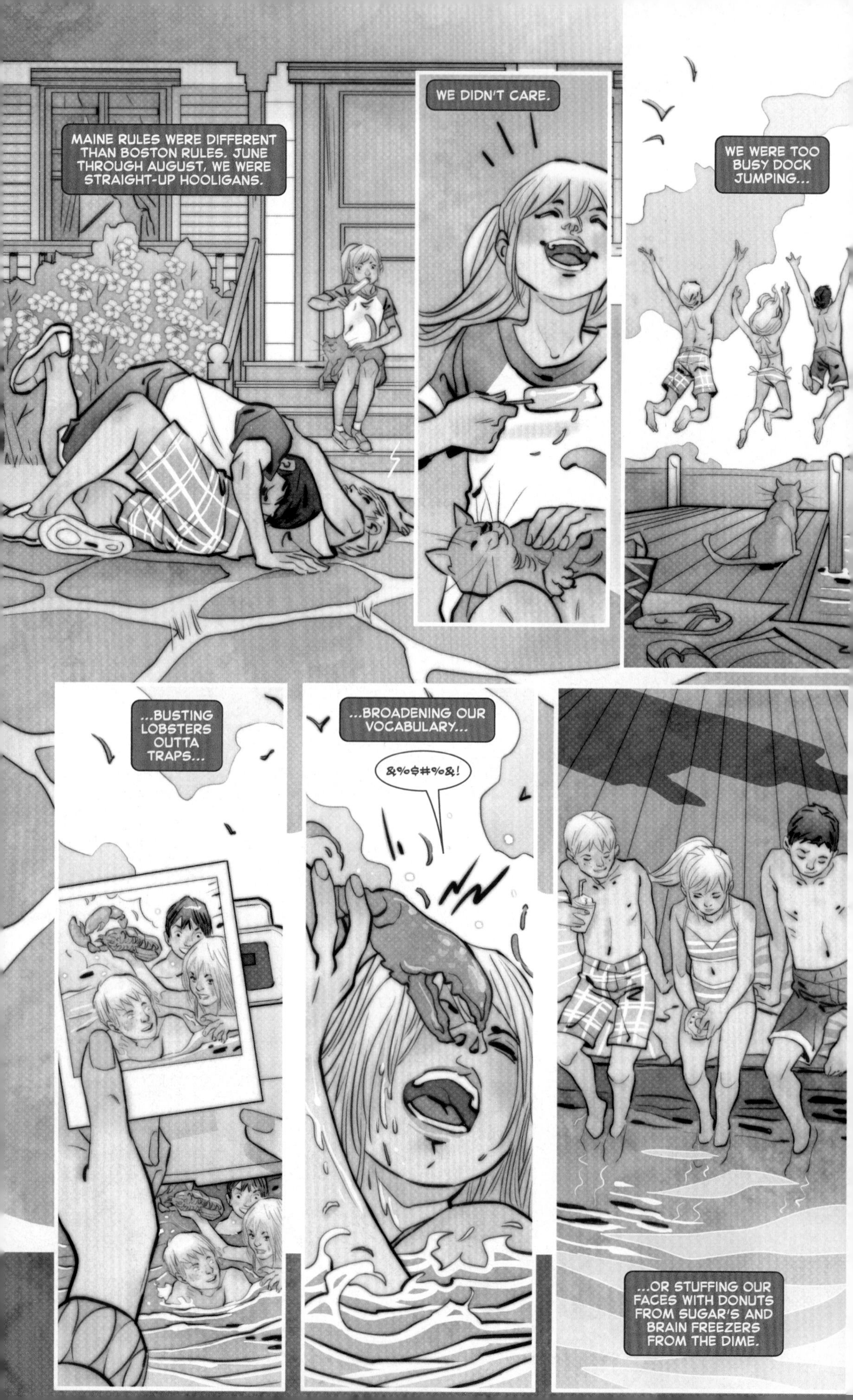
MAINE RULES WERE DIFFERENT THAN BOSTON RULES. JUNE THROUGH AUGUST, WE WERE STRAIGHT-UP HOOLIGANS.
WE DIDN'T CARE.
WE WERE TOO BUSY DOCK JUMPING...
...BUSTING LOBSTERS OUTTA TRAPS...
...BROADENING OUR VOCABULARY...
&%$#%&!
...OR STUFFING OUR FACES WITH DONUTS FROM SUGAR'S AND BRAIN FREEZERS FROM THE DIME.

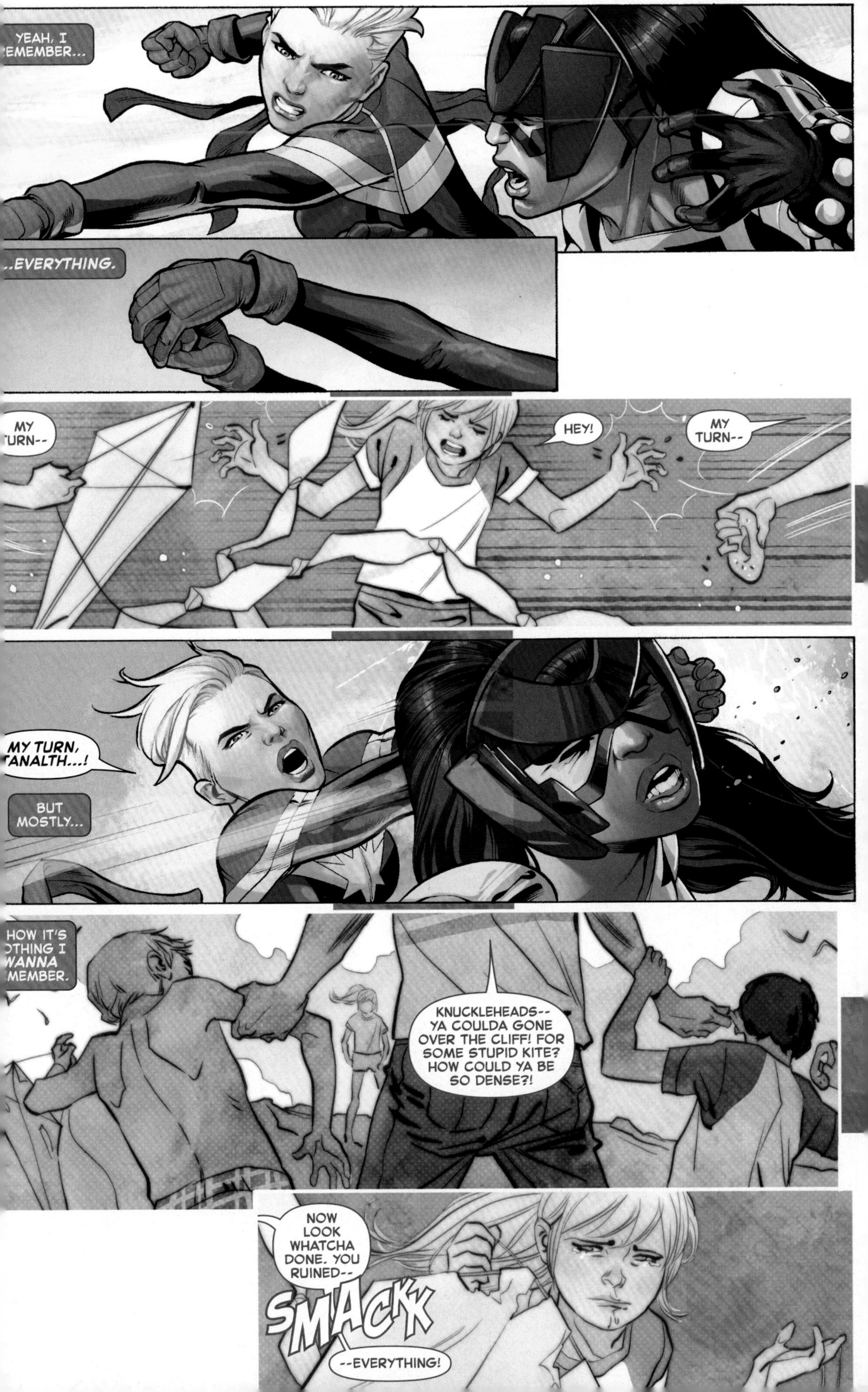
YEAH, I
EMEMBER...
..EVERYTHING.
MY
TURN--
HEY!
MY
TURN--
MY TURN,
TANALTH...!
BUT
MOSTLY...
HOW IT'S
OTHING I
WANNA
EMEMBER.
KNUCKLEHEADS--
YA COULDA GONE
OVER THE CLIFF! FOR
SOME STUPID KITE?
HOW COULD YA BE
SO DENSE?!
NOW
LOOK
WHATCHA
DONE. YOU
RUINED--
SMACK
--EVERYTHING!

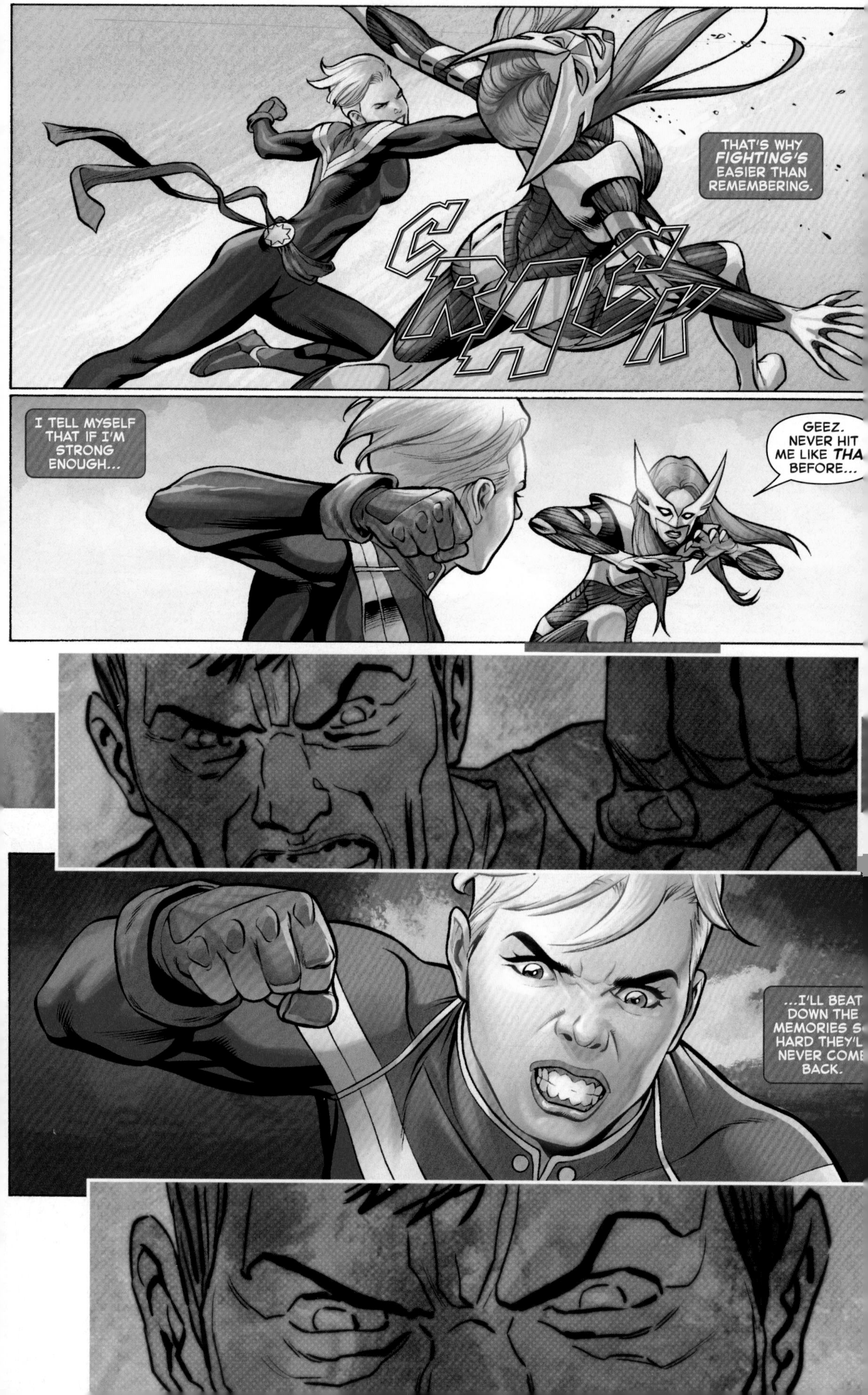

THAT'S WHY FIGHTING'S EASIER THAN REMEMBERING.
CRACK
I TELL MYSELF THAT IF I'M STRONG ENOUGH...
GEEZ. NEVER HIT ME LIKE THA BEFORE...
...I'LL BEAT DOWN THE MEMORIES S HARD THEY'L NEVER COME BACK.

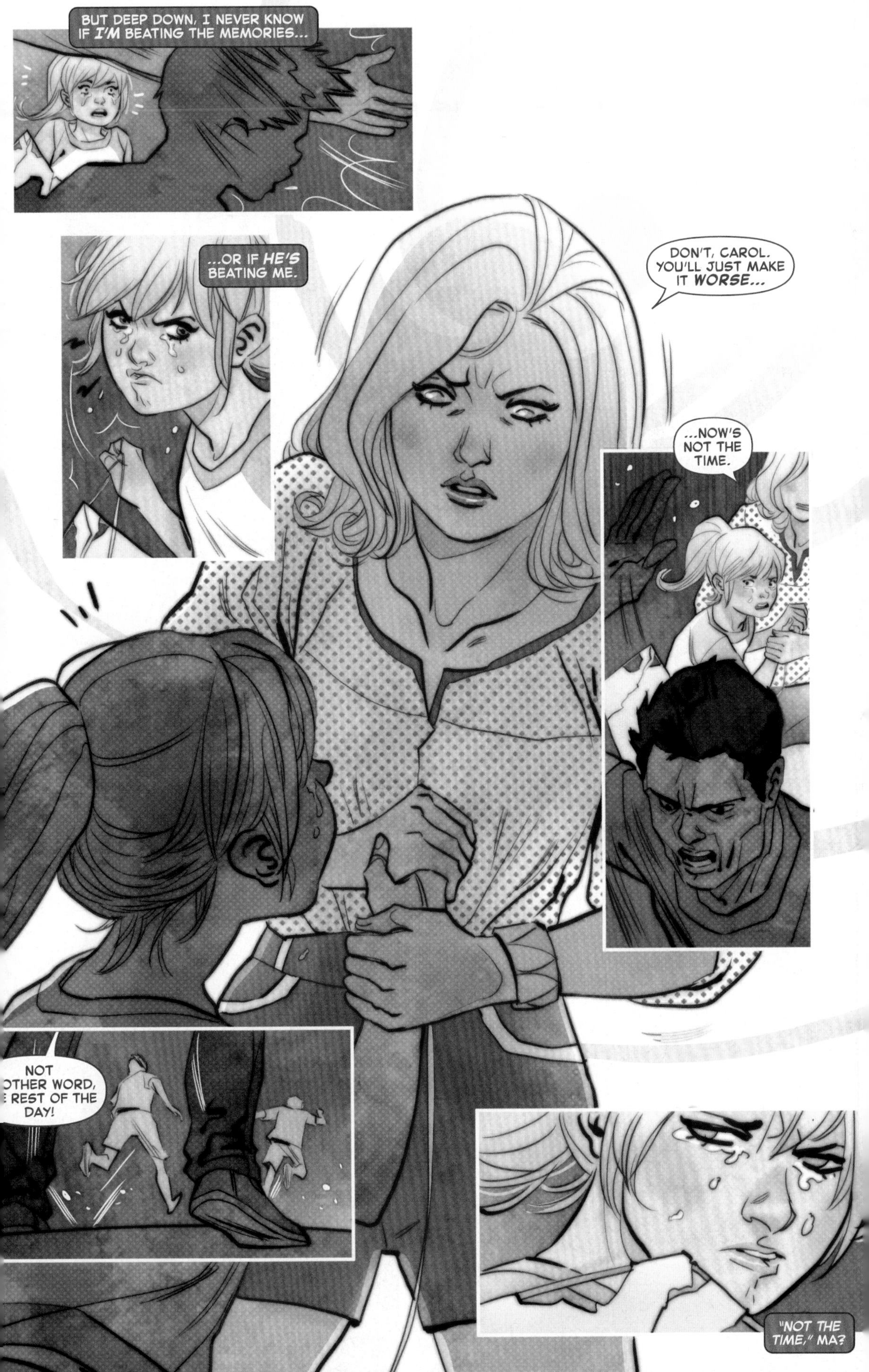
BUT DEEP DOWN, I NEVER KNOW IF I'M BEATING THE MEMORIES...
...OR IF HE'S BEATING ME.
DON'T, CAROL. YOU'LL JUST MAKE IT WORSE...
...NOW'S NOT THE TIME.
NOT OTHER WORD, E REST OF THE DAY!
"NOT THE TIME," MA?

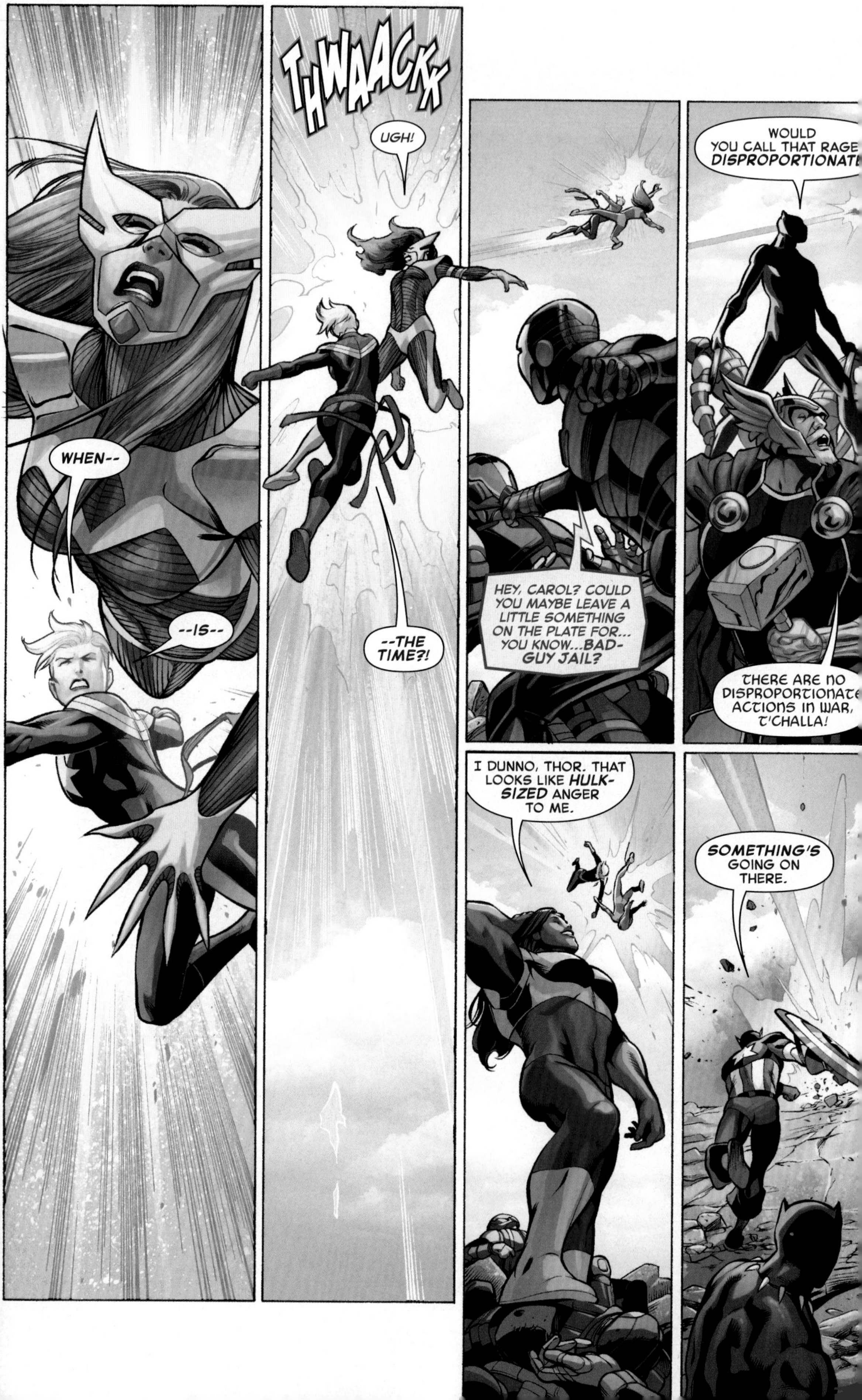
WHEN--
--IS--
THWAACKK
UGH!
--THE TIME?!
HEY, CAROL? COULD YOU MAYBE LEAVE A LITTLE SOMETHING ON THE PLATE FOR... YOU KNOW...BAD-GUY JAIL?
WOULD YOU CALL THAT RAGE DISPROPORTIONATE
THERE ARE NO DISPROPORTIONATE ACTIONS IN WAR, T'CHALLA!
I DUNNO, THOR. THAT LOOKS LIKE HULK-SIZED ANGER TO ME.
SOMETHING'S GOING ON THERE.

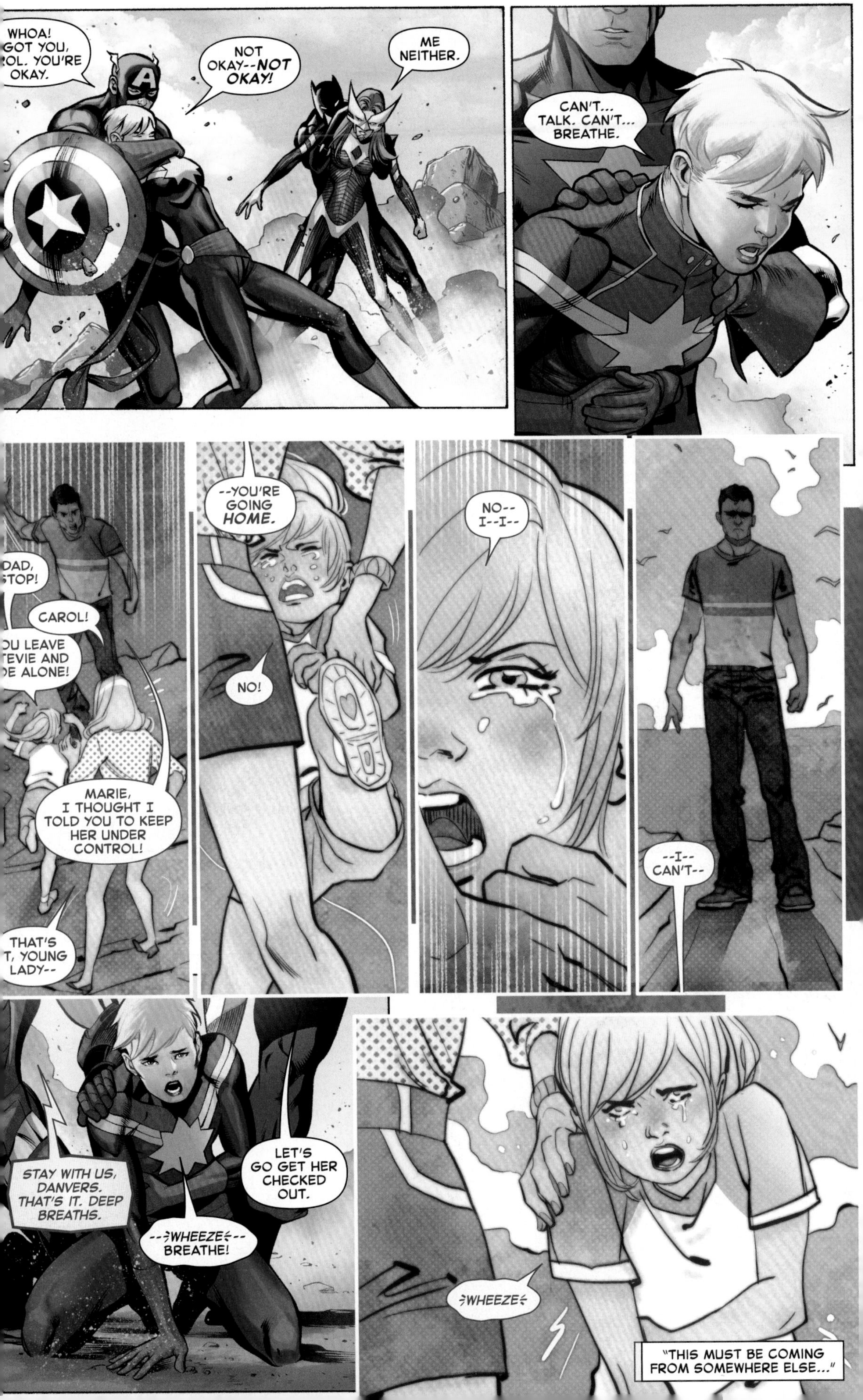
WHOA! GOT YOU, ROL. YOU'RE OKAY.
NOT OKAY--NOT OKAY!
ME NEITHER.
CAN'T... TALK. CAN'T... BREATHE.
DAD, STOP!
CAROL!
YOU LEAVE STEVIE AND JOE ALONE!
MARIE, I THOUGHT I TOLD YOU TO KEEP HER UNDER CONTROL!
THAT'S IT, YOUNG LADY--
--YOU'RE GOING HOME.
NO!
NO-- I--I--
--I-- CAN'T--
STAY WITH US, DANVERS. THAT'S IT. DEEP BREATHS.
--WHEEZE-- BREATHE!
LET'S GO GET HER CHECKED OUT.
WHEEZE
"THIS MUST BE COMING FROM SOMEWHERE ELSE..."

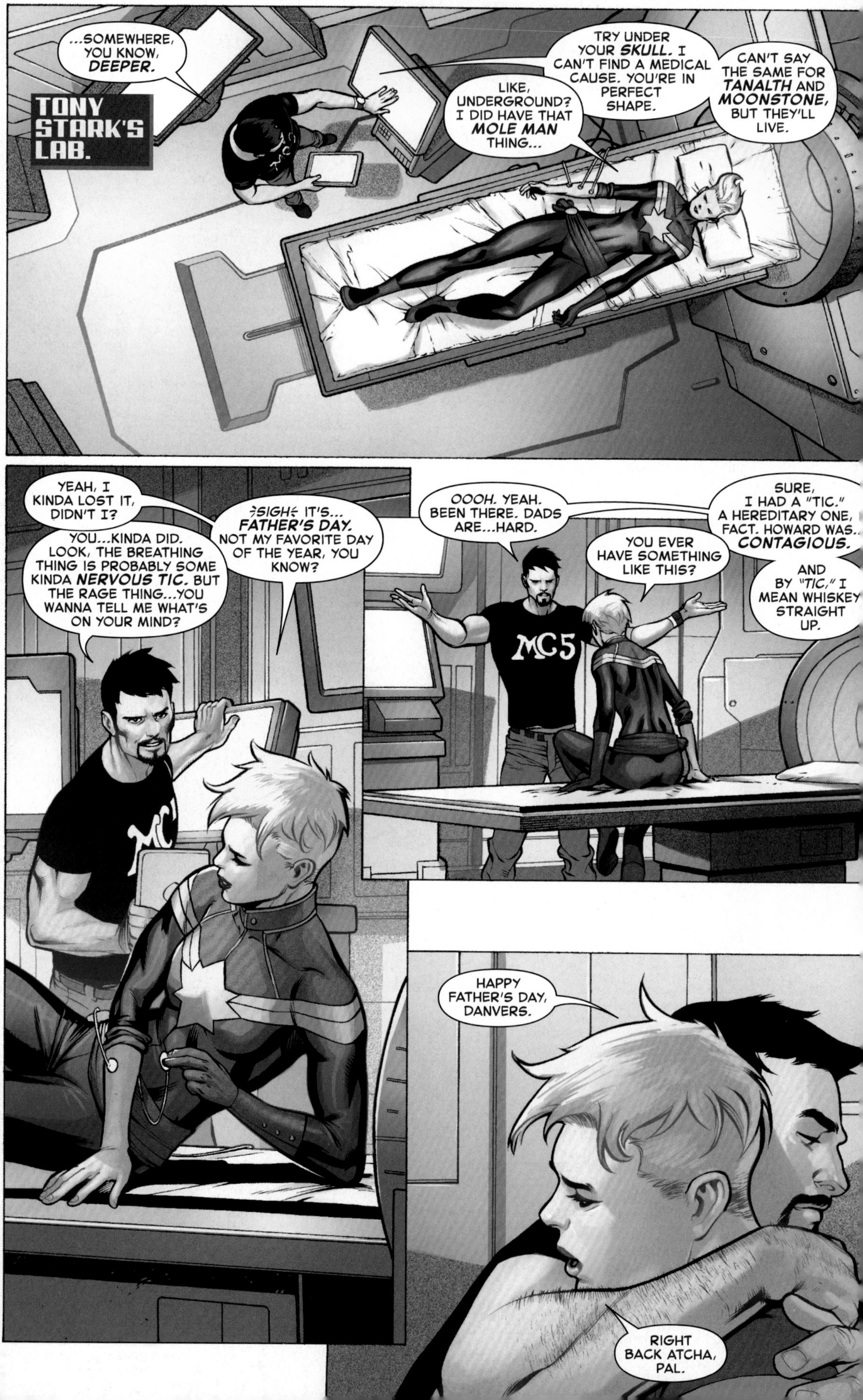

TONY STARK'S LAB.
...SOMEWHERE, YOU KNOW, DEEPER.
LIKE, UNDERGROUND? I DID HAVE THAT MOLE MAN THING...
TRY UNDER YOUR SKULL. I CAN'T FIND A MEDICAL CAUSE. YOU'RE IN PERFECT SHAPE.
CAN'T SAY THE SAME FOR TANALTH AND MOONSTONE, BUT THEY'LL LIVE.
YEAH, I KINDA LOST IT, DIDN'T I?
YOU...KINDA DID. LOOK, THE BREATHING THING IS PROBABLY SOME KINDA NERVOUS TIC. BUT THE RAGE THING...YOU WANNA TELL ME WHAT'S ON YOUR MIND?
SIGH IT'S... FATHER'S DAY. NOT MY FAVORITE DAY OF THE YEAR, YOU KNOW?
OOOH. YEAH. BEEN THERE. DADS ARE...HARD.
YOU EVER HAVE SOMETHING LIKE THIS?
SURE, I HAD A "TIC." A HEREDITARY ONE, FACT. HOWARD WAS... CONTAGIOUS.
AND BY "TIC," I MEAN WHISKEY STRAIGHT UP.
MC5
HAPPY FATHER'S DAY, DANVERS.
RIGHT BACK ATCHA, PAL.

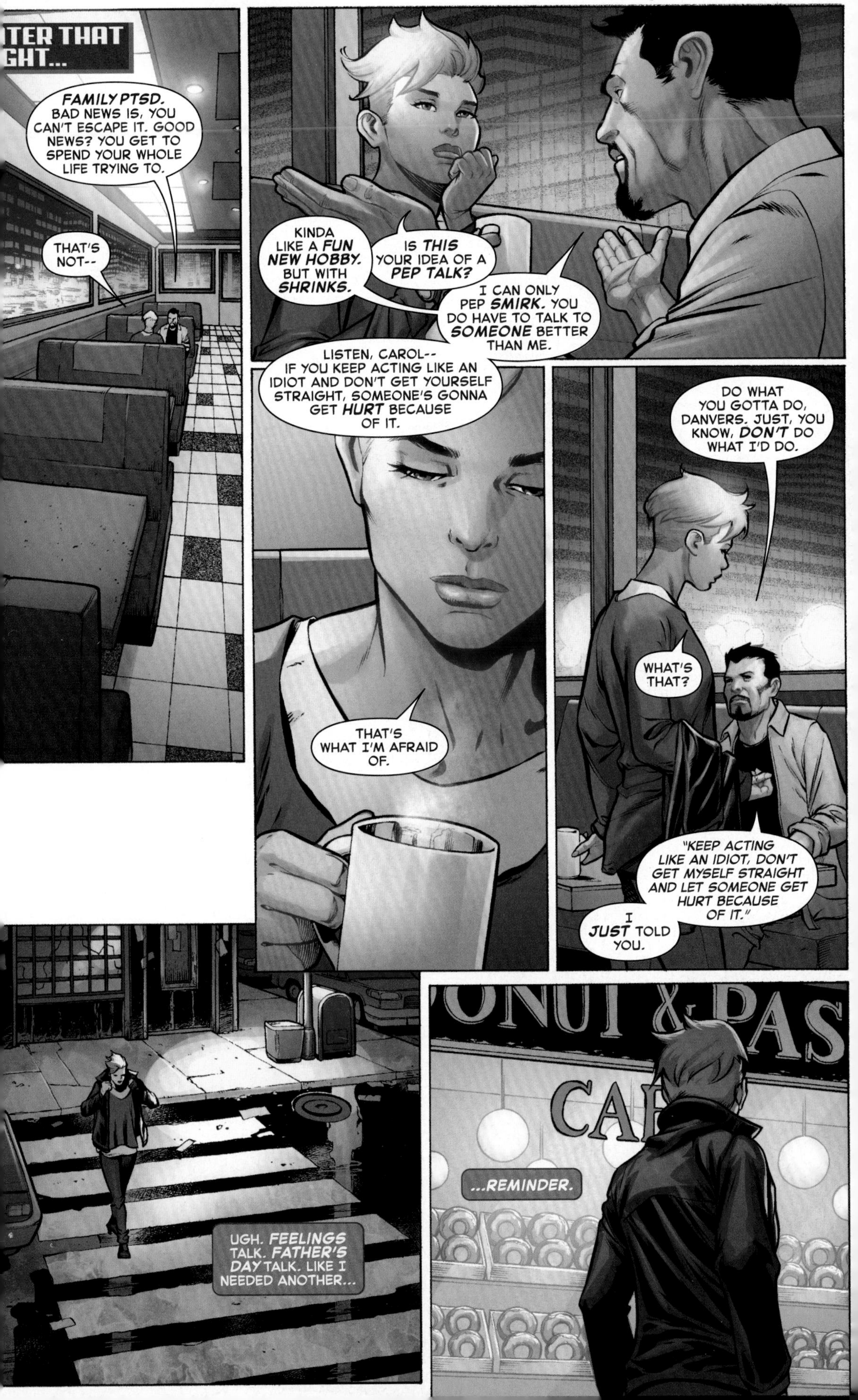

TER THAT GHT...
FAMILY PTSD. BAD NEWS IS, YOU CAN'T ESCAPE IT. GOOD NEWS? YOU GET TO SPEND YOUR WHOLE LIFE TRYING TO.
THAT'S NOT--
KINDA LIKE A FUN NEW HOBBY. BUT WITH SHRINKS.
IS THIS YOUR IDEA OF A PEP TALK?
I CAN ONLY PEP SMIRK. YOU DO HAVE TO TALK TO SOMEONE BETTER THAN ME.
LISTEN, CAROL-- IF YOU KEEP ACTING LIKE AN IDIOT AND DON'T GET YOURSELF STRAIGHT, SOMEONE'S GONNA GET HURT BECAUSE OF IT.
THAT'S WHAT I'M AFRAID OF.
DO WHAT YOU GOTTA DO, DANVERS. JUST, YOU KNOW, DON'T DO WHAT I'D DO.
WHAT'S THAT?
"KEEP ACTING LIKE AN IDIOT, DON'T GET MYSELF STRAIGHT AND LET SOMEONE GET HURT BECAUSE OF IT."
I JUST TOLD YOU.
UGH. FEELINGS TALK. FATHER'S DAY TALK. LIKE I NEEDED ANOTHER...
ONUT & PAS
CA
...REMINDER.

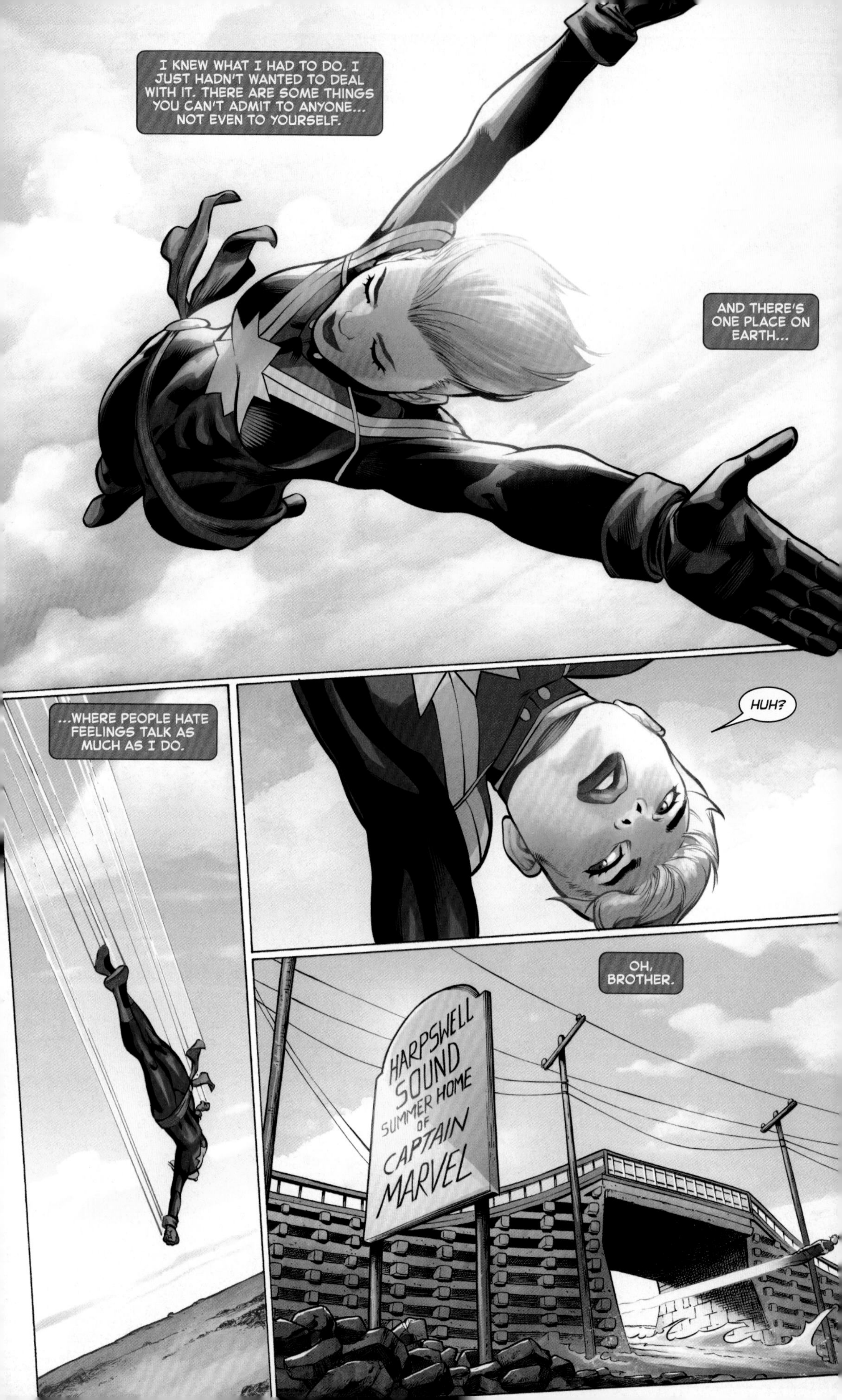
I KNEW WHAT I HAD TO DO. I JUST HADN'T WANTED TO DEAL WITH IT. THERE ARE SOME THINGS YOU CAN'T ADMIT TO ANYONE... NOT EVEN TO YOURSELF.
AND THERE'S ONE PLACE ON EARTH...
...WHERE PEOPLE HATE FEELINGS TALK AS MUCH AS I DO.
HUH?
OH, BROTHER.
HARPSWELL SOUND SUMMER HOME OF CAPTAIN MARVEL

SUGAR'S DONUTS

OFFICIAL DONUT OF CAPTAIN MAR...

LOST DOG
to draw
like a p...
486

RETRO BOOTLEG FESTIVAL
STARLAND VOCAL BAND
KC & SUNSHINE BAND
PLAYER
AMERICA

SUGAR'S DONUTS

OFFICIAL? I DON'T KNOW THAT WE'VE MADE IT OFFICIAL...

WHAT, YA GOT A THING FOR THE DUNKSTAH NOW?

BETTER KEEP THAT TO YAHSELF, S. DANVERS. WOULDN'T WANTITAH GET OUT THAT YAH CHEATIN' ON US...

US? YOU'RE NOT MRS. LEE. SHE'S THE OWNER OF SUGAR'S.

DUH. I'M LOUIS LEE.

LITTLE LOUIS?

THEY DON'T CALL ME THAT MUCH ANYMORE. NOT SINCE 'BOUT 6'4".

SUGAR'S DONUTS

OFFICIAL DONUT OF CAPTAIN MARVEL

Art
Lean to d...
LOST DOG
RETRO
FEST...

WHAT BRINGS YA BACK HEAH, CAROL?

I DON'T KNOW. THEY SAY YOU CAN NEVER GO HOME AGAIN, BUT HONESTLY...?

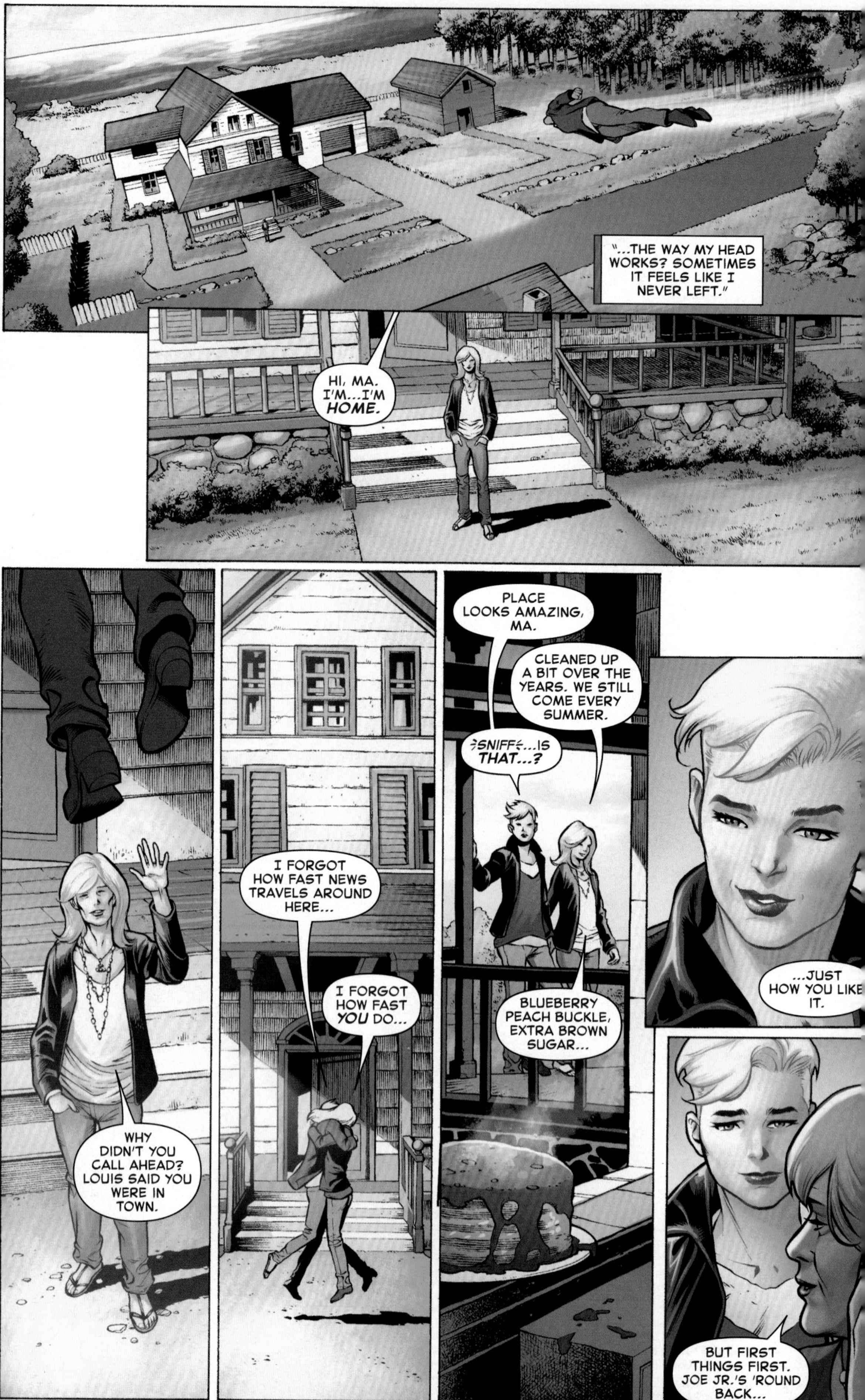
"...THE WAY MY HEAD WORKS? SOMETIMES IT FEELS LIKE I NEVER LEFT."
HI, MA. I'M...I'M HOME.
WHY DIDN'T YOU CALL AHEAD? LOUIS SAID YOU WERE IN TOWN.
I FORGOT HOW FAST NEWS TRAVELS AROUND HERE...
I FORGOT HOW FAST YOU DO...
PLACE LOOKS AMAZING, MA.
CLEANED UP A BIT OVER THE YEARS. WE STILL COME EVERY SUMMER.
SNIFF...IS THAT...?
BLUEBERRY PEACH BUCKLE, EXTRA BROWN SUGAR...
...JUST HOW YOU LIKE IT.
BUT FIRST THINGS FIRST. JOE JR.'S 'ROUND BACK...

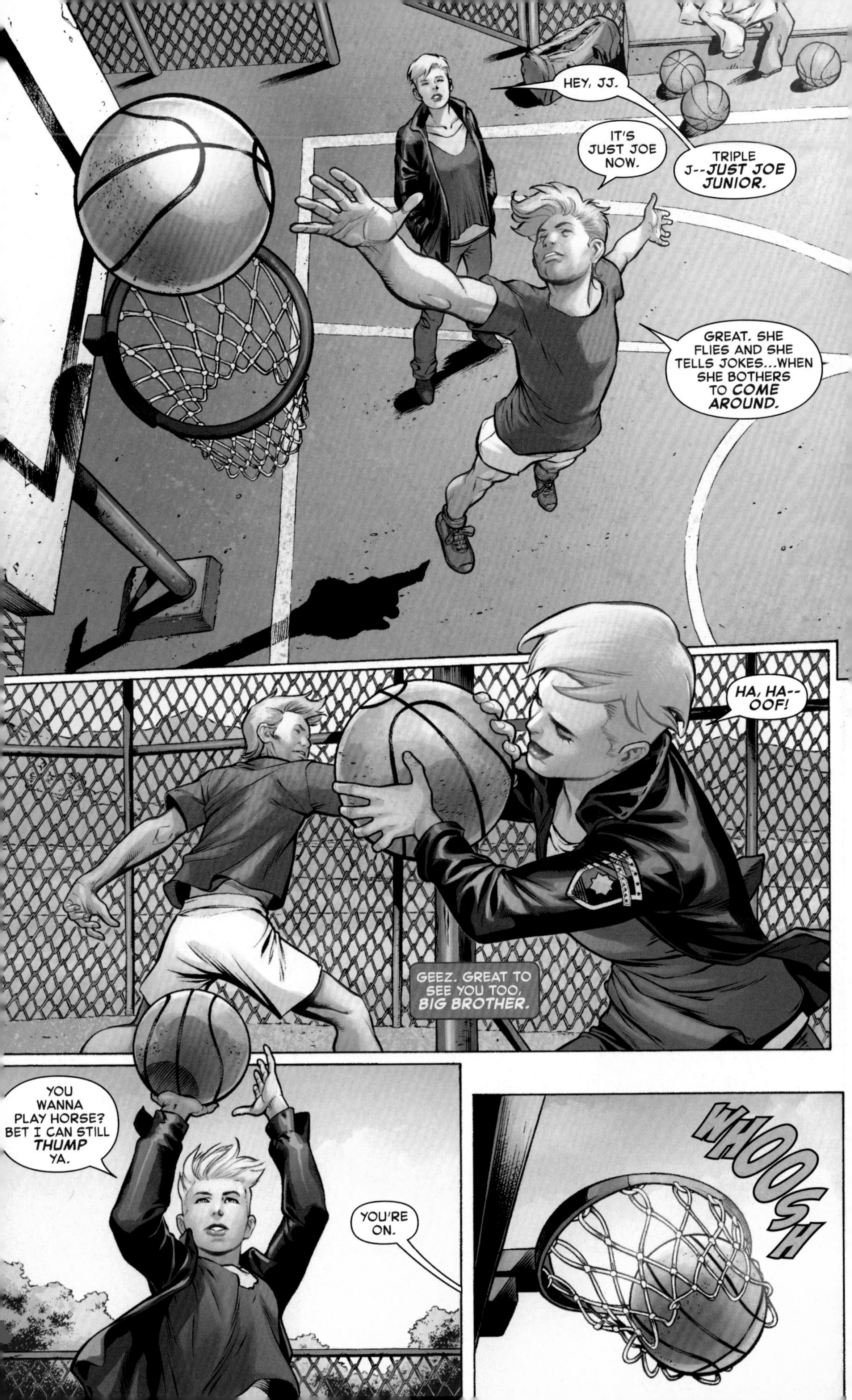
HEY, JJ.
IT'S JUST JOE NOW.
TRIPLE J--JUST JOE JUNIOR.
GREAT. SHE FLIES AND SHE TELLS JOKES...WHEN SHE BOTHERS TO COME AROUND.
HA, HA--OOF!
GEEZ. GREAT TO SEE YOU TOO, BIG BROTHER.
YOU WANNA PLAY HORSE? BET I CAN STILL THUMP YA.
YOU'RE ON.
WHOOOSH

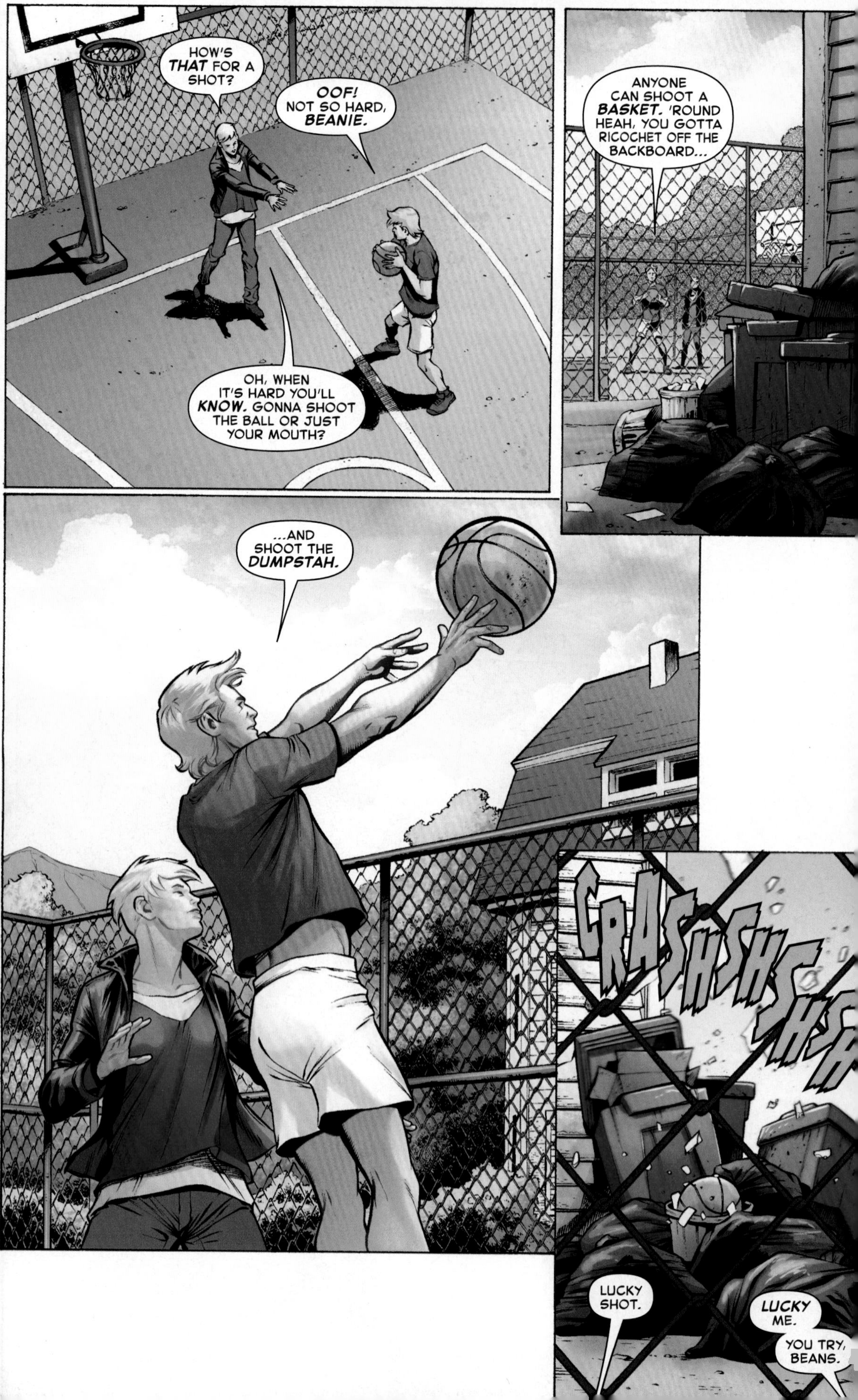
HOW'S THAT FOR A SHOT?
OOF! NOT SO HARD, BEANIE.
OH, WHEN IT'S HARD YOU'LL KNOW. GONNA SHOOT THE BALL OR JUST YOUR MOUTH?
ANYONE CAN SHOOT A BASKET. 'ROUND HEAH, YOU GOTTA RICOCHET OFF THE BACKBOARD...
...AND SHOOT THE DUMPSTAH.
CRASHSHSHSH
LUCKY SHOT.
LUCKY ME.
YOU TRY, BEANS.

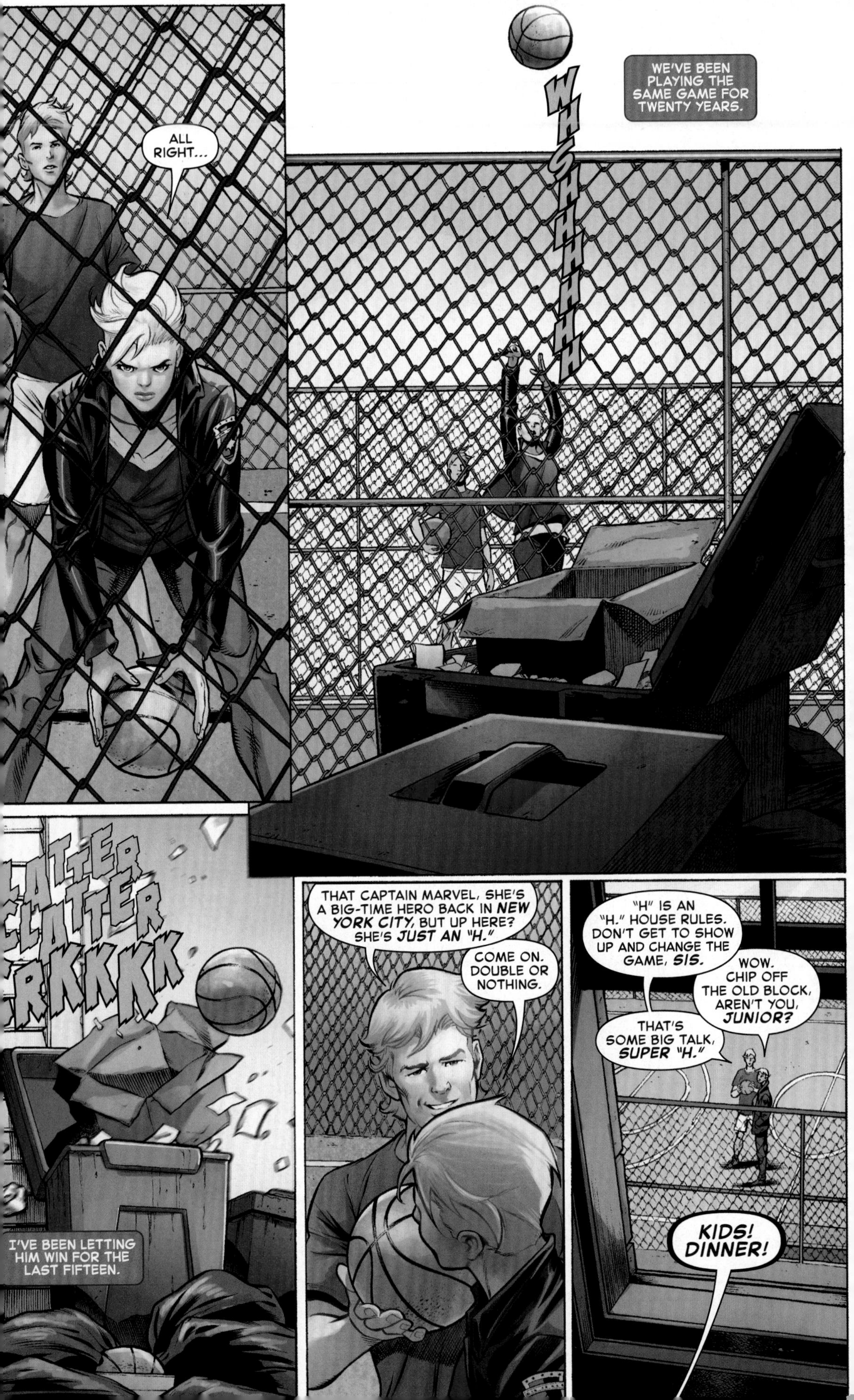

WE'VE BEEN PLAYING THE SAME GAME FOR TWENTY YEARS.
ALL RIGHT...
WHSHHHHHH
CLATTER CLATTER KRKKKK
I'VE BEEN LETTING HIM WIN FOR THE LAST FIFTEEN.
THAT CAPTAIN MARVEL, SHE'S A BIG-TIME HERO BACK IN NEW YORK CITY, BUT UP HERE? SHE'S JUST AN "H."
COME ON. DOUBLE OR NOTHING.
"H" IS AN "H." HOUSE RULES. DON'T GET TO SHOW UP AND CHANGE THE GAME, SIS.
WOW. CHIP OFF THE OLD BLOCK, AREN'T YOU, JUNIOR?
THAT'S SOME BIG TALK, SUPER "H."
KIDS! DINNER!

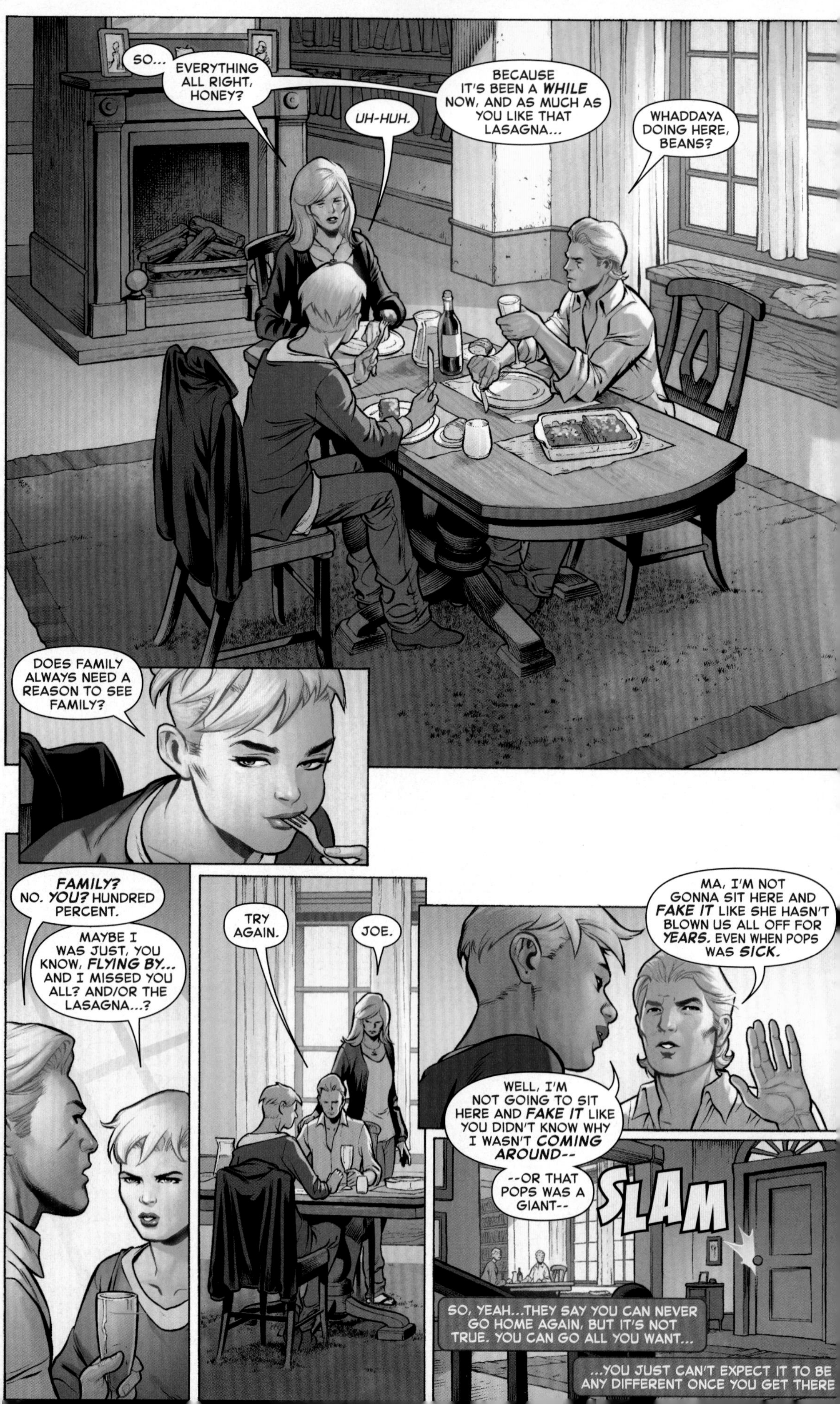

SO...
EVERYTHING ALL RIGHT, HONEY?
UH-HUH.
BECAUSE IT'S BEEN A WHILE NOW, AND AS MUCH AS YOU LIKE THAT LASAGNA...
WHADDAYA DOING HERE, BEANS?
DOES FAMILY ALWAYS NEED A REASON TO SEE FAMILY?
FAMILY? NO. YOU? HUNDRED PERCENT.
MAYBE I WAS JUST, YOU KNOW, FLYING BY... AND I MISSED YOU ALL? AND/OR THE LASAGNA...?
TRY AGAIN.
JOE.
MA, I'M NOT GONNA SIT HERE AND FAKE IT LIKE SHE HASN'T BLOWN US ALL OFF FOR YEARS. EVEN WHEN POPS WAS SICK.
WELL, I'M NOT GOING TO SIT HERE AND FAKE IT LIKE YOU DIDN'T KNOW WHY I WASN'T COMING AROUND--
--OR THAT POPS WAS A GIANT--
SLAM
SO, YEAH...THEY SAY YOU CAN NEVER GO HOME AGAIN, BUT IT'S NOT TRUE. YOU CAN GO ALL YOU WANT...
...YOU JUST CAN'T EXPECT IT TO BE ANY DIFFERENT ONCE YOU GET THERE

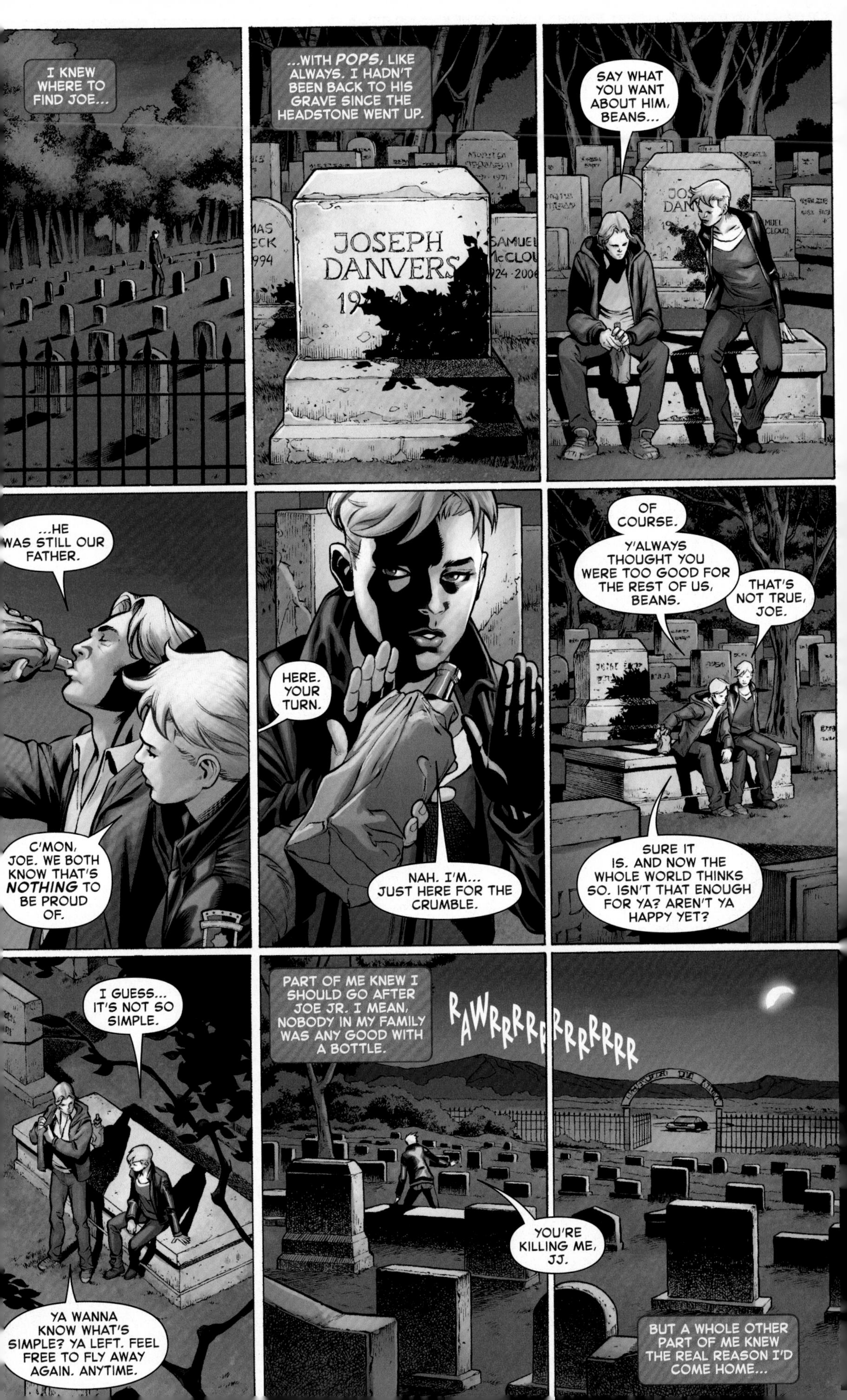
I KNEW WHERE TO FIND JOE...
...WITH POPS, LIKE ALWAYS. I HADN'T BEEN BACK TO HIS GRAVE SINCE THE HEADSTONE WENT UP.
JOSEPH DANVERS
SAY WHAT YOU WANT ABOUT HIM, BEANS...
...HE WAS STILL OUR FATHER.
C'MON, JOE. WE BOTH KNOW THAT'S NOTHING TO BE PROUD OF.
HERE. YOUR TURN.
NAH. I'M... JUST HERE FOR THE CRUMBLE.
OF COURSE.
Y'ALWAYS THOUGHT YOU WERE TOO GOOD FOR THE REST OF US, BEANS.
THAT'S NOT TRUE, JOE.
SURE IT IS. AND NOW THE WHOLE WORLD THINKS SO. ISN'T THAT ENOUGH FOR YA? AREN'T YA HAPPY YET?
I GUESS... IT'S NOT SO SIMPLE.
YA WANNA KNOW WHAT'S SIMPLE? YA LEFT. FEEL FREE TO FLY AWAY AGAIN. ANYTIME.
PART OF ME KNEW I SHOULD GO AFTER JOE JR. I MEAN, NOBODY IN MY FAMILY WAS ANY GOOD WITH A BOTTLE.
RAWRRRRRRRRRRRR
YOU'RE KILLING ME, JJ.
BUT A WHOLE OTHER PART OF ME KNEW THE REAL REASON I'D COME HOME...

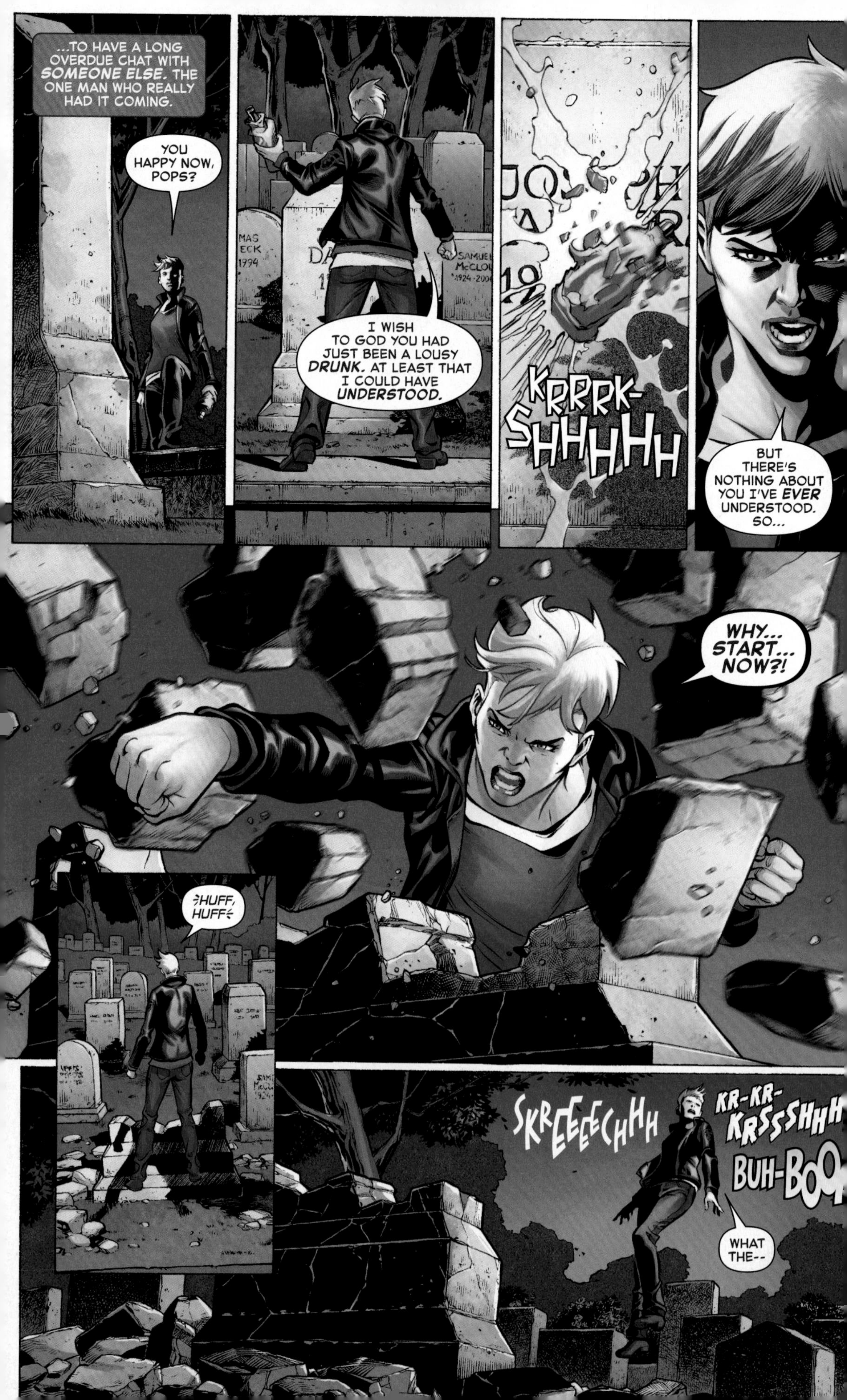
...TO HAVE A LONG OVERDUE CHAT WITH SOMEONE ELSE. THE ONE MAN WHO REALLY HAD IT COMING.
YOU HAPPY NOW, POPS?
I WISH TO GOD YOU HAD JUST BEEN A LOUSY DRUNK. AT LEAST THAT I COULD HAVE UNDERSTOOD.
KRRRK-SHHHHHH
BUT THERE'S NOTHING ABOUT YOU I'VE EVER UNDERSTOOD. SO...
WHY... START... NOW?!
HUFF, HUFF
SKREEEEECHHH
KR-KR-KRSSSHHH
BUH-BOO
WHAT THE--

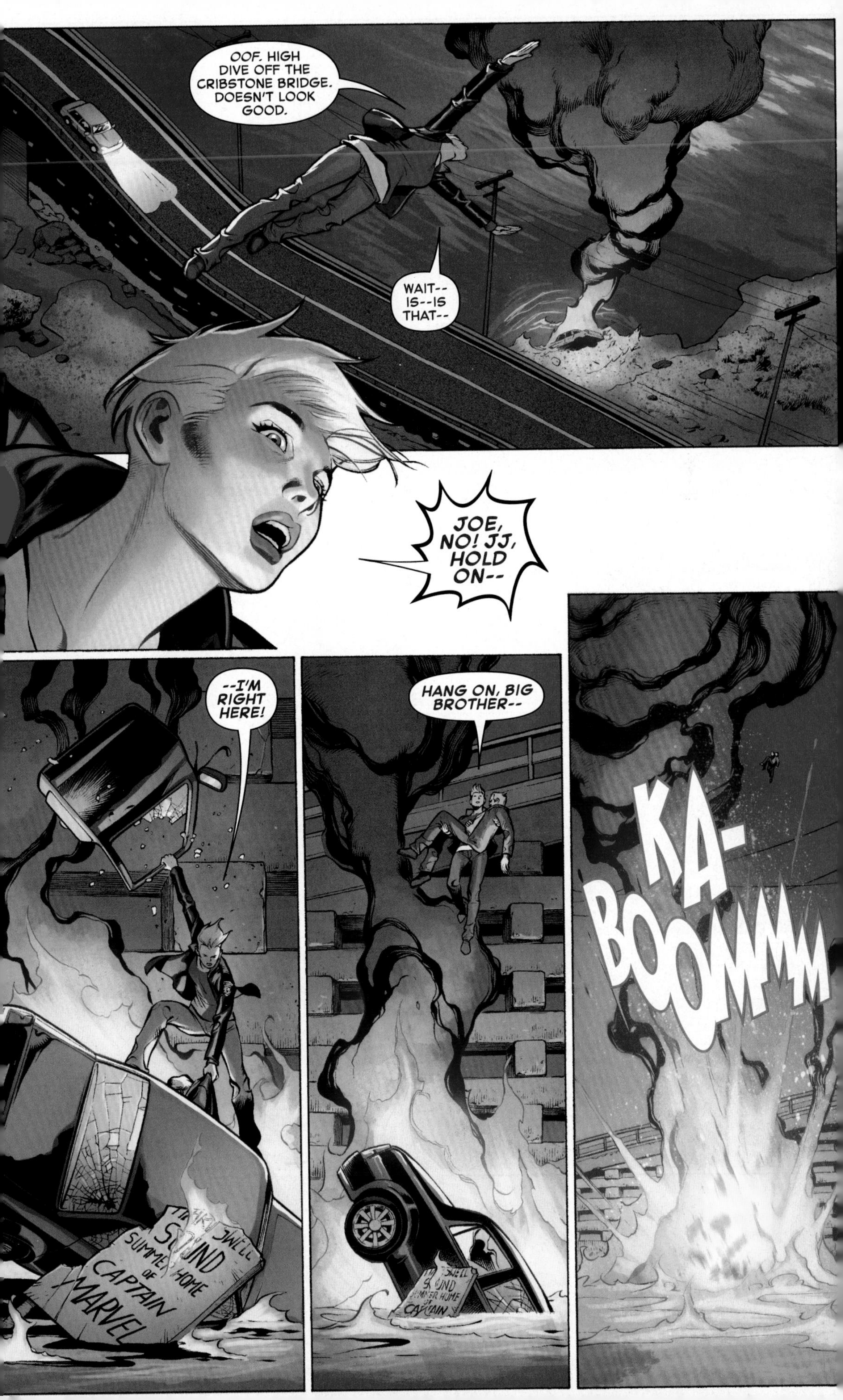
OOF. HIGH DIVE OFF THE CRIBSTONE BRIDGE. DOESN'T LOOK GOOD.
WAIT-- IS--IS THAT--
JOE, NO! JJ, HOLD ON--
--I'M RIGHT HERE!
SUMMER HOME OF CAPTAIN MARVEL
HANG ON, BIG BROTHER--
KA-BOOMMMM

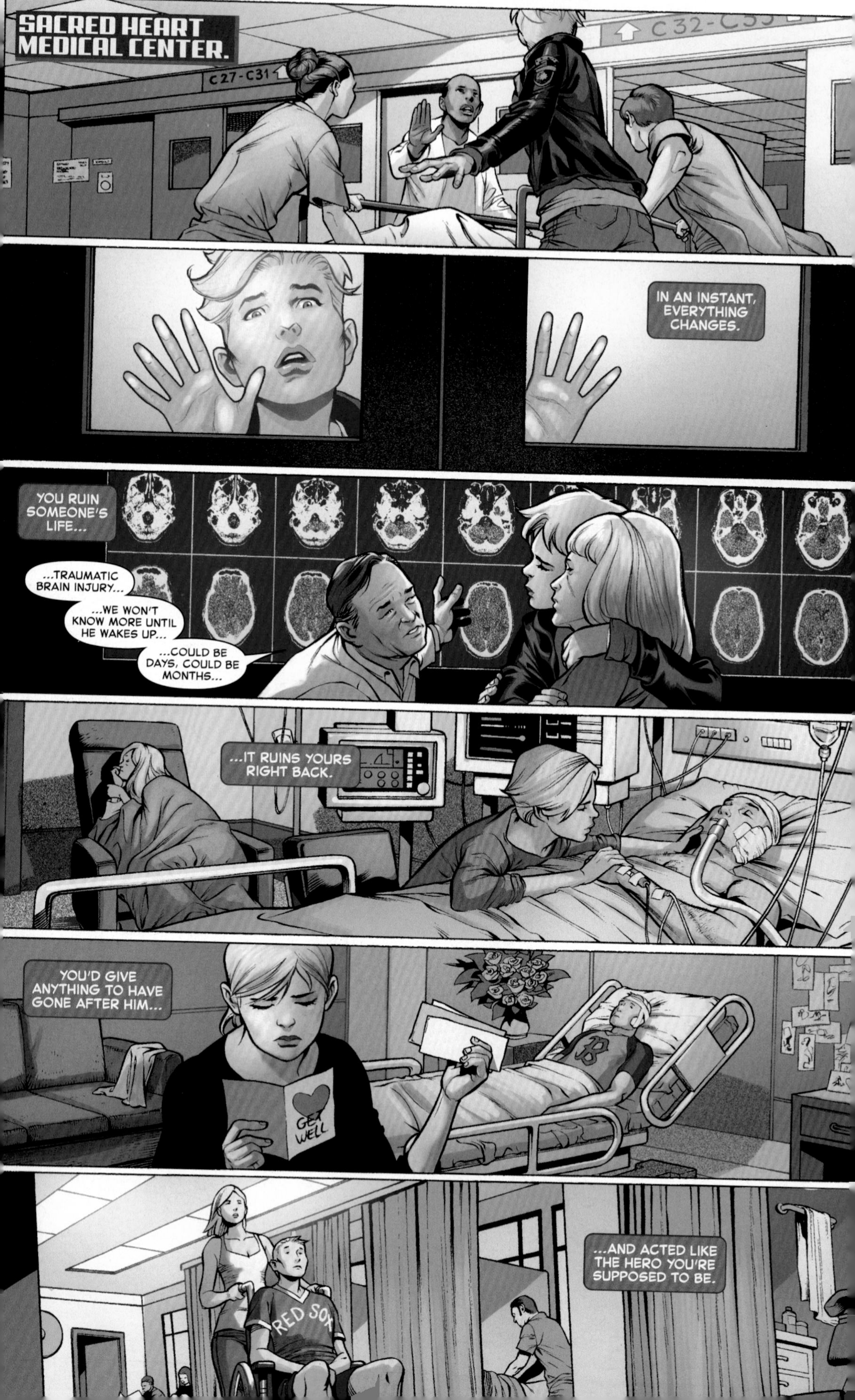
SACRED HEART MEDICAL CENTER.
C27-C31
C32-C35
IN AN INSTANT, EVERYTHING CHANGES.
YOU RUIN SOMEONE'S LIFE...
...TRAUMATIC BRAIN INJURY...
...WE WON'T KNOW MORE UNTIL HE WAKES UP...
...COULD BE DAYS, COULD BE MONTHS...
...IT RUINS YOURS RIGHT BACK.
YOU'D GIVE ANYTHING TO HAVE GONE AFTER HIM...
GET WELL
...AND ACTED LIKE THE HERO YOU'RE SUPPOSED TO BE.
RED SOX

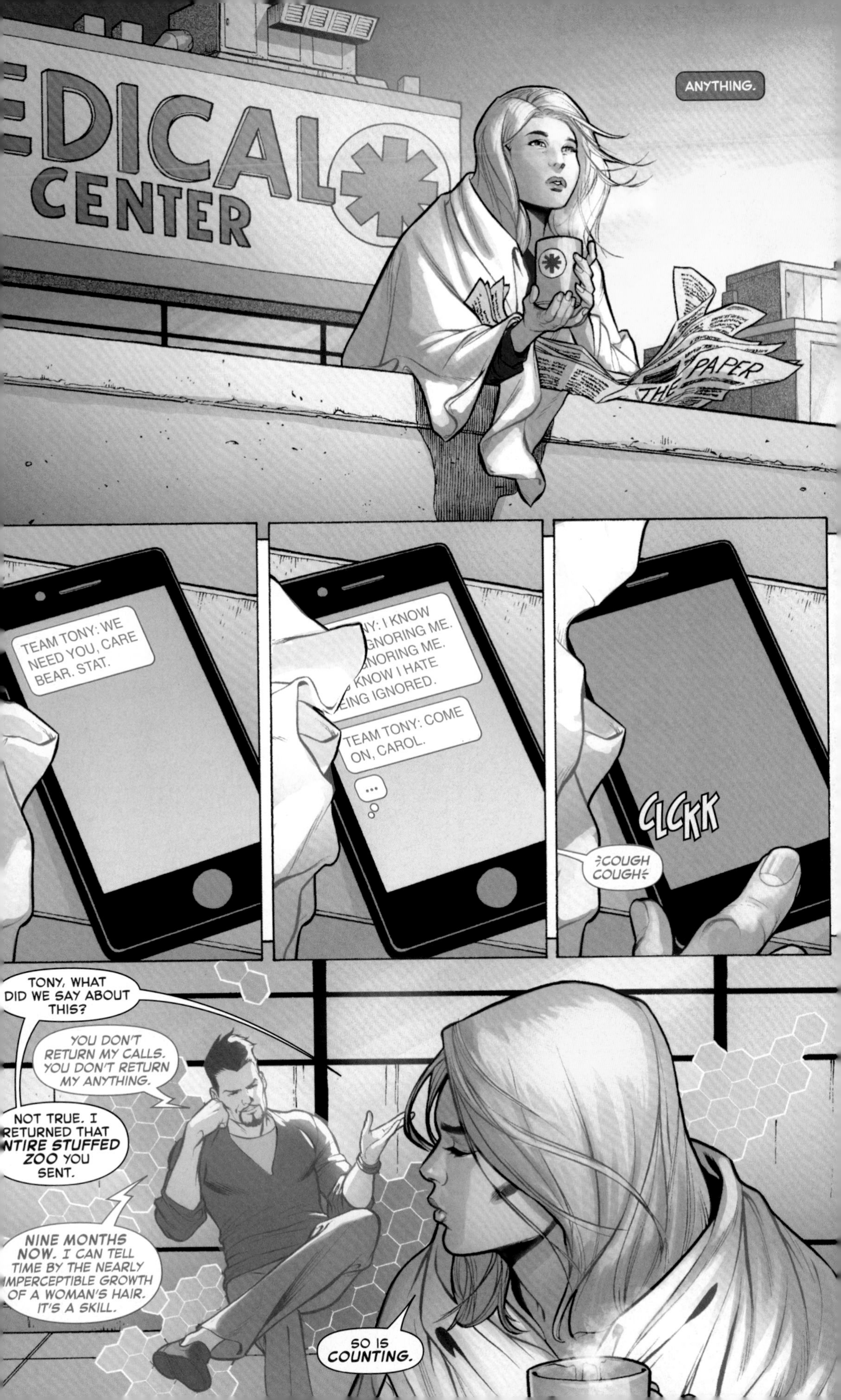

EDICAL CENTER
ANYTHING.
THE PAPER
TEAM TONY: WE NEED YOU, CARE BEAR. STAT.
NY: I KNOW GNORING ME. GNORING ME. KNOW I HATE EING IGNORED.
TEAM TONY: COME ON, CAROL.
...
CLCKK
COUGH COUGH
TONY, WHAT DID WE SAY ABOUT THIS?
YOU DON'T RETURN MY CALLS. YOU DON'T RETURN MY ANYTHING.
NOT TRUE. I RETURNED THAT NTIRE STUFFED ZOO YOU SENT.
NINE MONTHS NOW. I CAN TELL TIME BY THE NEARLY MPERCEPTIBLE GROWTH OF A WOMAN'S HAIR. IT'S A SKILL.
SO IS COUNTING.

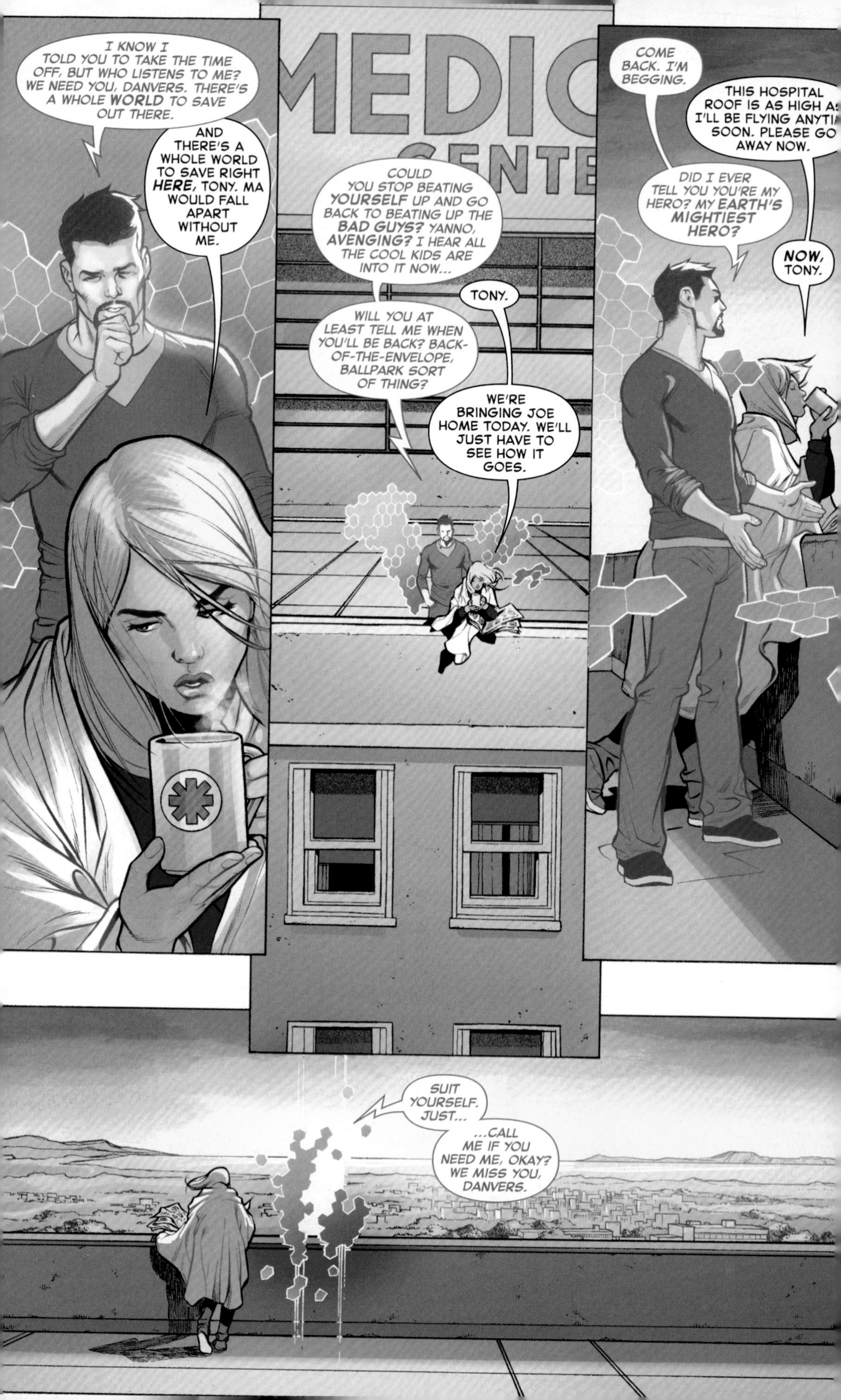

MEDIC CENTE
I KNOW I TOLD YOU TO TAKE THE TIME OFF, BUT WHO LISTENS TO ME? WE NEED YOU, DANVERS. THERE'S A WHOLE WORLD TO SAVE OUT THERE.
AND THERE'S A WHOLE WORLD TO SAVE RIGHT HERE, TONY. MA WOULD FALL APART WITHOUT ME.
COULD YOU STOP BEATING YOURSELF UP AND GO BACK TO BEATING UP THE BAD GUYS? YANNO, AVENGING? I HEAR ALL THE COOL KIDS ARE INTO IT NOW...
WILL YOU AT LEAST TELL ME WHEN YOU'LL BE BACK? BACK-OF-THE-ENVELOPE, BALLPARK SORT OF THING?
TONY.
WE'RE BRINGING JOE HOME TODAY. WE'LL JUST HAVE TO SEE HOW IT GOES.
COME BACK. I'M BEGGING.
THIS HOSPITAL ROOF IS AS HIGH A I'LL BE FLYING ANYTI SOON. PLEASE GO AWAY NOW.
DID I EVER TELL YOU YOU'RE MY HERO? MY EARTH'S MIGHTIEST HERO?
NOW, TONY.
SUIT YOURSELF. JUST...
...CALL ME IF YOU NEED ME, OKAY? WE MISS YOU, DANVERS.

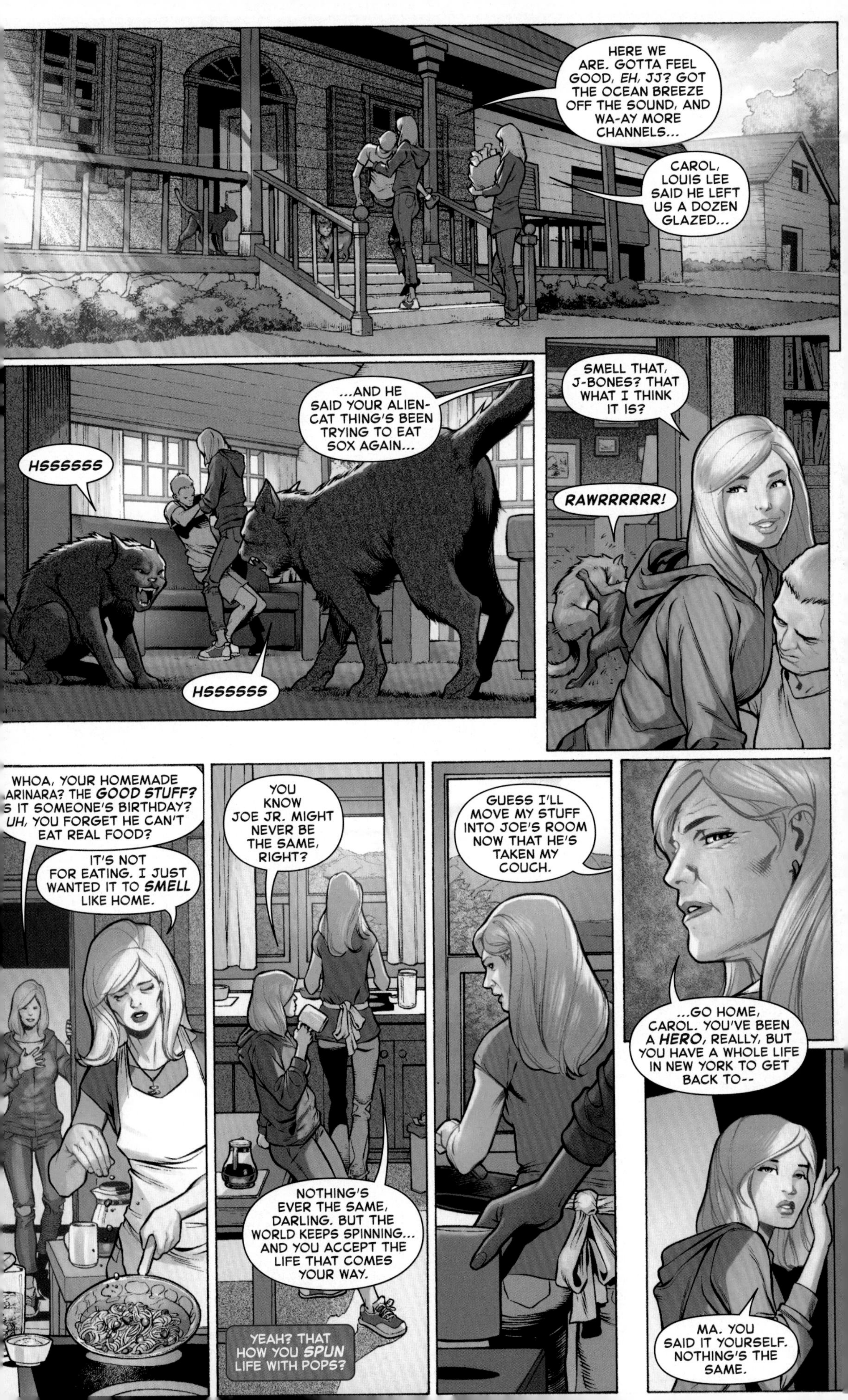
HERE WE ARE. GOTTA FEEL GOOD, EH, JJ? GOT THE OCEAN BREEZE OFF THE SOUND, AND WA-AY MORE CHANNELS...
CAROL, LOUIS LEE SAID HE LEFT US A DOZEN GLAZED...
...AND HE SAID YOUR ALIEN-CAT THING'S BEEN TRYING TO EAT SOX AGAIN...
HSSSSSS
HSSSSSS
SMELL THAT, J-BONES? THAT WHAT I THINK IT IS?
RAWRRRRRR!
WHOA, YOUR HOMEMADE
ARINARA? THE GOOD STUFF?
S IT SOMEONE'S BIRTHDAY?
UH, YOU FORGET HE CAN'T EAT REAL FOOD?
IT'S NOT FOR EATING. I JUST WANTED IT TO SMELL LIKE HOME.
YOU KNOW JOE JR. MIGHT NEVER BE THE SAME, RIGHT?
NOTHING'S EVER THE SAME, DARLING. BUT THE WORLD KEEPS SPINNING... AND YOU ACCEPT THE LIFE THAT COMES YOUR WAY.
YEAH? THAT HOW YOU SPUN LIFE WITH POPS?
GUESS I'LL MOVE MY STUFF INTO JOE'S ROOM NOW THAT HE'S TAKEN MY COUCH.
...GO HOME, CAROL. YOU'VE BEEN A HERO, REALLY, BUT YOU HAVE A WHOLE LIFE IN NEW YORK TO GET BACK TO--
MA. YOU SAID IT YOURSELF. NOTHING'S THE SAME.

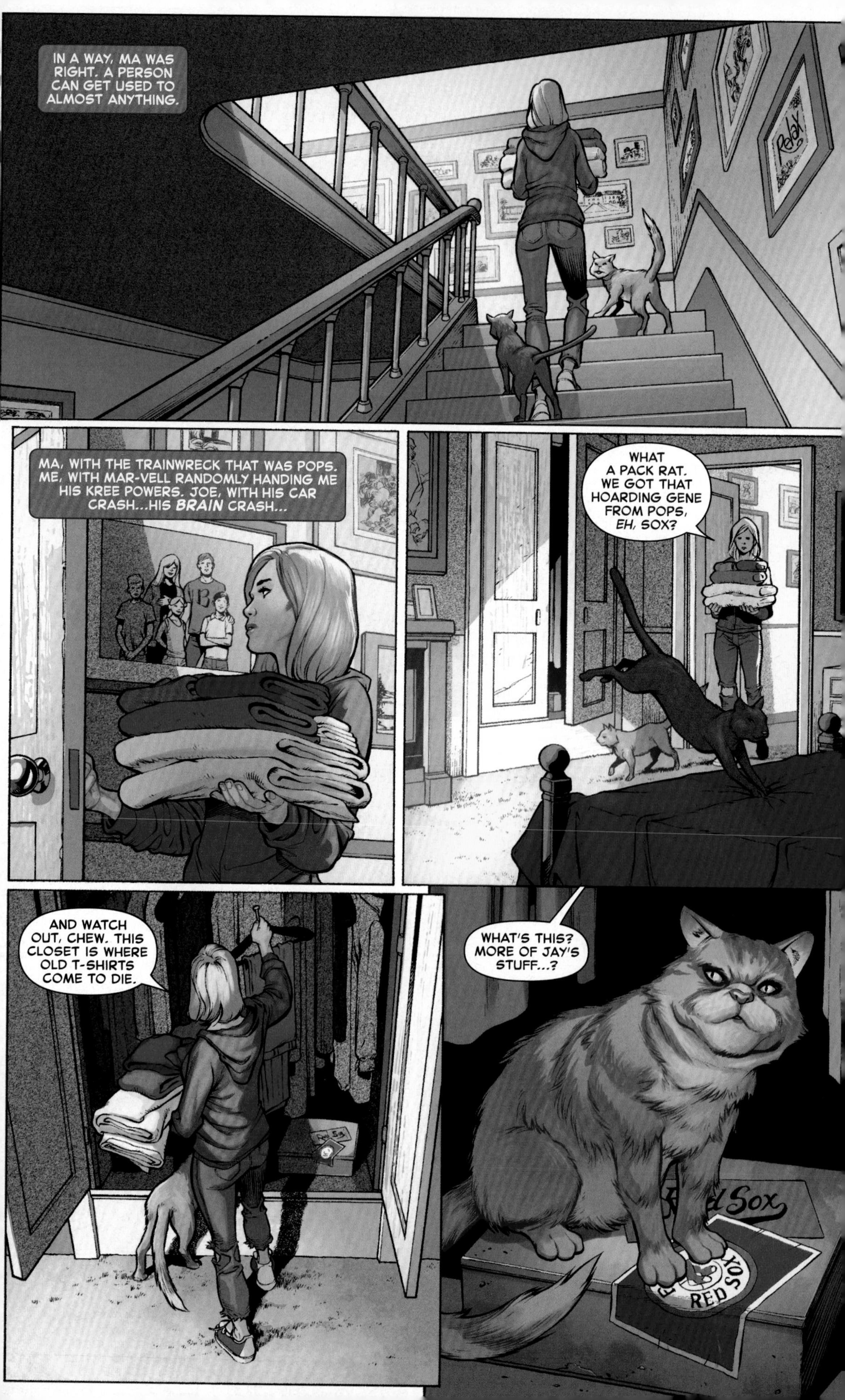
IN A WAY, MA WAS RIGHT. A PERSON CAN GET USED TO ALMOST ANYTHING.
Relax
MA, WITH THE TRAINWRECK THAT WAS POPS. ME, WITH MAR-VELL RANDOMLY HANDING ME HIS KREE POWERS. JOE, WITH HIS CAR CRASH...HIS *BRAIN* CRASH...
WHAT A PACK RAT. WE GOT THAT HOARDING GENE FROM POPS, *EH,* SOX?
AND WATCH OUT, CHEW. THIS CLOSET IS WHERE OLD T-SHIRTS COME TO DIE.
WHAT'S THIS? MORE OF JAY'S STUFF...?
Red Sox
RED SOX

THIS LOOKS TOO OLD TO BE JJ'S OR STEVIE'S OR MINE.

MA MUST HAVE BEEN CLEANING OUT THE ATTIC.

WHAT'S...

"...I'm ripped apart when I'm not with you, but I'm gutted when I am. I'm afraid of you and I'm afraid of losing you. And nobody in the universe but you knows how I feel.

My love,

I have to make a confession...I'm ripped apart when I'm not with you, but I'm gutted when I am. I'm afraid of you and I'm afraid of losing you. And nobody in the universe but you knows how I feel.

I'm not an idiot. I know there's no this turns out well, not for either I know we're not meant to be. I hat people will say if they find maybe you're right, and we op seeing each other...

be you're wrong, because top seeing each other, we're stop feeling each other, not I have a family and ot you don't.

eason we found each other, it's this: You are my can't give up on that, and me to.

All my love
Joseph

WHAT IS THIS? WHO WROTE THIS? THE HANDWRITING IS SO FAMILIAR. POPS? MA? CAN'T IMAGINE EITHER...

"...I'm not an idiot. I know there's no way this turns out well, not for either of s. I know we're not meant to be. I know what people will say if they find ut. So maybe you're right, and we should top seeing each other...

"...but maybe you're wrong, because even if we stop seeing each other, we're never gonna stop feeling each other, whether or not I have a family and whether or not you don't.

"There's a reason we found each other, my love, and it's this: You are my soulmate. I can't give up on that, and you can't ask me to.

"All my love...

"...Joseph."

HOLY--POPS WAS HAVING AN AFFAIR?

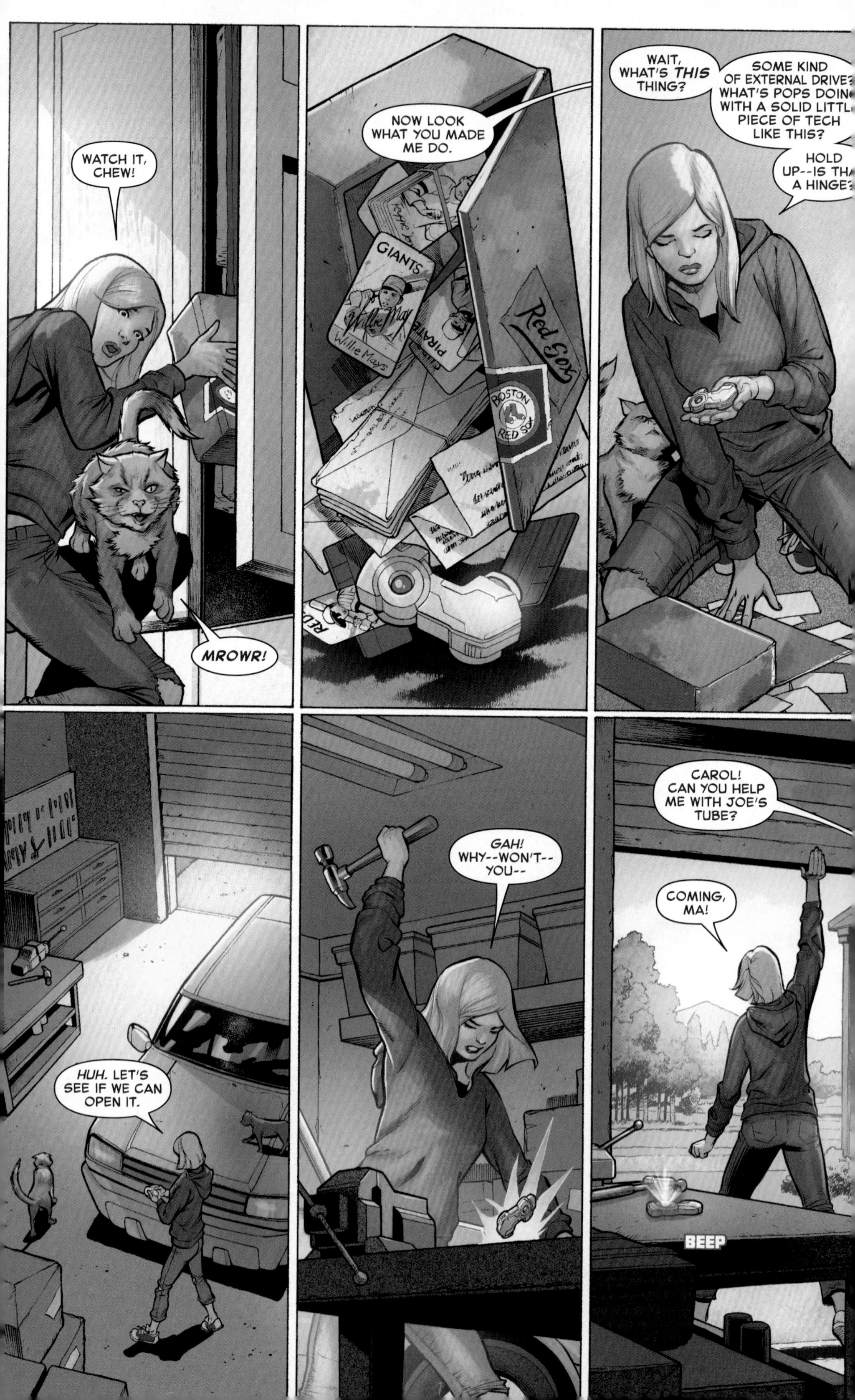
WATCH IT, CHEW!
MROWR!
NOW LOOK WHAT YOU MADE ME DO.
GIANTS
Willie Mays
PIRATE
Red Sox
BOSTON RED SOX
WAIT, WHAT'S *THIS* THING?
SOME KIND OF EXTERNAL DRIVE? WHAT'S POPS DOIN WITH A SOLID LITTL PIECE OF TECH LIKE THIS?
HOLD UP--IS THA A HINGE?
HUH. LET'S SEE IF WE CAN OPEN IT.
GAH! WHY--WON'T--YOU--
CAROL! CAN YOU HELP ME WITH JOE'S TUBE?
COMING, MA!
BEEP

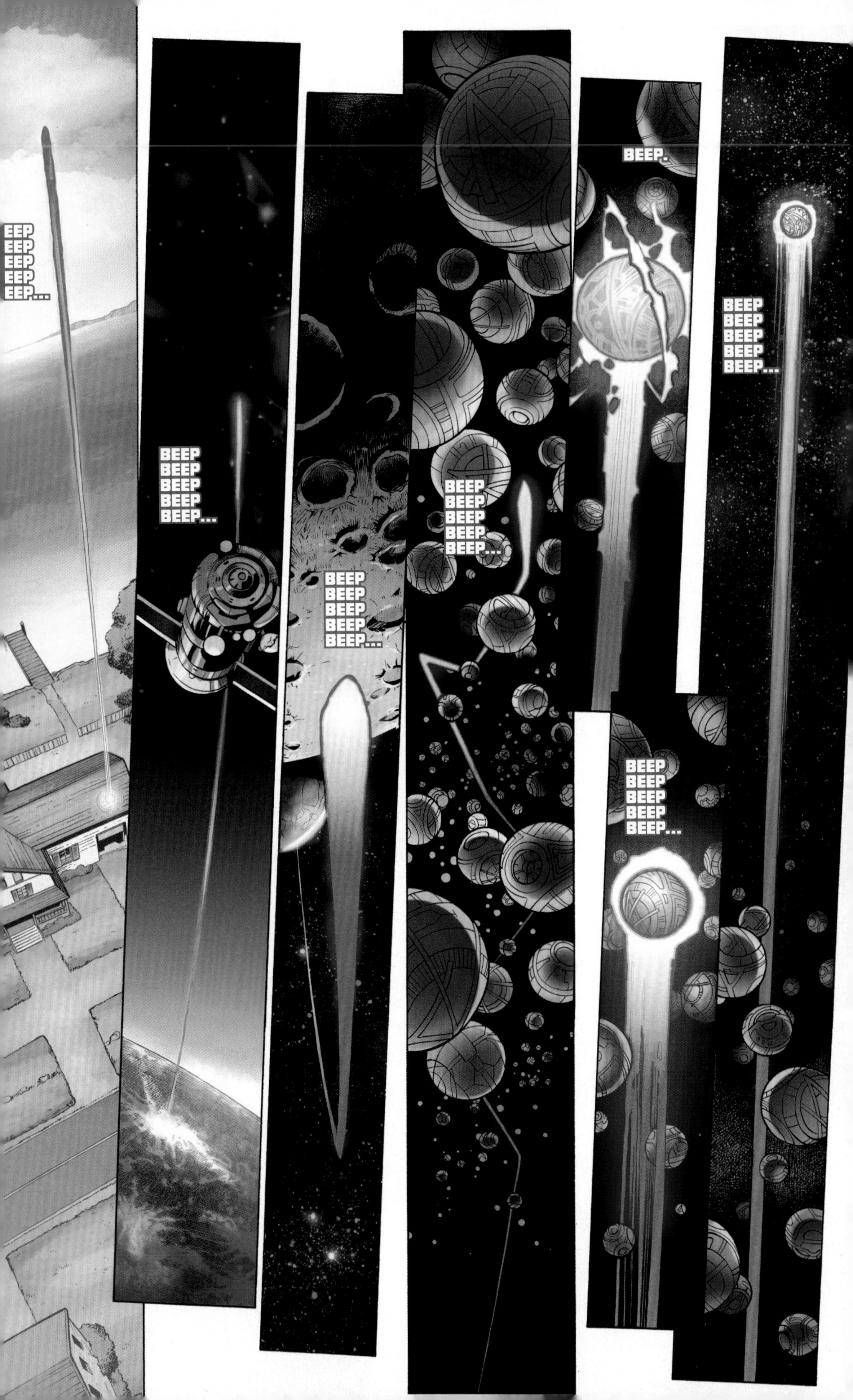
EEP
EEP
EEP
EEP
EEP...
BEEP
BEEP
BEEP
BEEP
BEEP...
BEEP
BEEP
BEEP
BEEP
BEEP...
BEEP
BEEP
BEEP
BEEP
BEEP...
BEEP.
BEEP
BEEP
BEEP
BEEP
BEEP...
BEEP
BEEP
BEEP
BEEP
BEEP...

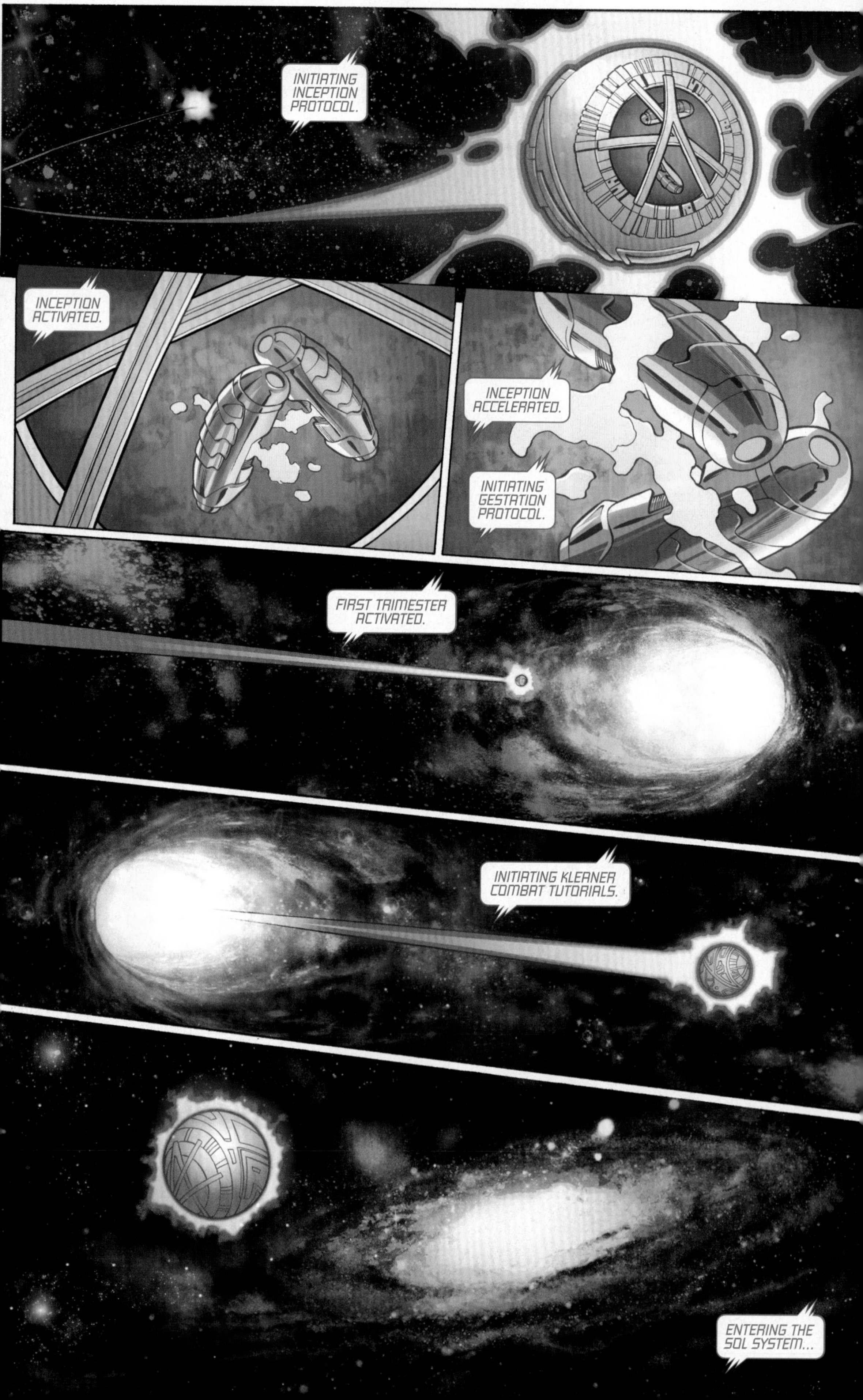
INITIATING INCEPTION PROTOCOL.
INCEPTION ACTIVATED.
INCEPTION ACCELERATED.
INITIATING GESTATION PROTOCOL.
FIRST TRIMESTER ACTIVATED.
INITIATING KLEANER COMBAT TUTORIALS.
ENTERING THE SOL SYSTEM...

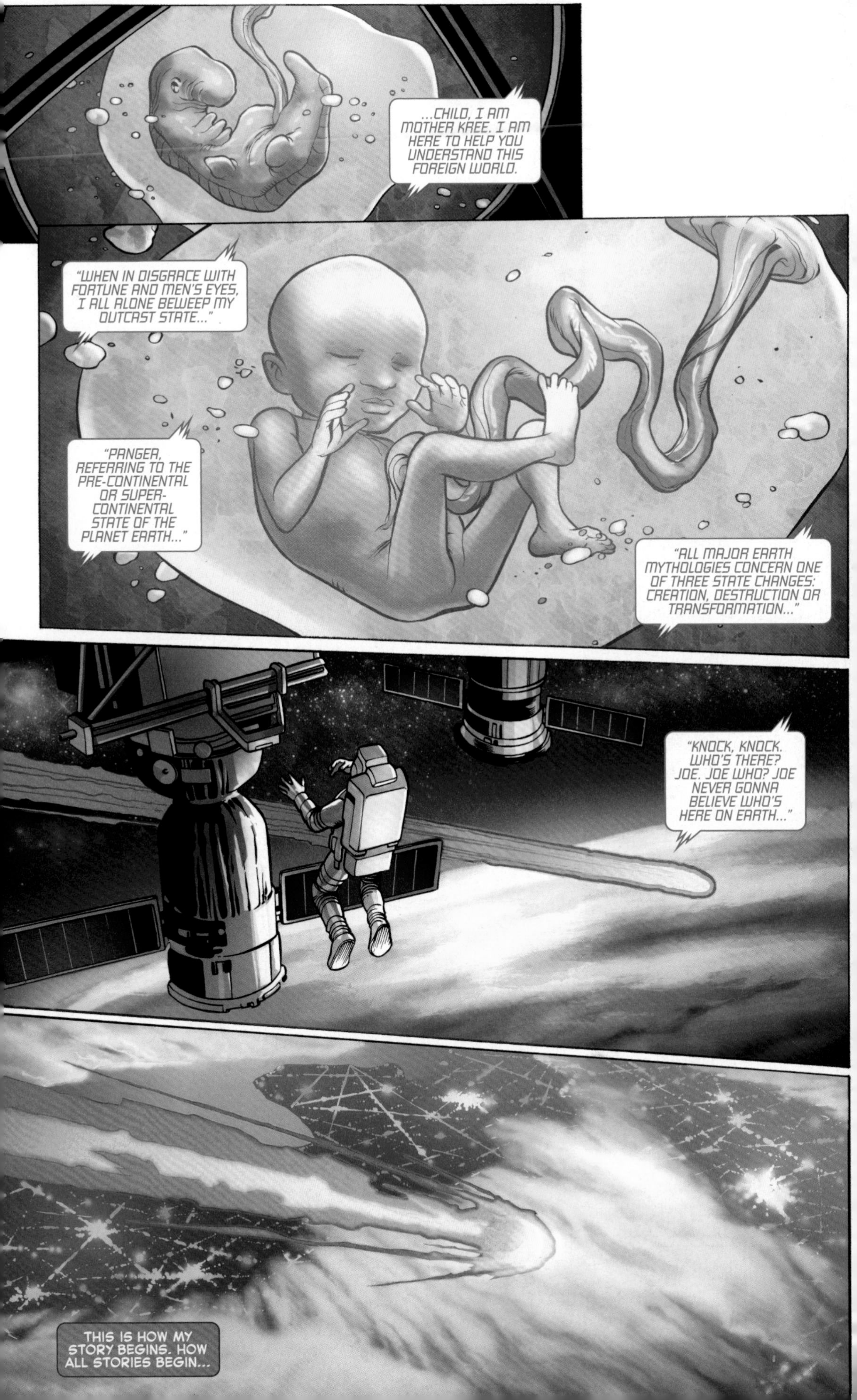
...CHILD, I AM MOTHER KREE. I AM HERE TO HELP YOU UNDERSTAND THIS FOREIGN WORLD.
"WHEN IN DISGRACE WITH FORTUNE AND MEN'S EYES, I ALL ALONE BEWEEP MY OUTCAST STATE..."
"PANGER, REFERRING TO THE PRE-CONTINENTAL OR SUPER-CONTINENTAL STATE OF THE PLANET EARTH..."
"ALL MAJOR EARTH MYTHOLOGIES CONCERN ONE OF THREE STATE CHANGES: CREATION, DESTRUCTION OR TRANSFORMATION..."
"KNOCK, KNOCK. WHO'S THERE? JOE. JOE WHO? JOE NEVER GONNA BELIEVE WHO'S HERE ON EARTH..."
THIS IS HOW MY STORY BEGINS. HOW ALL STORIES BEGIN...

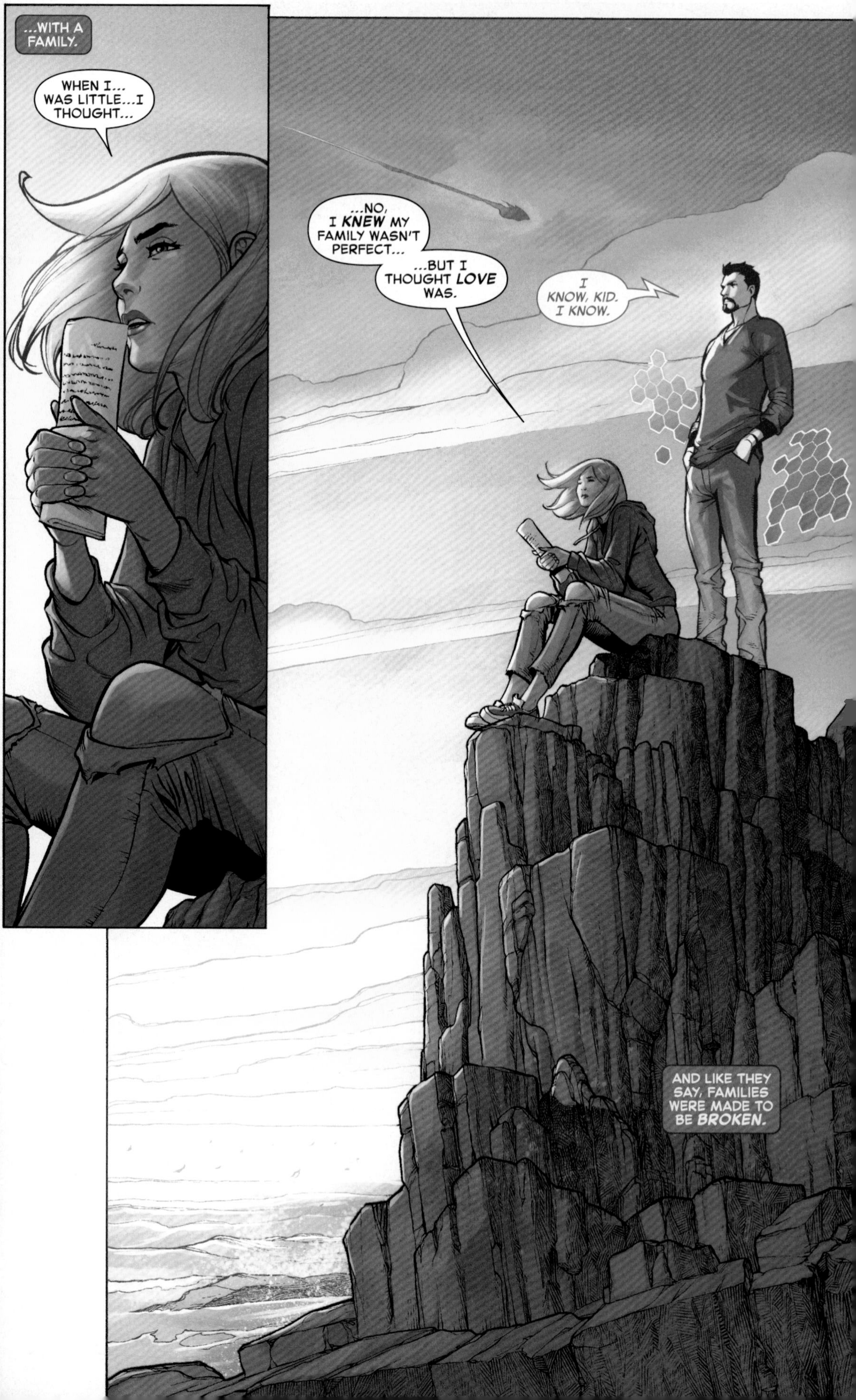
...WITH A FAMILY.
WHEN I... WAS LITTLE...I THOUGHT...
...NO, I KNEW MY FAMILY WASN'T PERFECT...
...BUT I THOUGHT LOVE WAS.
I KNOW, KID. I KNOW.
AND LIKE THEY SAY, FAMILIES WERE MADE TO BE BROKEN.

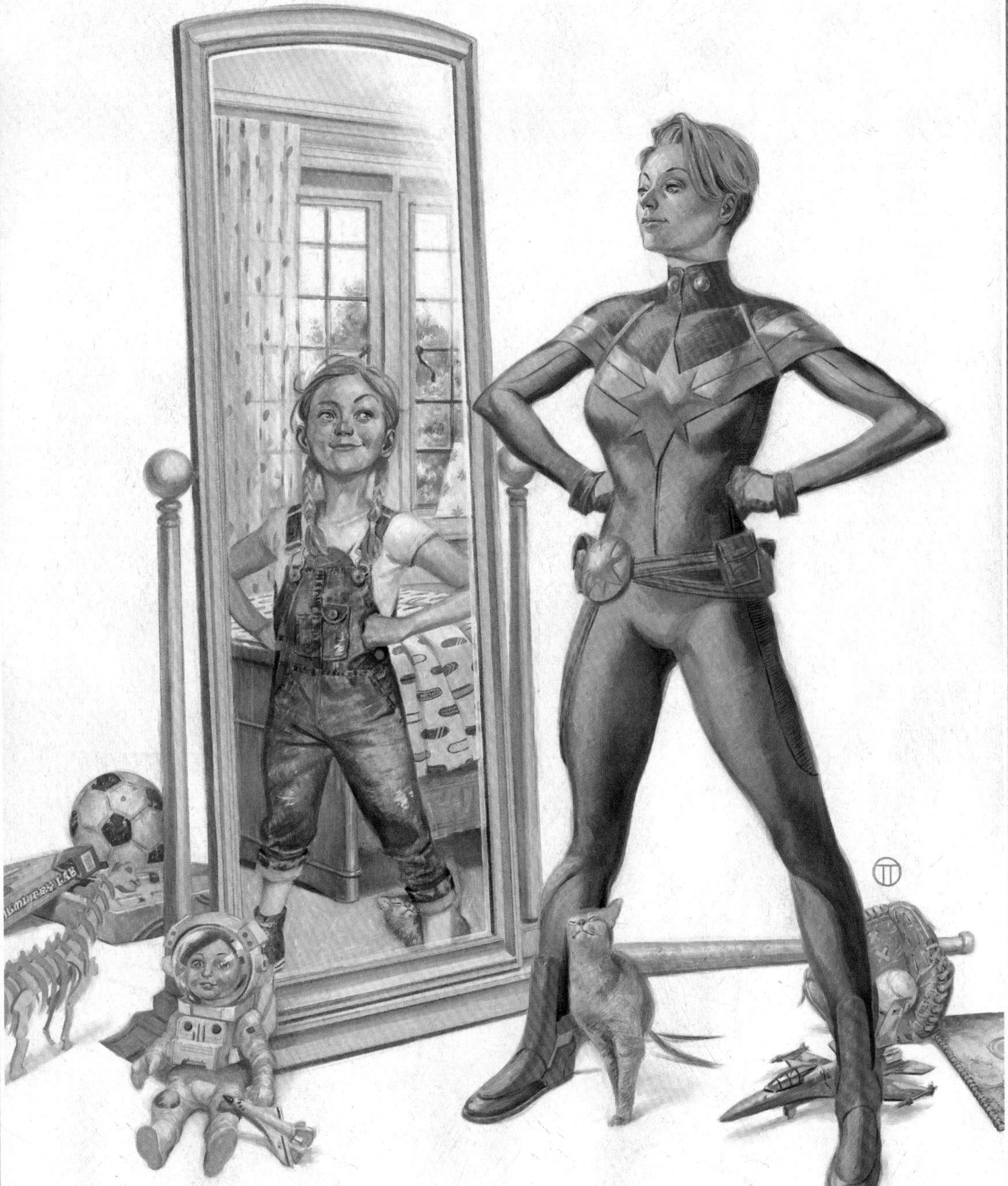

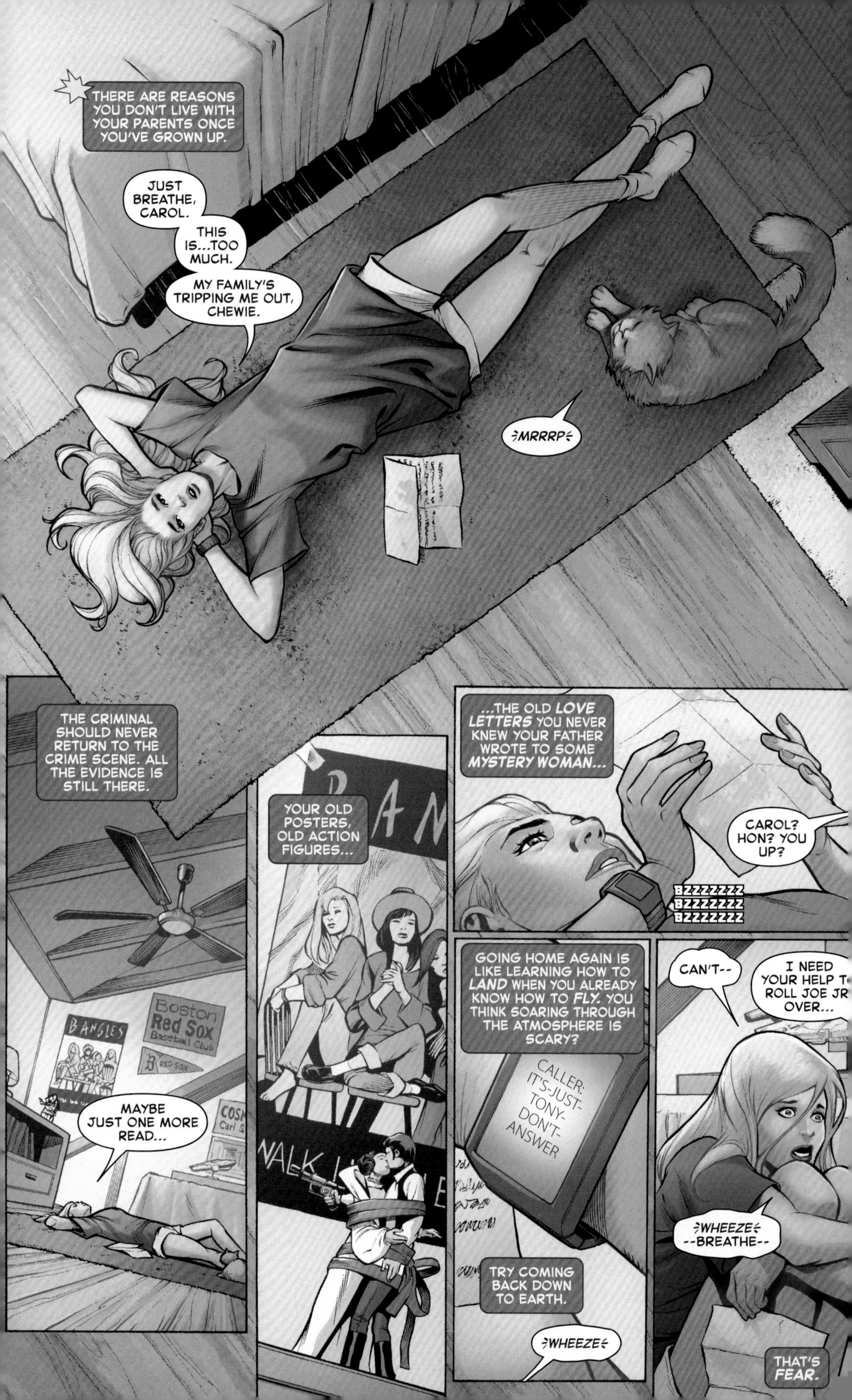
THERE ARE REASONS YOU DON'T LIVE WITH YOUR PARENTS ONCE YOU'VE GROWN UP.
JUST BREATHE, CAROL.
THIS IS...TOO MUCH.
MY FAMILY'S TRIPPING ME OUT, CHEWIE.
MRRRP
THE CRIMINAL SHOULD NEVER RETURN TO THE CRIME SCENE. ALL THE EVIDENCE IS STILL THERE.
Boston Red Sox Baseball Club
BANGLES
MAYBE JUST ONE MORE READ...
YOUR OLD POSTERS, OLD ACTION FIGURES...
...THE OLD LOVE LETTERS YOU NEVER KNEW YOUR FATHER WROTE TO SOME MYSTERY WOMAN...
CAROL? HON? YOU UP?
BZZZZZZZ
BZZZZZZZ
BZZZZZZZ
GOING HOME AGAIN IS LIKE LEARNING HOW TO LAND WHEN YOU ALREADY KNOW HOW TO FLY. YOU THINK SOARING THROUGH THE ATMOSPHERE IS SCARY?
CALLER: IT'S-JUST-TONY-DON'T-ANSWER
TRY COMING BACK DOWN TO EARTH.
WHEEZE
CAN'T--
I NEED YOUR HELP TO ROLL JOE JR OVER...
WHEEZE --BREATHE--
THAT'S FEAR.

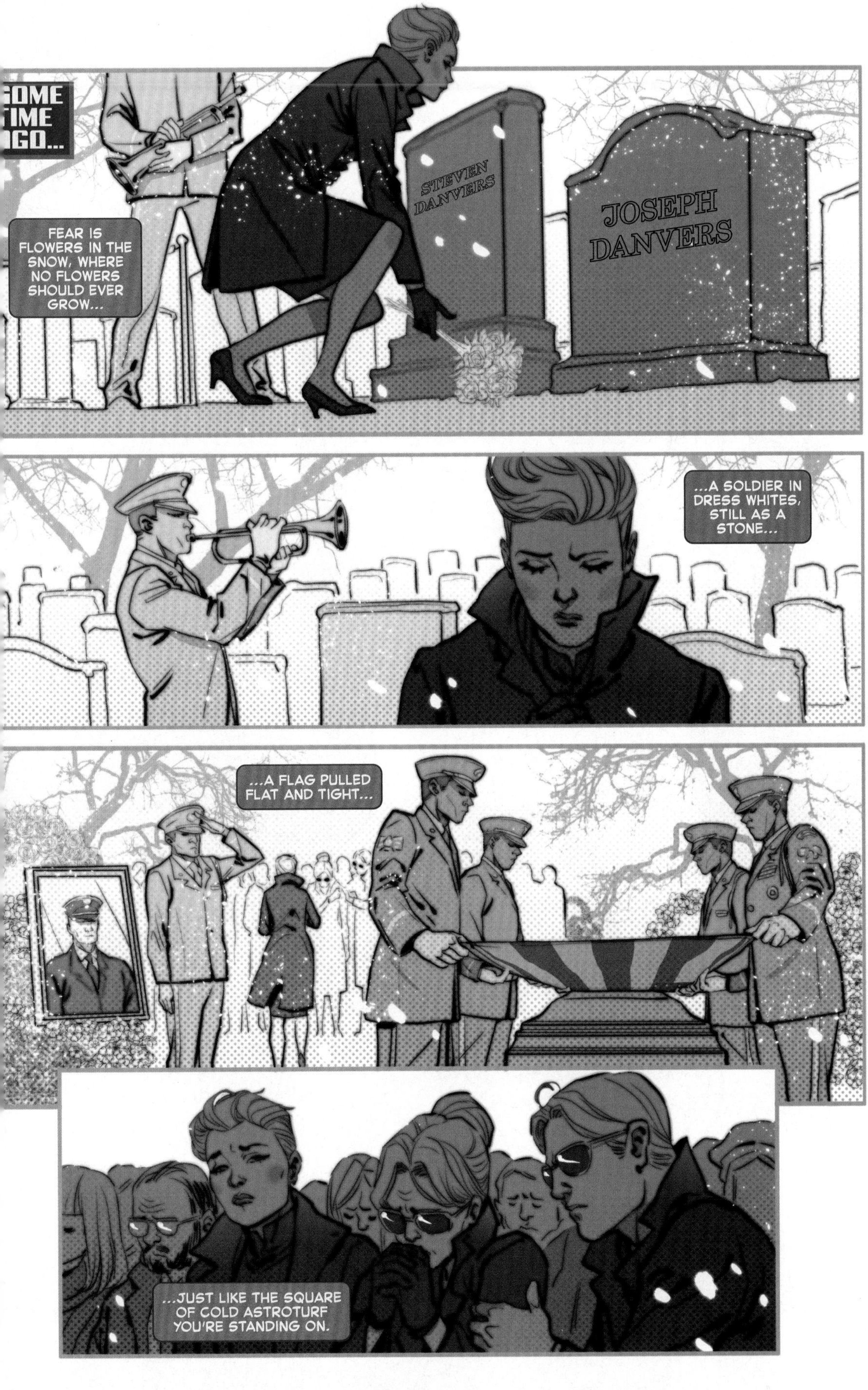
SOME TIME AGO...
FEAR IS FLOWERS IN THE SNOW, WHERE NO FLOWERS SHOULD EVER GROW...
STEVEN DANVERS
JOSEPH DANVERS
...A SOLDIER IN DRESS WHITES, STILL AS A STONE...
...A FLAG PULLED FLAT AND TIGHT...
...JUST LIKE THE SQUARE OF COLD ASTROTURF YOU'RE STANDING ON.

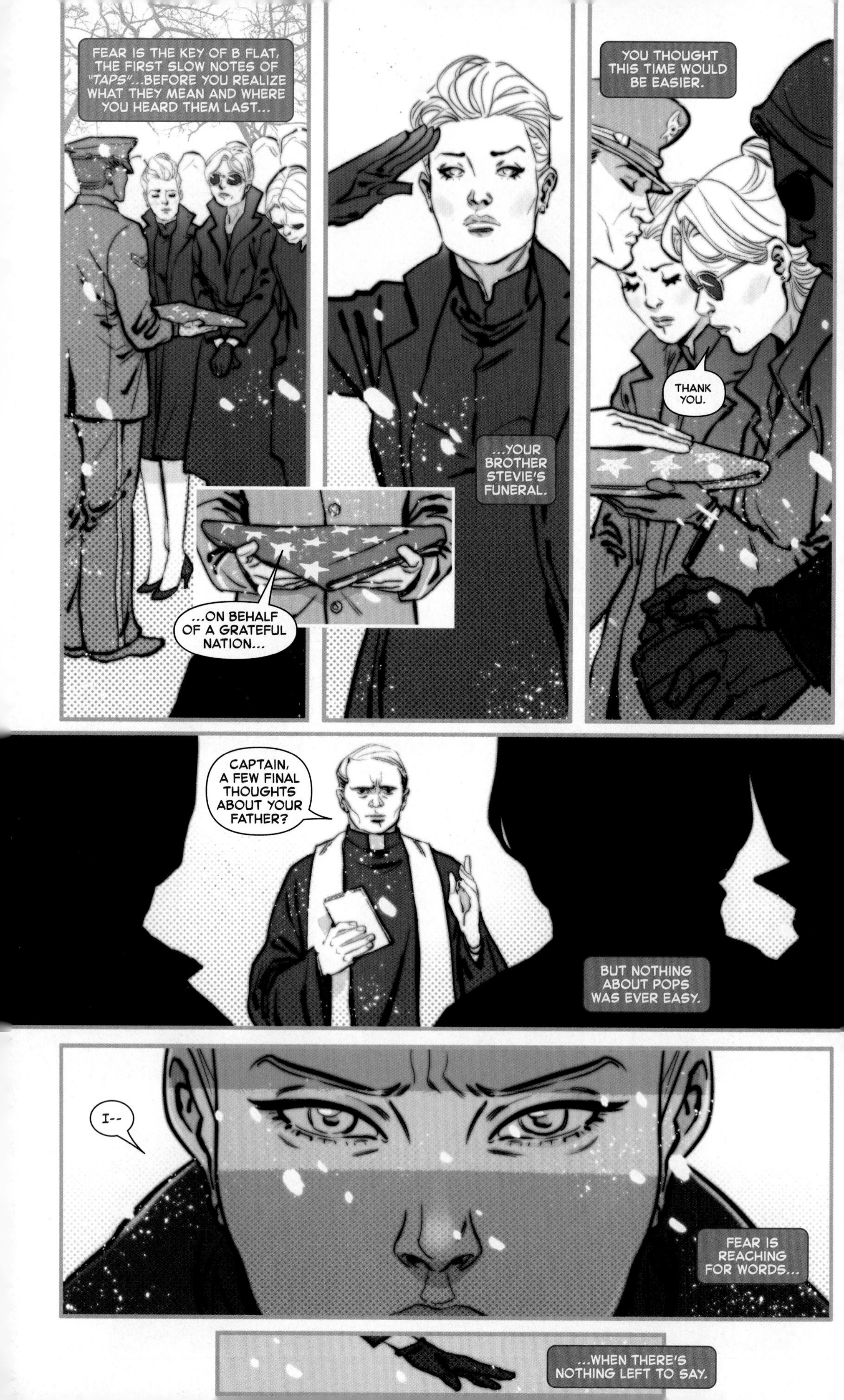
FEAR IS THE KEY OF B FLAT, THE FIRST SLOW NOTES OF "TAPS"...BEFORE YOU REALIZE WHAT THEY MEAN AND WHERE YOU HEARD THEM LAST...
...ON BEHALF OF A GRATEFUL NATION...
...YOUR BROTHER STEVIE'S FUNERAL.
YOU THOUGHT THIS TIME WOULD BE EASIER.
THANK YOU.
CAPTAIN, A FEW FINAL THOUGHTS ABOUT YOUR FATHER?
BUT NOTHING ABOUT POPS WAS EVER EASY.
I--
FEAR IS REACHING FOR WORDS...
...WHEN THERE'S NOTHING LEFT TO SAY.

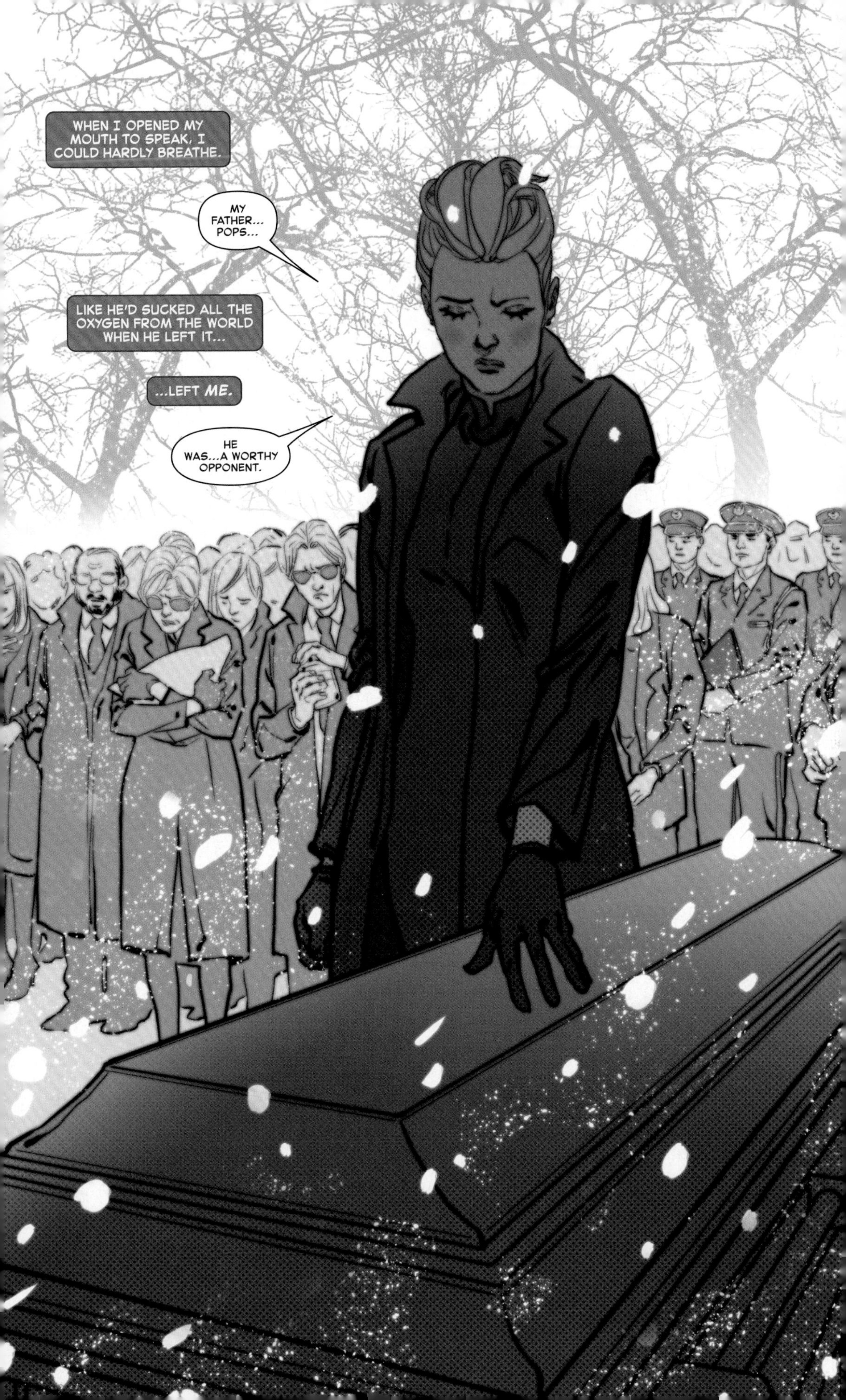
WHEN I OPENED MY MOUTH TO SPEAK, I COULD HARDLY BREATHE.
MY FATHER... POPS...
LIKE HE'D SUCKED ALL THE OXYGEN FROM THE WORLD WHEN HE LEFT IT...
...LEFT *ME.*
HE WAS...A WORTHY OPPONENT.

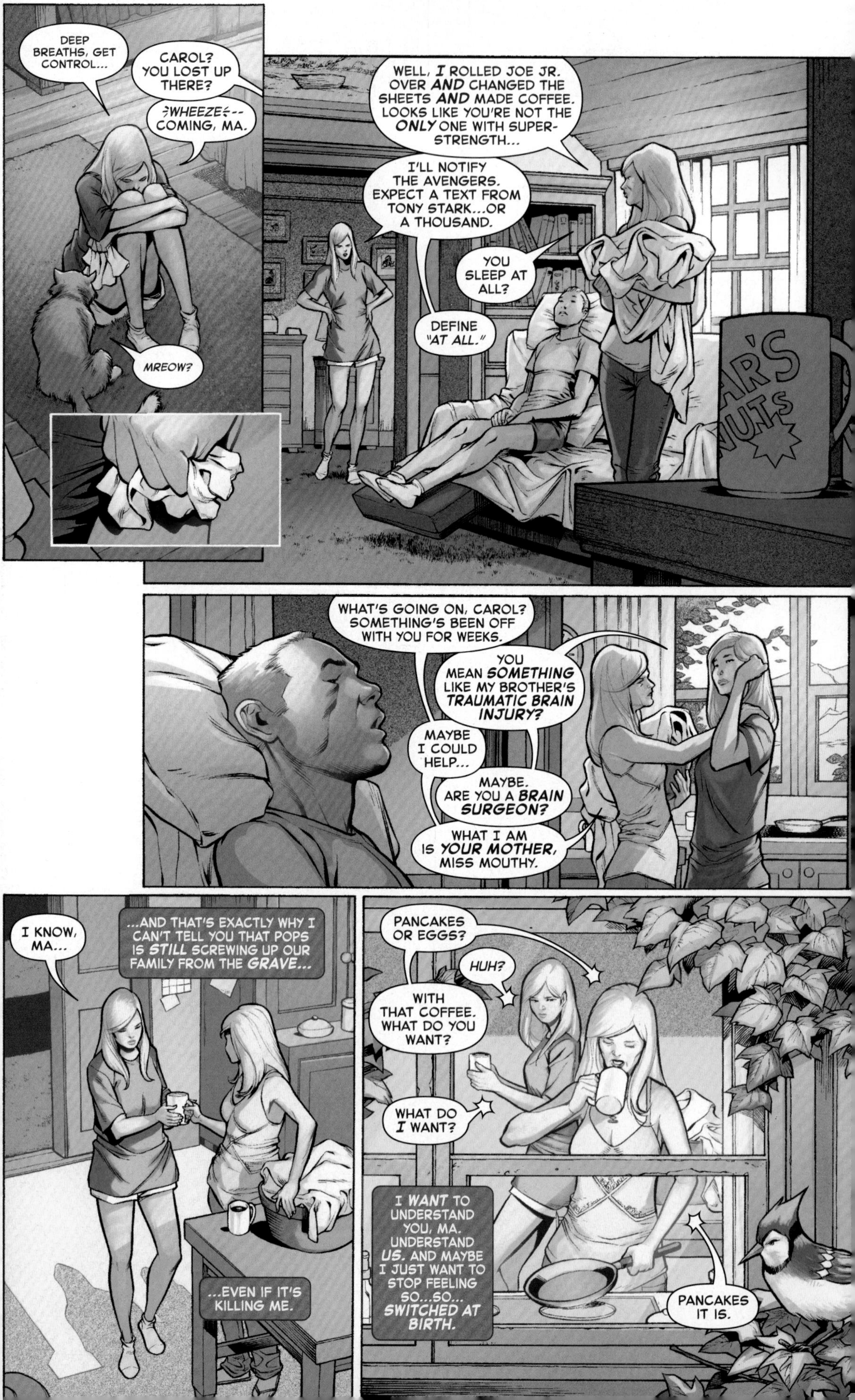
DEEP BREATHS, GET CONTROL...
CAROL? YOU LOST UP THERE?
⇒WHEEZE⇐-- COMING, MA.
MREOW?
WELL, I ROLLED JOE JR. OVER AND CHANGED THE SHEETS AND MADE COFFEE. LOOKS LIKE YOU'RE NOT THE ONLY ONE WITH SUPER-STRENGTH...
I'LL NOTIFY THE AVENGERS. EXPECT A TEXT FROM TONY STARK...OR A THOUSAND.
YOU SLEEP AT ALL?
DEFINE "AT ALL."
WHAT'S GOING ON, CAROL? SOMETHING'S BEEN OFF WITH YOU FOR WEEKS.
YOU MEAN SOMETHING LIKE MY BROTHER'S TRAUMATIC BRAIN INJURY?
MAYBE I COULD HELP...
MAYBE. ARE YOU A BRAIN SURGEON?
WHAT I AM IS YOUR MOTHER, MISS MOUTHY.
I KNOW, MA...
...AND THAT'S EXACTLY WHY I CAN'T TELL YOU THAT POPS IS STILL SCREWING UP OUR FAMILY FROM THE GRAVE...
...EVEN IF IT'S KILLING ME.
PANCAKES OR EGGS?
HUH?
WITH THAT COFFEE. WHAT DO YOU WANT?
WHAT DO I WANT?
I WANT TO UNDERSTAND YOU, MA. UNDERSTAND US. AND MAYBE I JUST WANT TO STOP FEELING SO...SO... SWITCHED AT BIRTH.
PANCAKES IT IS.

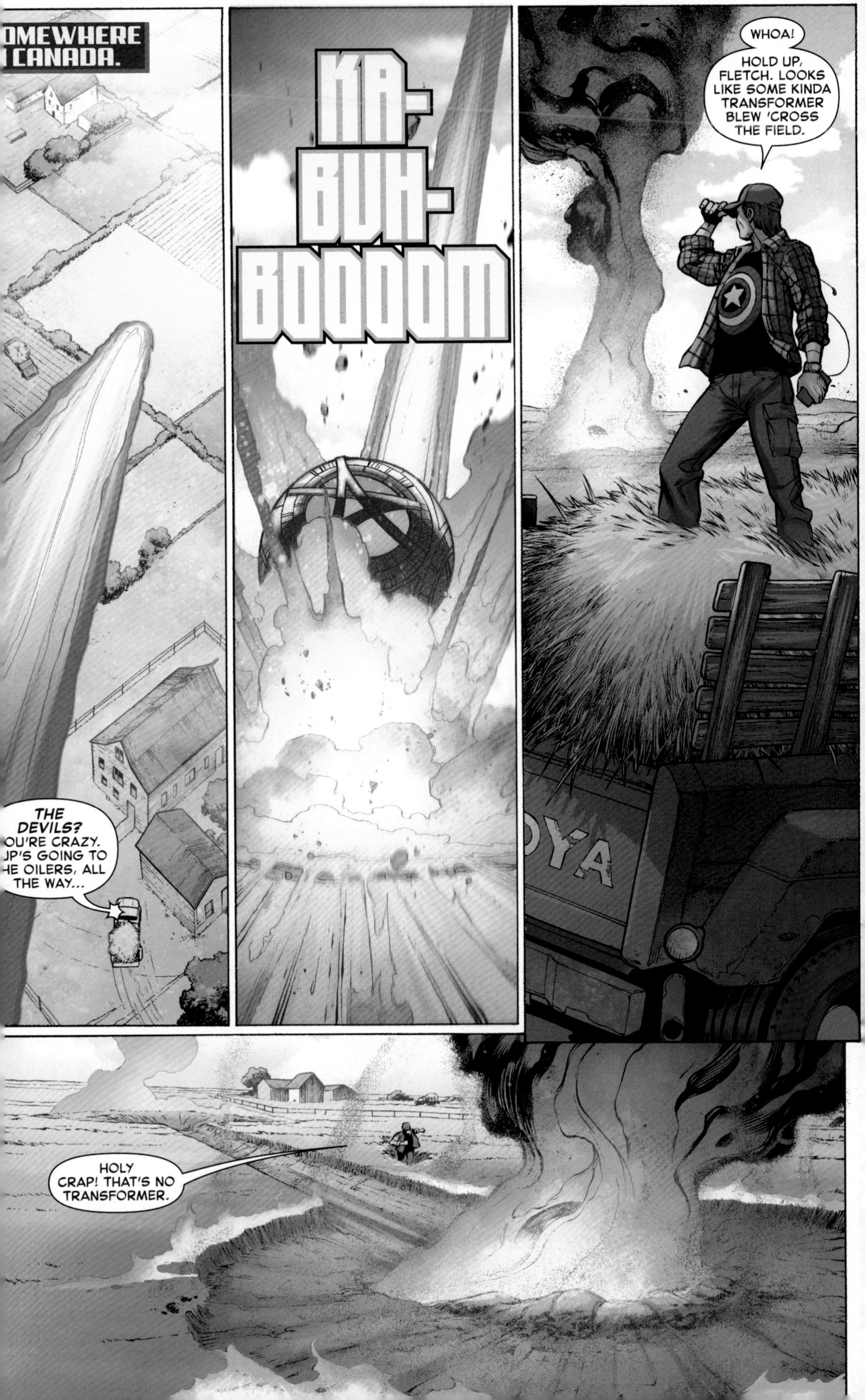

OMEWHERE
CANADA.
KA-BUH-BOOOOM
WHOA!
HOLD UP, FLETCH. LOOKS LIKE SOME KINDA TRANSFORMER BLEW 'CROSS THE FIELD.
THE DEVILS? OU'RE CRAZY. P'S GOING TO HE OILERS, ALL THE WAY...
OYA
HOLY CRAP! THAT'S NO TRANSFORMER.

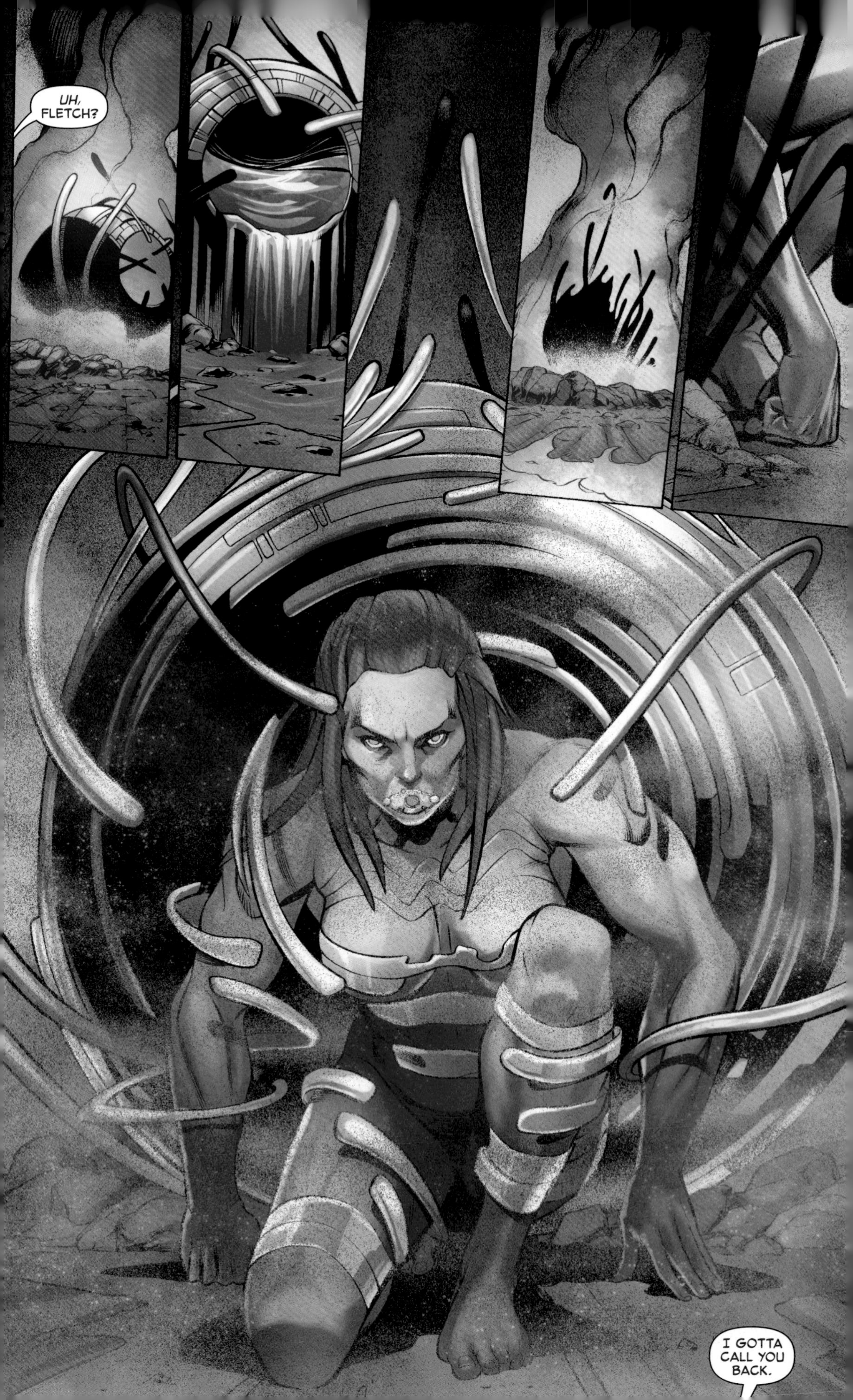
UH, FLETCH?
I GOTTA CALL YOU BACK.

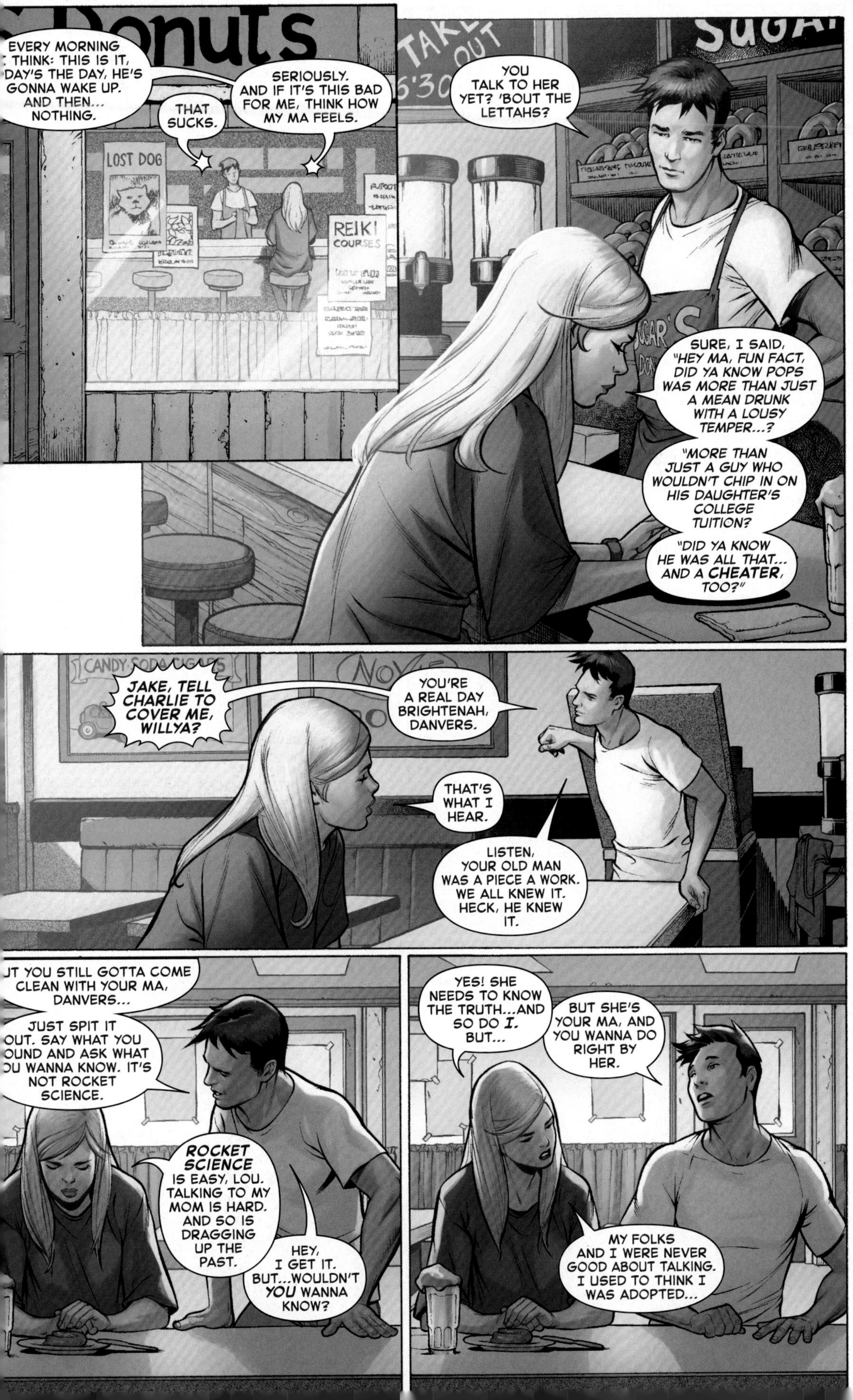
Donuts
EVERY MORNING I THINK: THIS IS IT, TODAY'S THE DAY, HE'S GONNA WAKE UP. AND THEN... NOTHING.
THAT SUCKS.
SERIOUSLY. AND IF IT'S THIS BAD FOR ME, THINK HOW MY MA FEELS.
LOST DOG
REIKI COURSES
TAKE OUT
SUGAR
YOU TALK TO HER YET? 'BOUT THE LETTAHS?
SURE, I SAID, "HEY MA, FUN FACT, DID YA KNOW POPS WAS MORE THAN JUST A MEAN DRUNK WITH A LOUSY TEMPER...?
"MORE THAN JUST A GUY WHO WOULDN'T CHIP IN ON HIS DAUGHTER'S COLLEGE TUITION?
"DID YA KNOW HE WAS ALL THAT... AND A CHEATER, TOO?"
CANDY·SODA·CIGARS
JAKE, TELL CHARLIE TO COVER ME, WILLYA?
YOU'RE A REAL DAY BRIGHTENAH, DANVERS.
THAT'S WHAT I HEAR.
LISTEN, YOUR OLD MAN WAS A PIECE A WORK. WE ALL KNEW IT. HECK, HE KNEW IT.
UT YOU STILL GOTTA COME CLEAN WITH YOUR MA, DANVERS...
JUST SPIT IT OUT. SAY WHAT YOU OUND AND ASK WHAT OU WANNA KNOW. IT'S NOT ROCKET SCIENCE.
ROCKET SCIENCE IS EASY, LOU. TALKING TO MY MOM IS HARD. AND SO IS DRAGGING UP THE PAST.
HEY, I GET IT. BUT...WOULDN'T YOU WANNA KNOW?
YES! SHE NEEDS TO KNOW THE TRUTH...AND SO DO I. BUT...
BUT SHE'S YOUR MA, AND YOU WANNA DO RIGHT BY HER.
MY FOLKS AND I WERE NEVER GOOD ABOUT TALKING. I USED TO THINK I WAS ADOPTED...

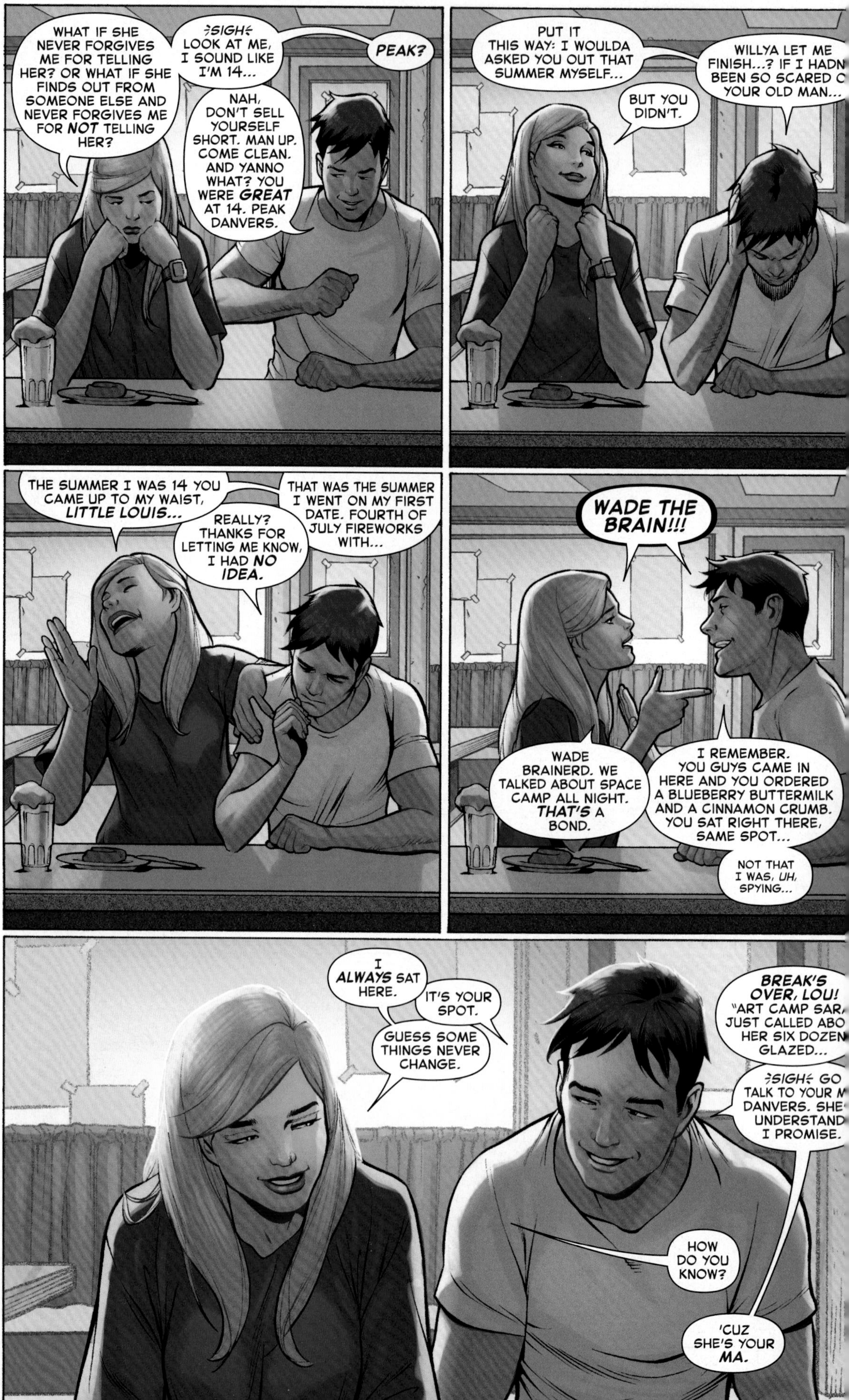
WHAT IF SHE NEVER FORGIVES ME FOR TELLING HER? OR WHAT IF SHE FINDS OUT FROM SOMEONE ELSE AND NEVER FORGIVES ME FOR NOT TELLING HER?
⸗SIGH⸗ LOOK AT ME, I SOUND LIKE I'M 14...
NAH, DON'T SELL YOURSELF SHORT. MAN UP. COME CLEAN. AND YANNO WHAT? YOU WERE GREAT AT 14. PEAK DANVERS.
PEAK?
PUT IT THIS WAY: I WOULDA ASKED YOU OUT THAT SUMMER MYSELF...
BUT YOU DIDN'T.
WILLYA LET ME FINISH...? IF I HADN BEEN SO SCARED O YOUR OLD MAN...
THE SUMMER I WAS 14 YOU CAME UP TO MY WAIST, LITTLE LOUIS...
REALLY? THANKS FOR LETTING ME KNOW, I HAD NO IDEA.
THAT WAS THE SUMMER I WENT ON MY FIRST DATE. FOURTH OF JULY FIREWORKS WITH...
WADE THE BRAIN!!!
WADE BRAINERD. WE TALKED ABOUT SPACE CAMP ALL NIGHT. THAT'S A BOND.
I REMEMBER. YOU GUYS CAME IN HERE AND YOU ORDERED A BLUEBERRY BUTTERMILK AND A CINNAMON CRUMB. YOU SAT RIGHT THERE, SAME SPOT...
NOT THAT I WAS, UH, SPYING...
I ALWAYS SAT HERE.
IT'S YOUR SPOT.
GUESS SOME THINGS NEVER CHANGE.
BREAK'S OVER, LOU! "ART CAMP SAR JUST CALLED ABO HER SIX DOZEN GLAZED...
⸗SIGH⸗ GO TALK TO YOUR M DANVERS. SHE UNDERSTAND I PROMISE.
HOW DO YOU KNOW?
'CUZ SHE'S YOUR MA.

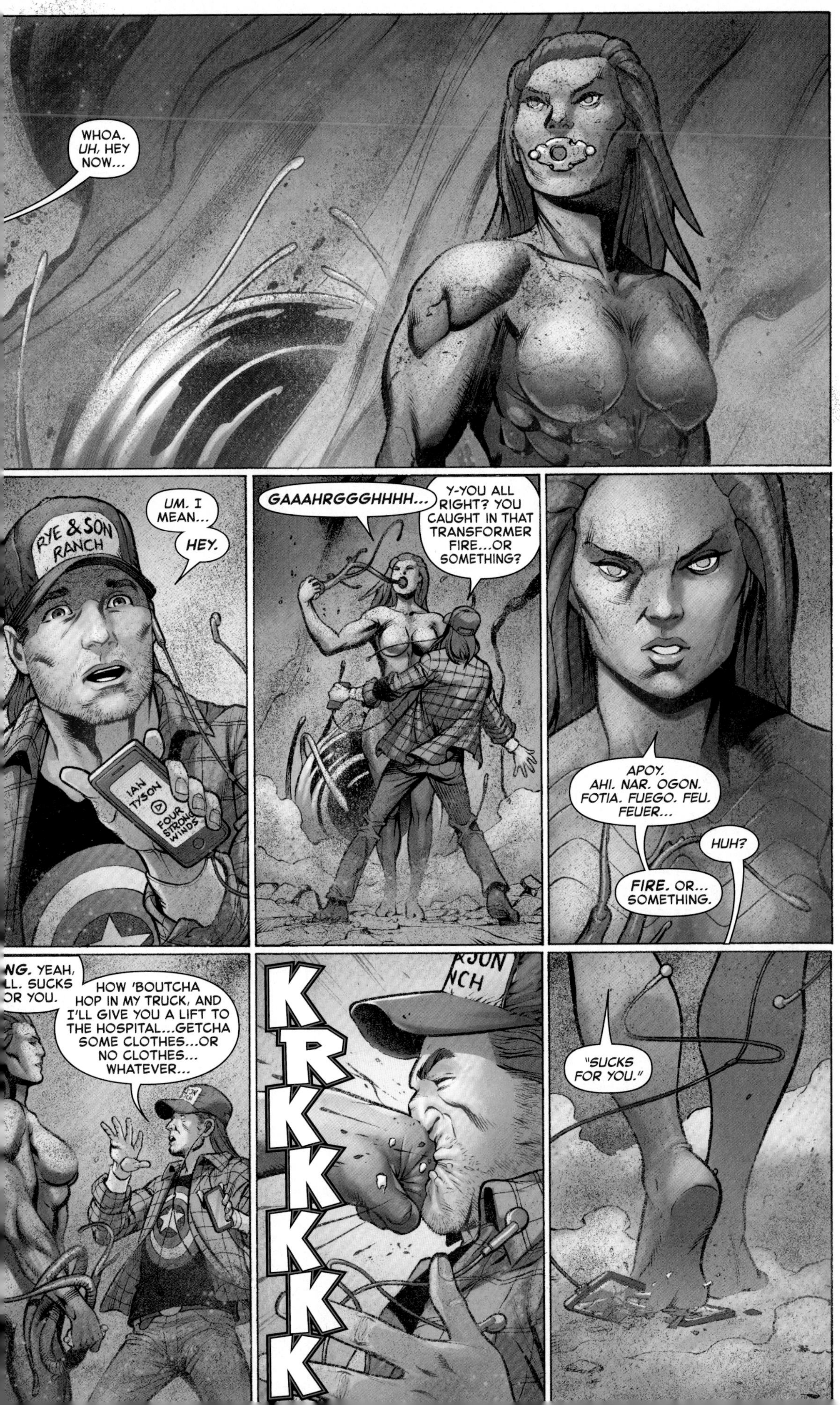
WHOA. UH, HEY NOW...
UM. I MEAN... HEY.
RYE & SON RANCH
IAN TYSON FOUR STRONG WINDS
GAAAHRGGGHHHH...
Y-YOU ALL RIGHT? YOU CAUGHT IN THAT TRANSFORMER FIRE...OR SOMETHING?
APOY. AHI. NAR. OGON. FOTIA. FUEGO. FEU. FEUER...
HUH?
FIRE. OR... SOMETHING.
NG. YEAH, LL. SUCKS OR YOU.
HOW 'BOUTCHA HOP IN MY TRUCK, AND I'LL GIVE YOU A LIFT TO THE HOSPITAL...GETCHA SOME CLOTHES...OR NO CLOTHES... WHATEVER...
KRKKKK
"SUCKS FOR YOU."

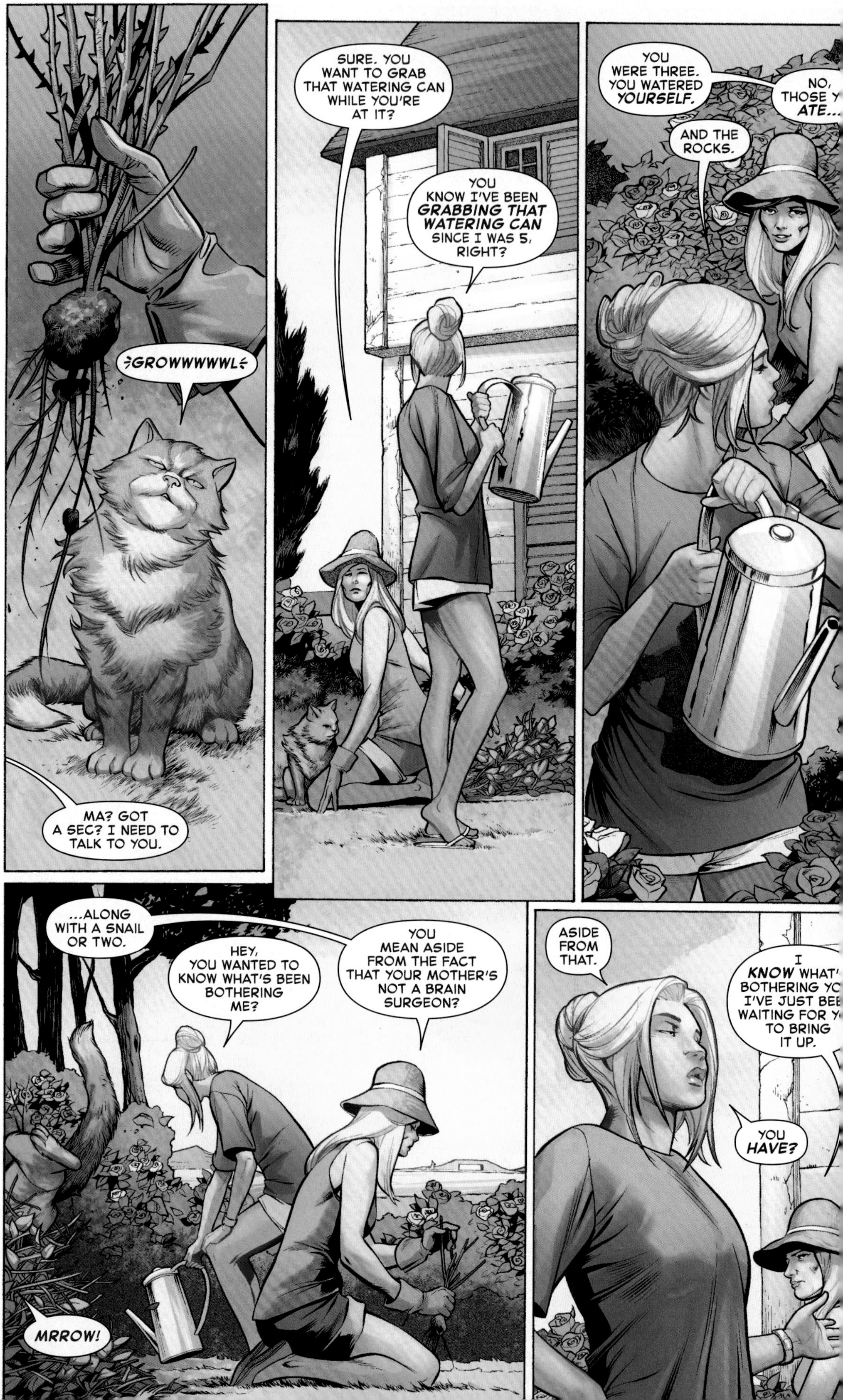
GROWWWWWL
MA? GOT A SEC? I NEED TO TALK TO YOU.
SURE. YOU WANT TO GRAB THAT WATERING CAN WHILE YOU'RE AT IT?
YOU KNOW I'VE BEEN GRABBING THAT WATERING CAN SINCE I WAS 5, RIGHT?
YOU WERE THREE. YOU WATERED YOURSELF.
NO, THOSE Y ATE...
AND THE ROCKS.
...ALONG WITH A SNAIL OR TWO.
HEY, YOU WANTED TO KNOW WHAT'S BEEN BOTHERING ME?
YOU MEAN ASIDE FROM THE FACT THAT YOUR MOTHER'S NOT A BRAIN SURGEON?
MRROW!
ASIDE FROM THAT.
I KNOW WHAT' BOTHERING YO I'VE JUST BEE WAITING FOR Y TO BRING IT UP.
YOU HAVE?

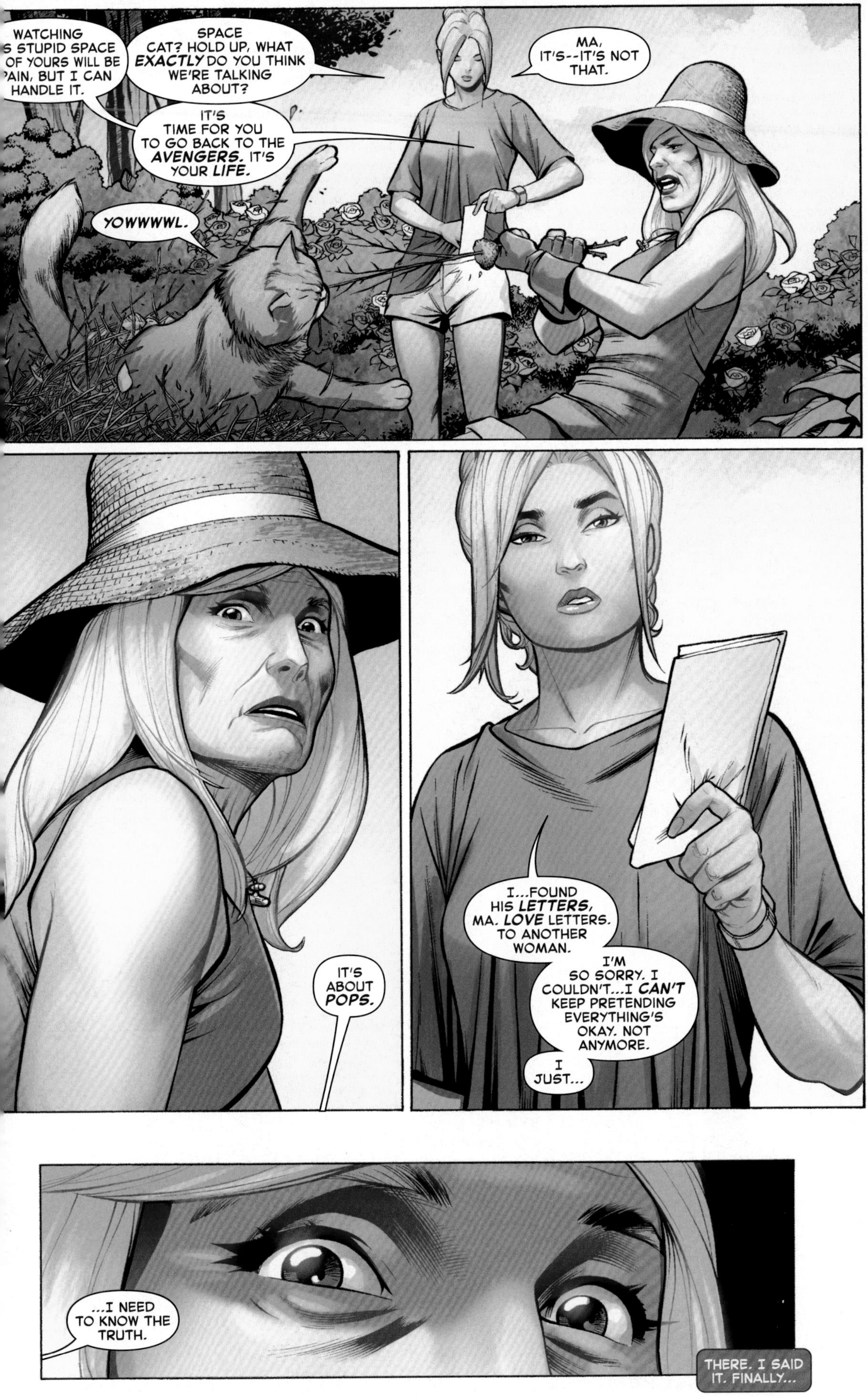
WATCHING S STUPID SPACE OF YOURS WILL BE PAIN, BUT I CAN HANDLE IT.
SPACE CAT? HOLD UP, WHAT EXACTLY DO YOU THINK WE'RE TALKING ABOUT?
MA, IT'S--IT'S NOT THAT.
IT'S TIME FOR YOU TO GO BACK TO THE AVENGERS. IT'S YOUR LIFE.
YOWWWWL.
IT'S ABOUT POPS.
I...FOUND HIS LETTERS, MA. LOVE LETTERS. TO ANOTHER WOMAN.
I'M SO SORRY. I COULDN'T...I CAN'T KEEP PRETENDING EVERYTHING'S OKAY. NOT ANYMORE.
I JUST...
...I NEED TO KNOW THE TRUTH.
THERE. I SAID IT. FINALLY...

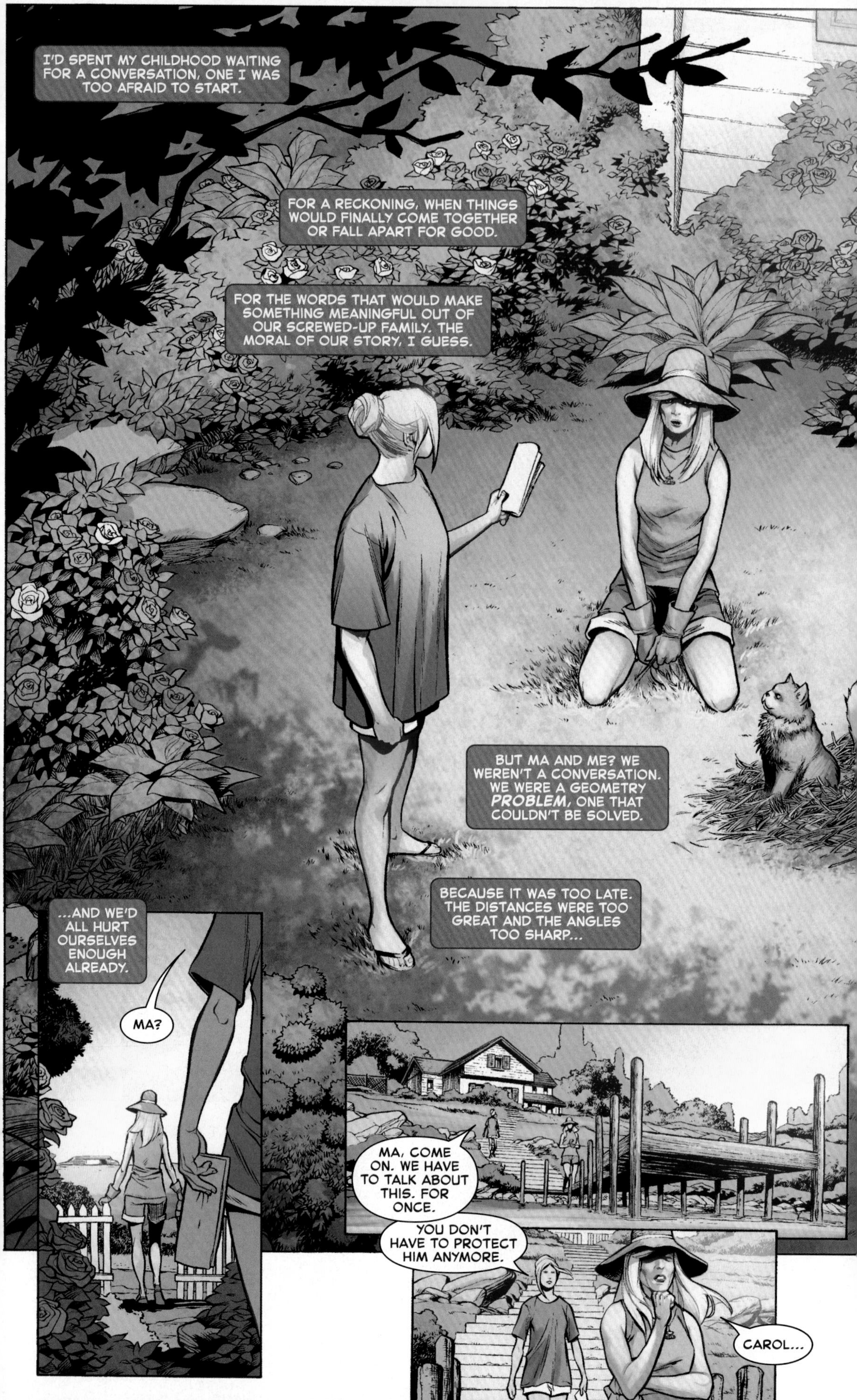
I'D SPENT MY CHILDHOOD WAITING FOR A CONVERSATION, ONE I WAS TOO AFRAID TO START.
FOR A RECKONING, WHEN THINGS WOULD FINALLY COME TOGETHER OR FALL APART FOR GOOD.
FOR THE WORDS THAT WOULD MAKE SOMETHING MEANINGFUL OUT OF OUR SCREWED-UP FAMILY. THE MORAL OF OUR STORY, I GUESS.
BUT MA AND ME? WE WEREN'T A CONVERSATION. WE WERE A GEOMETRY *PROBLEM,* ONE THAT COULDN'T BE SOLVED.
BECAUSE IT WAS TOO LATE. THE DISTANCES WERE TOO GREAT AND THE ANGLES TOO SHARP...
...AND WE'D ALL HURT OURSELVES ENOUGH ALREADY.
MA?
MA, COME ON. WE HAVE TO TALK ABOUT THIS. FOR ONCE.
YOU DON'T HAVE TO PROTECT HIM ANYMORE.
CAROL...

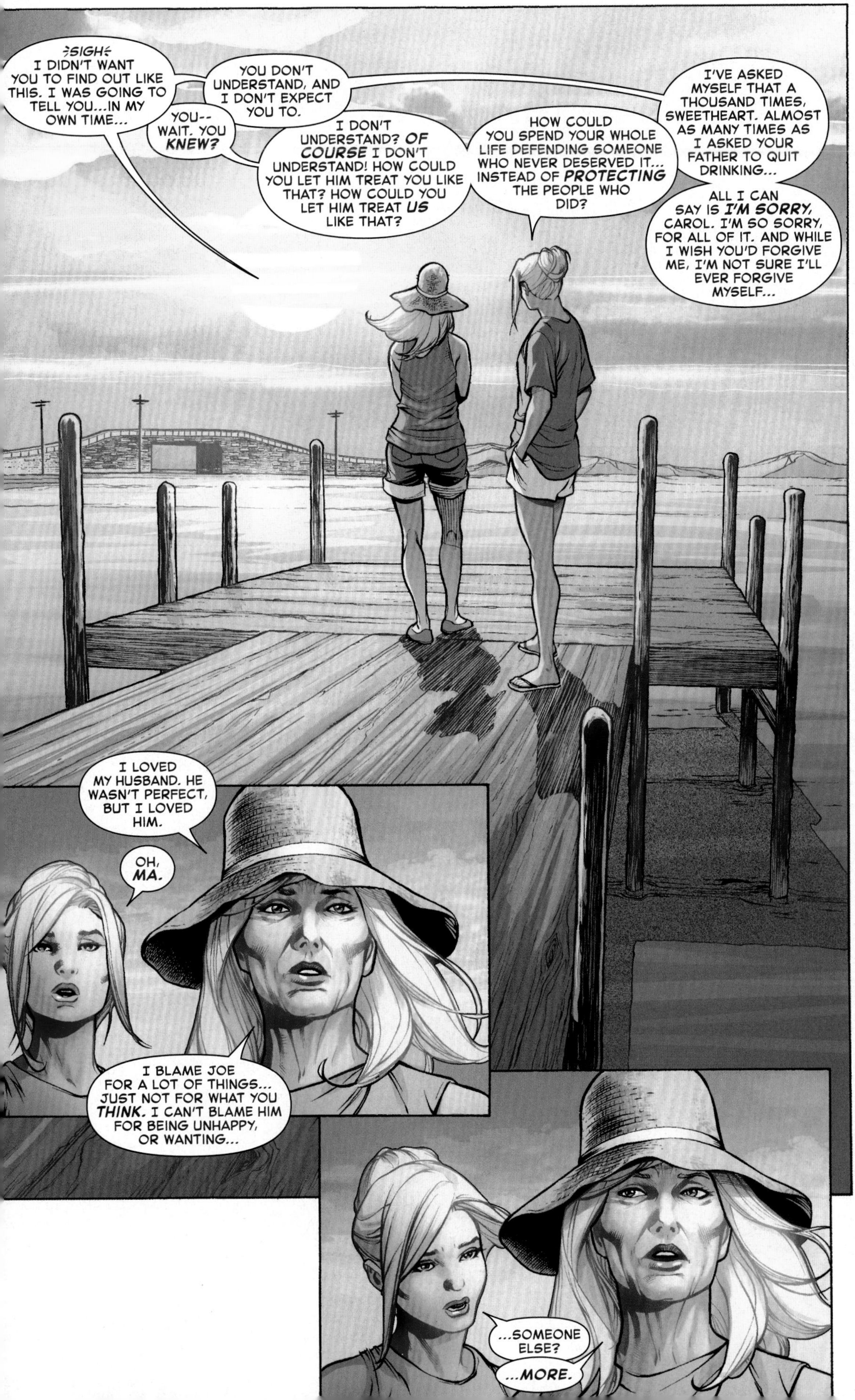

SIGH I DIDN'T WANT YOU TO FIND OUT LIKE THIS. I WAS GOING TO TELL YOU...IN MY OWN TIME...
YOU DON'T UNDERSTAND, AND I DON'T EXPECT YOU TO.
YOU-- WAIT. YOU KNEW?
I DON'T UNDERSTAND? OF COURSE I DON'T UNDERSTAND! HOW COULD YOU LET HIM TREAT YOU LIKE THAT? HOW COULD YOU LET HIM TREAT US LIKE THAT?
HOW COULD YOU SPEND YOUR WHOLE LIFE DEFENDING SOMEONE WHO NEVER DESERVED IT... INSTEAD OF PROTECTING THE PEOPLE WHO DID?
I'VE ASKED MYSELF THAT A THOUSAND TIMES, SWEETHEART. ALMOST AS MANY TIMES AS I ASKED YOUR FATHER TO QUIT DRINKING...
ALL I CAN SAY IS I'M SORRY, CAROL. I'M SO SORRY, FOR ALL OF IT. AND WHILE I WISH YOU'D FORGIVE ME, I'M NOT SURE I'LL EVER FORGIVE MYSELF...
I LOVED MY HUSBAND. HE WASN'T PERFECT, BUT I LOVED HIM.
OH, MA.
I BLAME JOE FOR A LOT OF THINGS... JUST NOT FOR WHAT YOU THINK. I CAN'T BLAME HIM FOR BEING UNHAPPY, OR WANTING...
...SOMEONE ELSE?
...MORE.

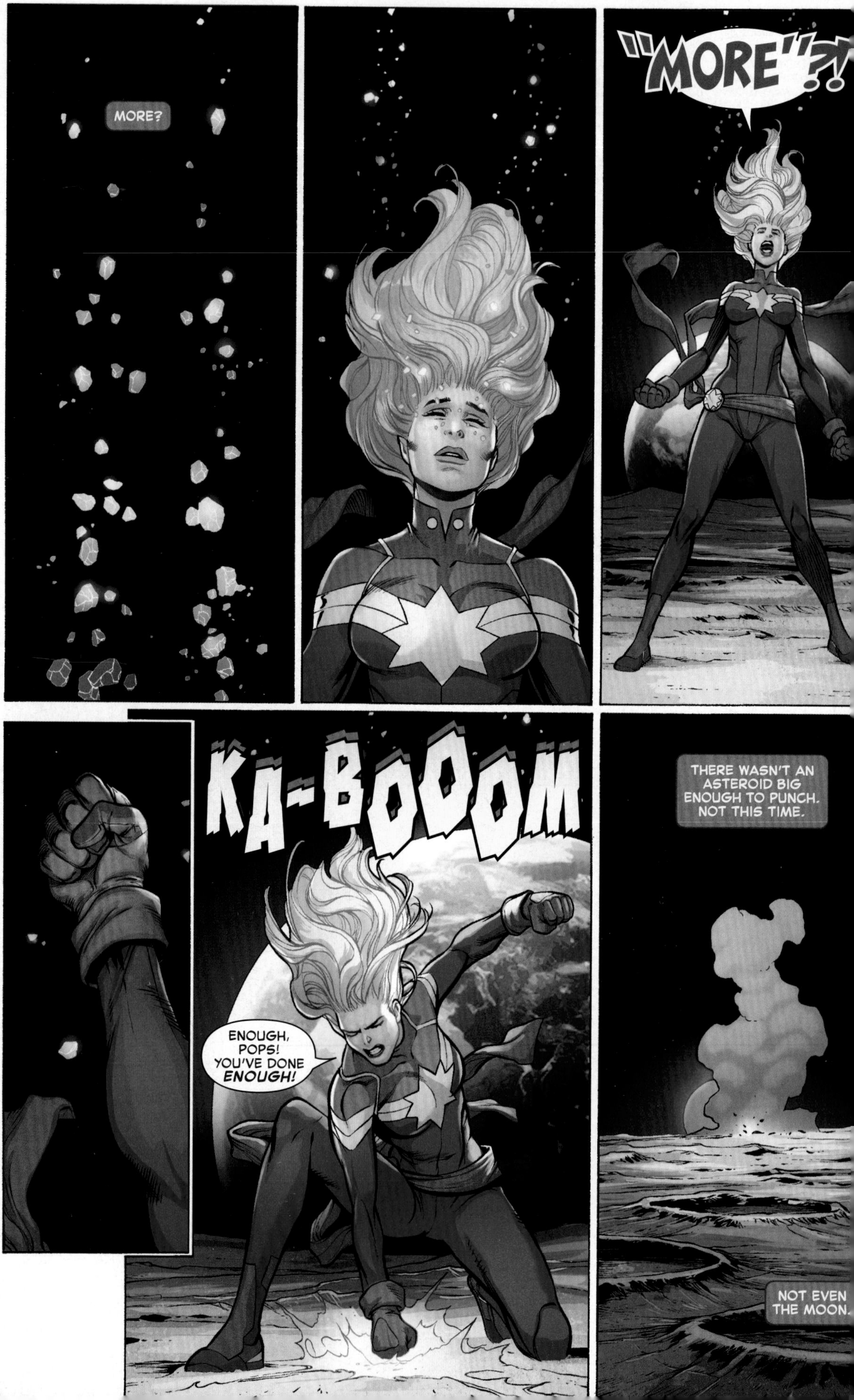
MORE?
"MORE"?!
KA-BOOOM
ENOUGH, POPS! YOU'VE DONE *ENOUGH!*
THERE WASN'T AN ASTEROID BIG ENOUGH TO PUNCH. NOT THIS TIME.
NOT EVEN THE MOON.

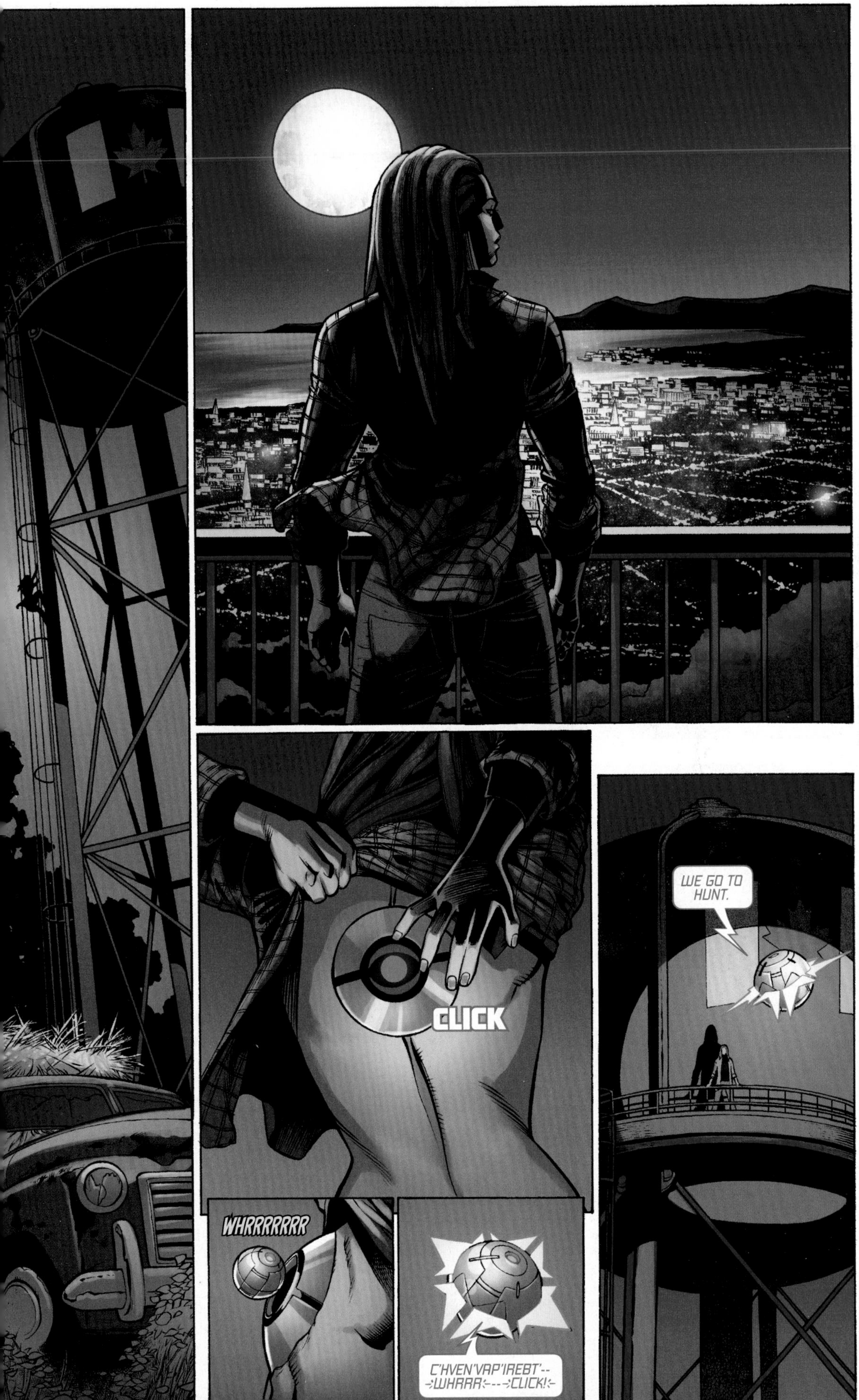
CLICK
WHRRRRRRR
C'HVEN'VAP'IREBT'--
--WHRRR---CLICK!-
WE GO TO HUNT.

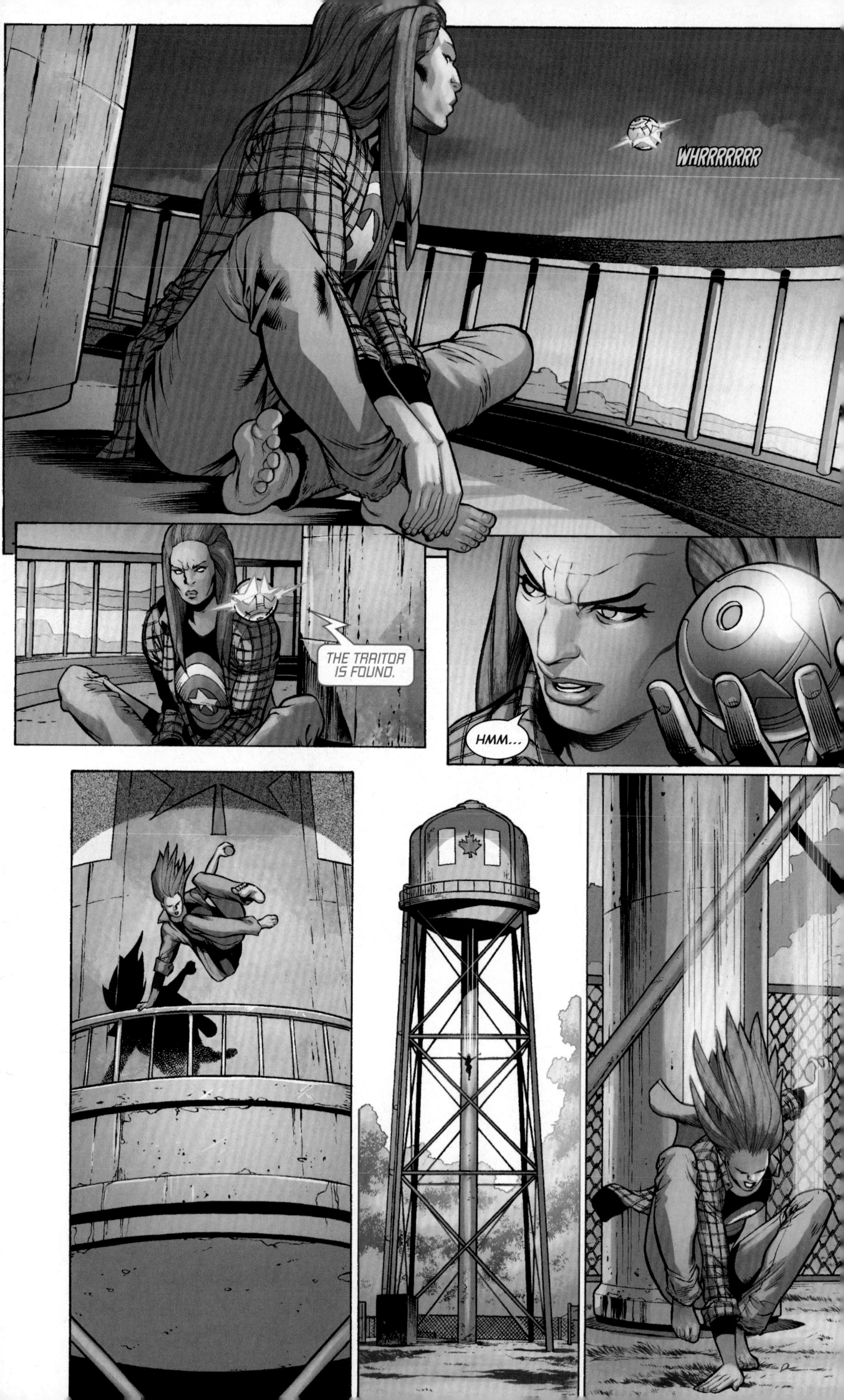
WHRRRRRRR
THE TRAITOR IS FOUND.
HMM...

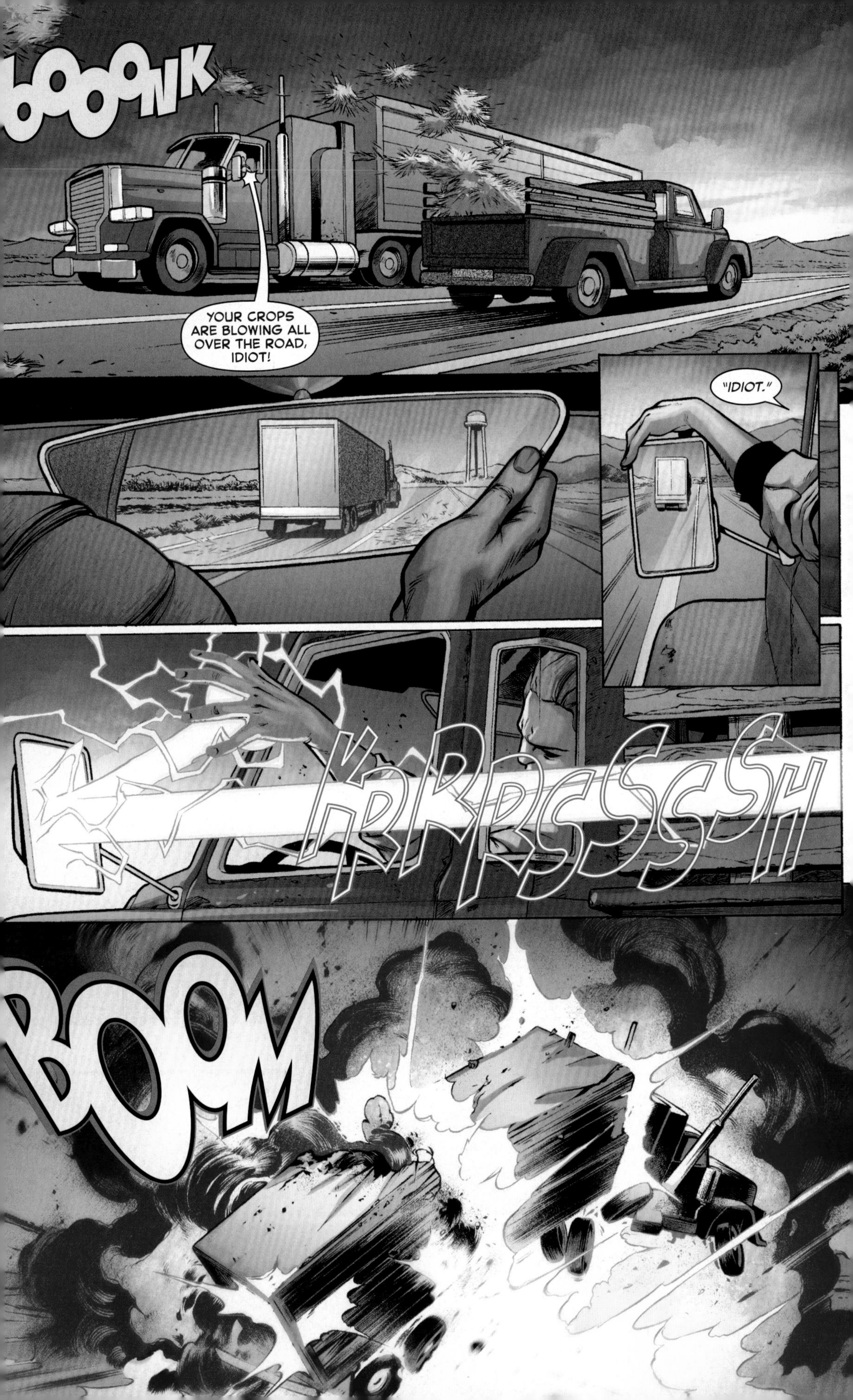
BOOONK
YOUR CROPS ARE BLOWING ALL OVER THE ROAD, IDIOT!
"IDIOT."
KRRRSSSSH
BOOM

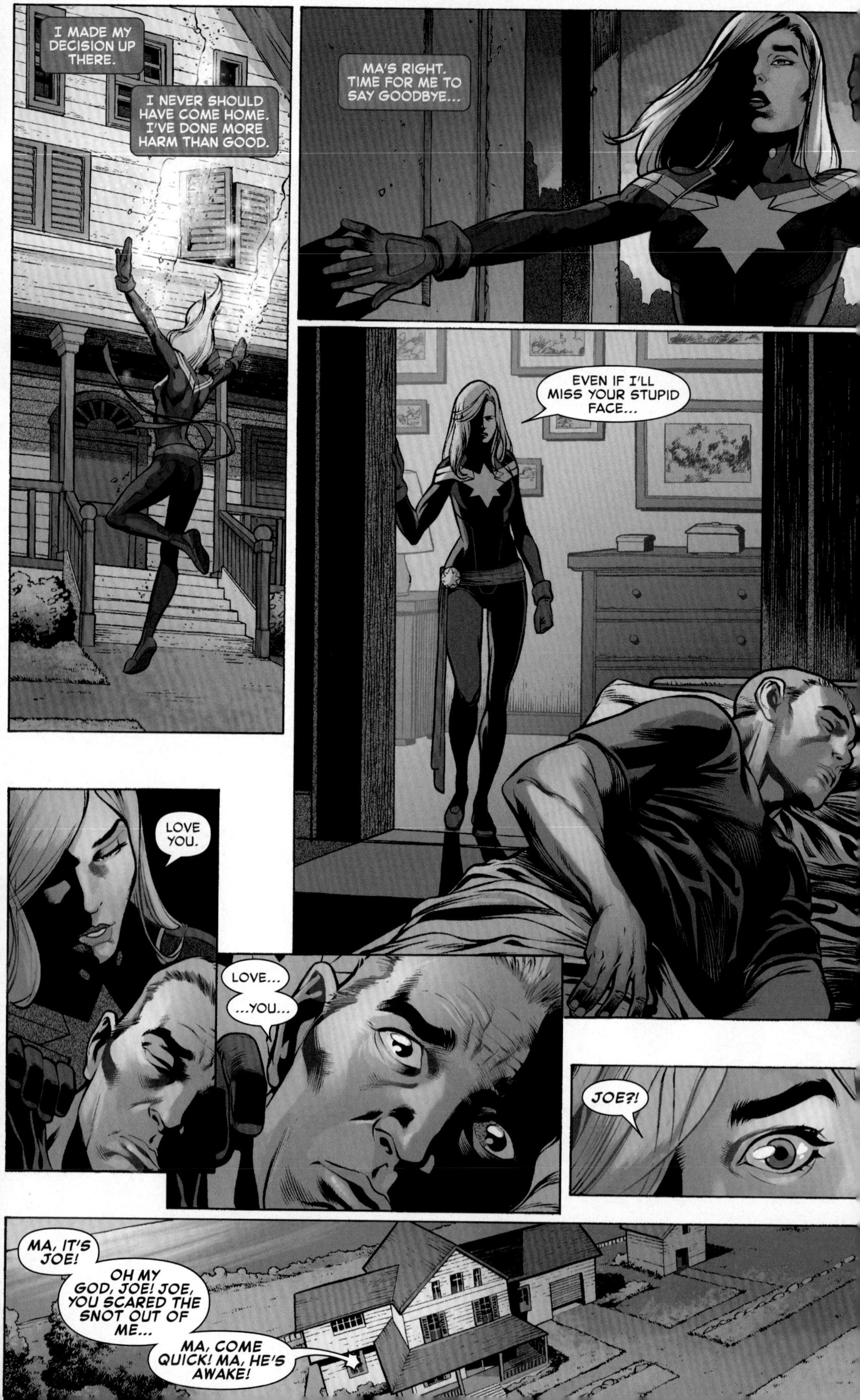
I MADE MY DECISION UP THERE.
I NEVER SHOULD HAVE COME HOME. I'VE DONE MORE HARM THAN GOOD.
MA'S RIGHT. TIME FOR ME TO SAY GOODBYE...
EVEN IF I'LL MISS YOUR STUPID FACE...
LOVE YOU.
LOVE...
...YOU...
JOE?!
MA, IT'S JOE!
OH MY GOD, JOE! JOE, YOU SCARED THE SNOT OUT OF ME...
MA, COME QUICK! MA, HE'S AWAKE!

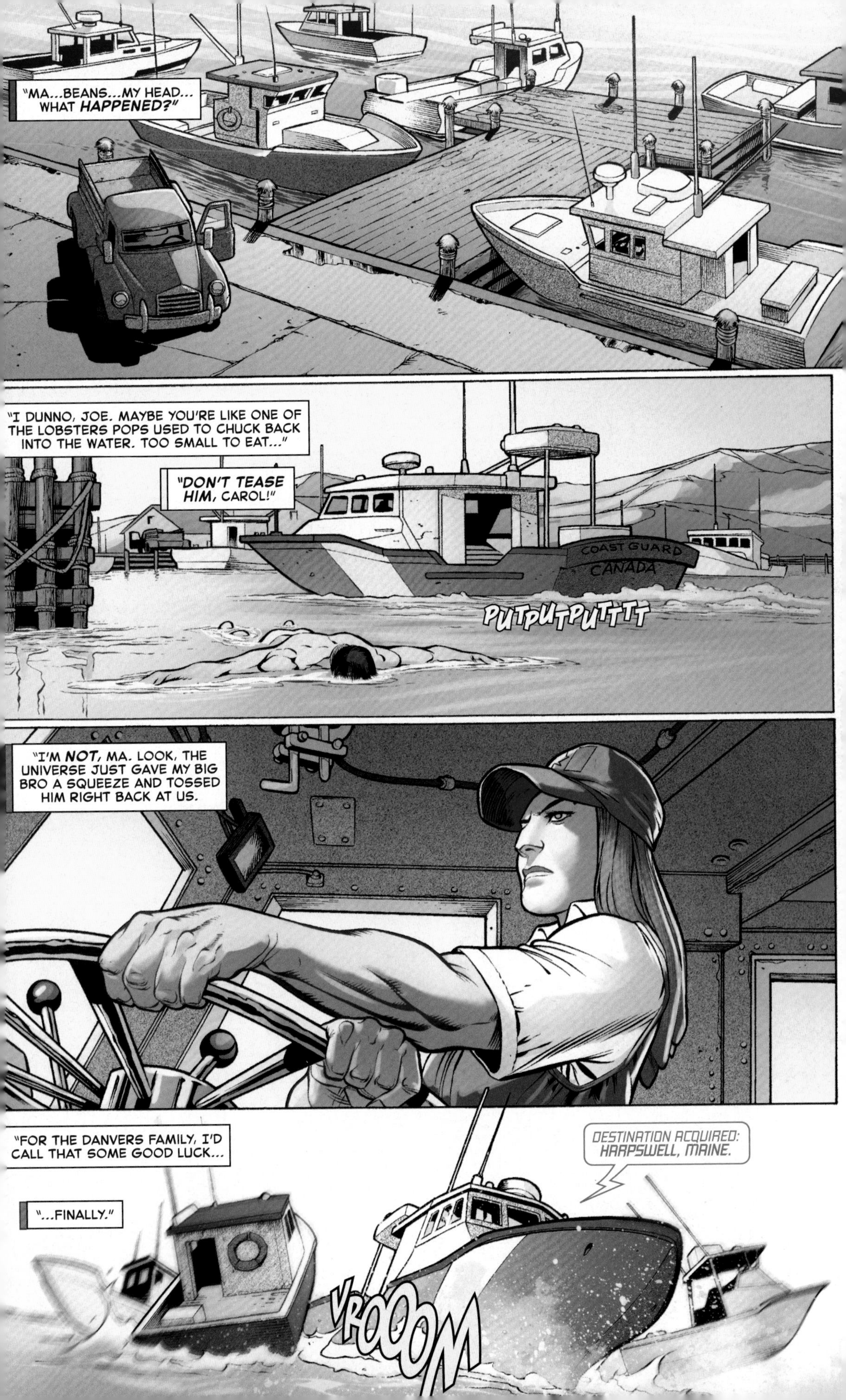
"MA...BEANS...MY HEAD... WHAT HAPPENED?"
"I DUNNO, JOE. MAYBE YOU'RE LIKE ONE OF THE LOBSTERS POPS USED TO CHUCK BACK INTO THE WATER. TOO SMALL TO EAT..."
"DON'T TEASE HIM, CAROL!"
COAST GUARD
CANADA
PUTPUTPUTTTT
"I'M NOT, MA. LOOK, THE UNIVERSE JUST GAVE MY BIG BRO A SQUEEZE AND TOSSED HIM RIGHT BACK AT US.
"FOR THE DANVERS FAMILY, I'D CALL THAT SOME GOOD LUCK...
DESTINATION ACQUIRED: HARPSWELL, MAINE.
"...FINALLY."
VROOOM

PART 3: CAUGHT

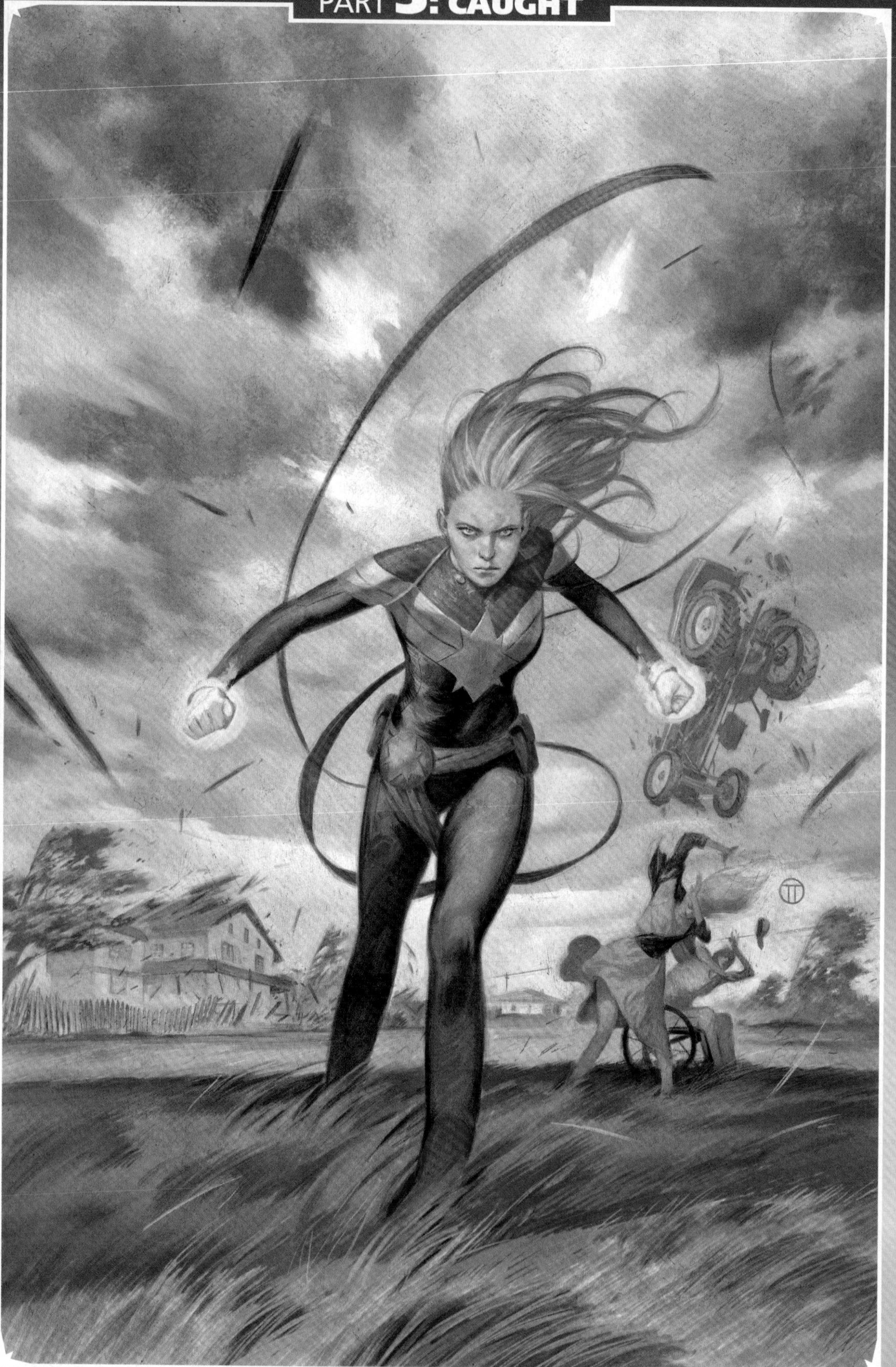

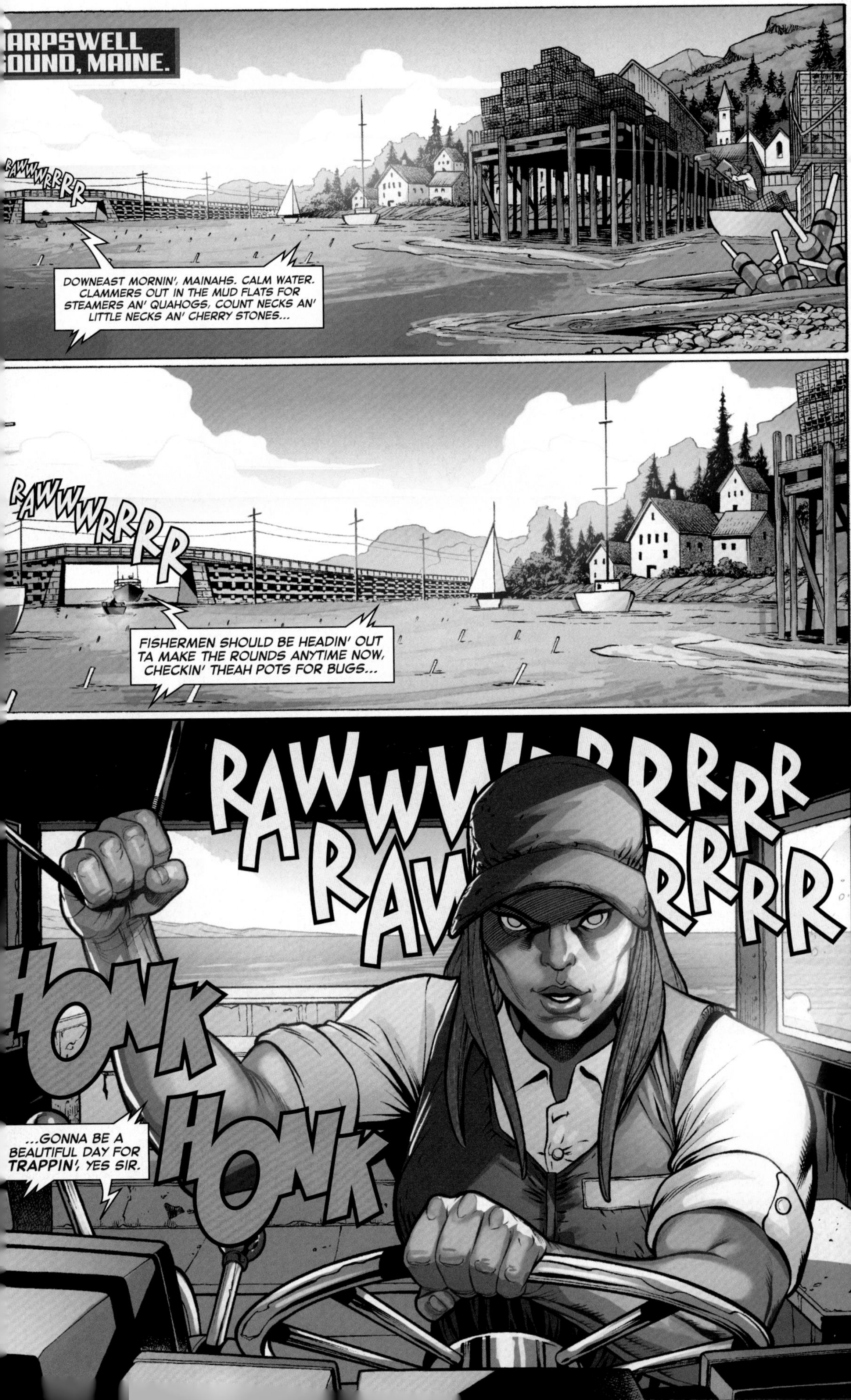
ARPSWELL
OUND, MAINE.
RAWWWRRRR
DOWNEAST MORNIN', MAINAHS. CALM WATER. CLAMMERS OUT IN THE MUD FLATS FOR STEAMERS AN' QUAHOGS, COUNT NECKS AN' LITTLE NECKS AN' CHERRY STONES...
RAWWWRRRRR
FISHERMEN SHOULD BE HEADIN' OUT TA MAKE THE ROUNDS ANYTIME NOW, CHECKIN' THEAH POTS FOR BUGS...
HONK
HONK
...GONNA BE A BEAUTIFUL DAY FOR **TRAPPIN'**, YES SIR.

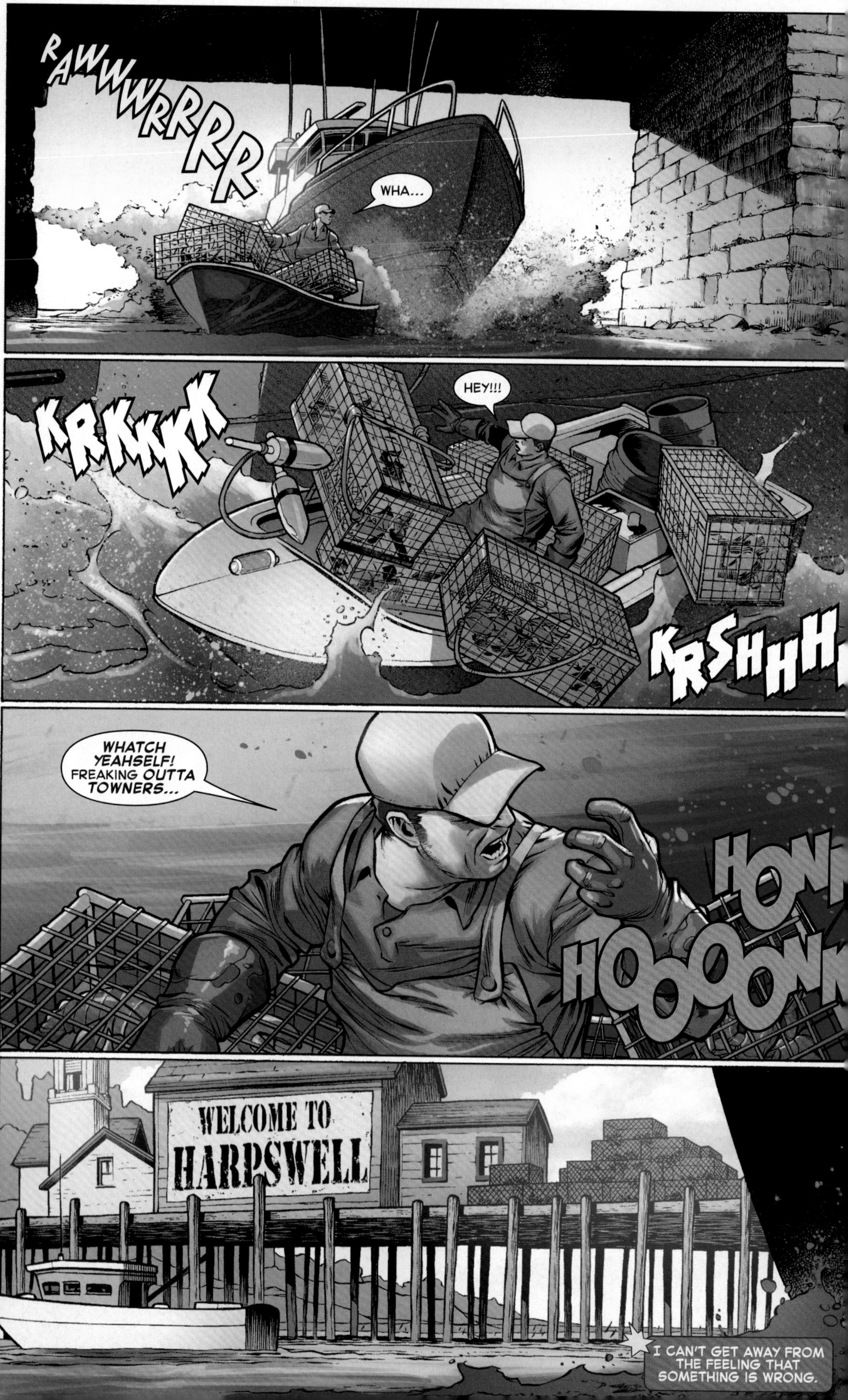
RAWWWRRRR
WHA...
KRKKKKK
HEY!!!
KRSHHH
WHATCH YEAHSELF! FREAKING OUTTA TOWNERS...
HON
HOOOONK
WELCOME TO HARPSWELL
I CAN'T GET AWAY FROM THE FEELING THAT SOMETHING IS WRONG.

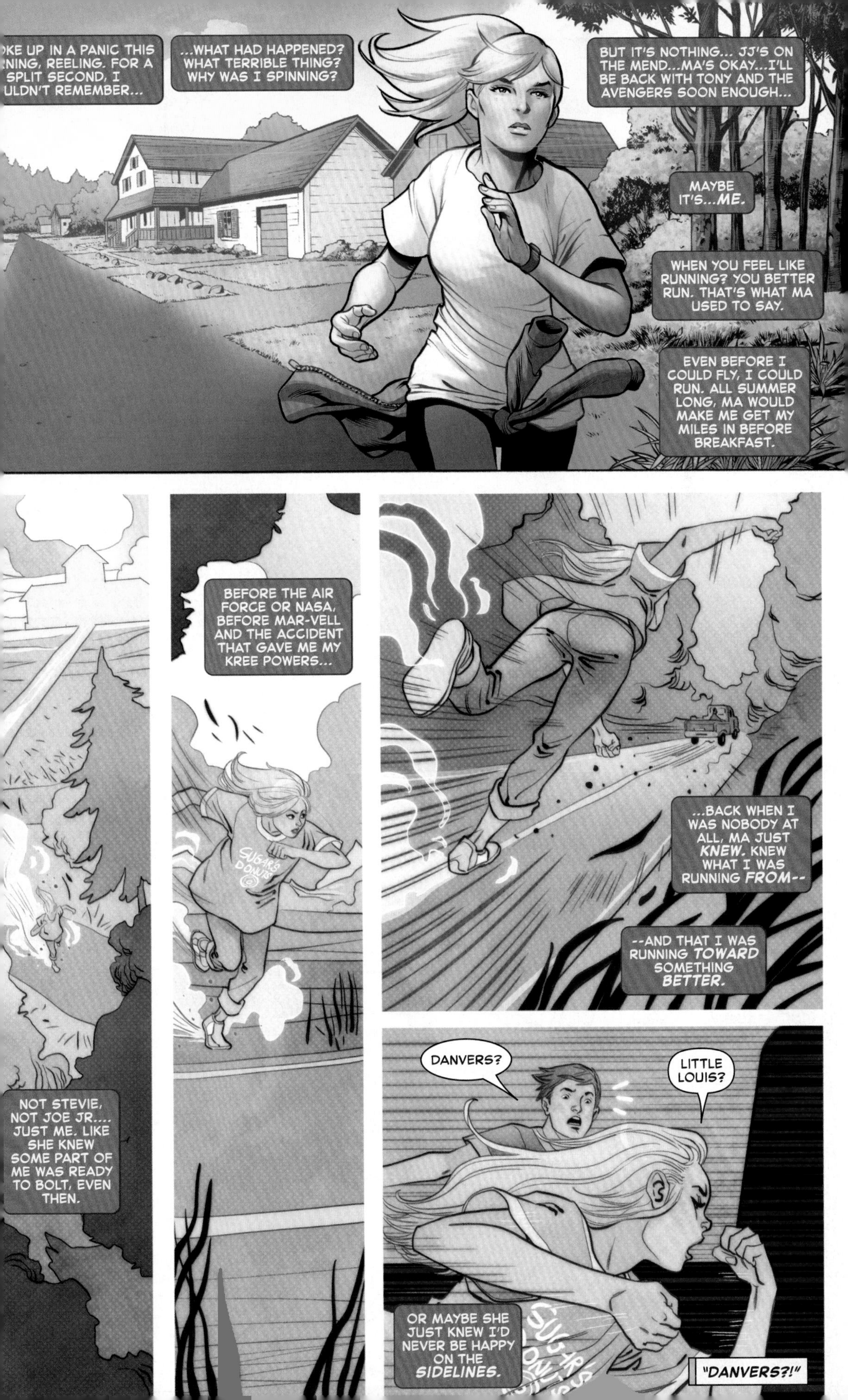

OKE UP IN A PANIC THIS RNING, REELING. FOR A SPLIT SECOND, I ULDN'T REMEMBER...
...WHAT HAD HAPPENED? WHAT TERRIBLE THING? WHY WAS I SPINNING?
BUT IT'S NOTHING... JJ'S ON THE MEND...MA'S OKAY...I'LL BE BACK WITH TONY AND THE AVENGERS SOON ENOUGH...
MAYBE IT'S...ME.
WHEN YOU FEEL LIKE RUNNING? YOU BETTER RUN. THAT'S WHAT MA USED TO SAY.
EVEN BEFORE I COULD FLY, I COULD RUN. ALL SUMMER LONG, MA WOULD MAKE ME GET MY MILES IN BEFORE BREAKFAST.
BEFORE THE AIR FORCE OR NASA, BEFORE MAR-VELL AND THE ACCIDENT THAT GAVE ME MY KREE POWERS...
SUGAR'S DONUTS
...BACK WHEN I WAS NOBODY AT ALL, MA JUST KNEW. KNEW WHAT I WAS RUNNING FROM--
--AND THAT I WAS RUNNING TOWARD SOMETHING BETTER.
NOT STEVIE, NOT JOE JR.... JUST ME. LIKE SHE KNEW SOME PART OF ME WAS READY TO BOLT, EVEN THEN.
DANVERS?
LITTLE LOUIS?
OR MAYBE SHE JUST KNEW I'D NEVER BE HAPPY ON THE SIDELINES.
"DANVERS?!"

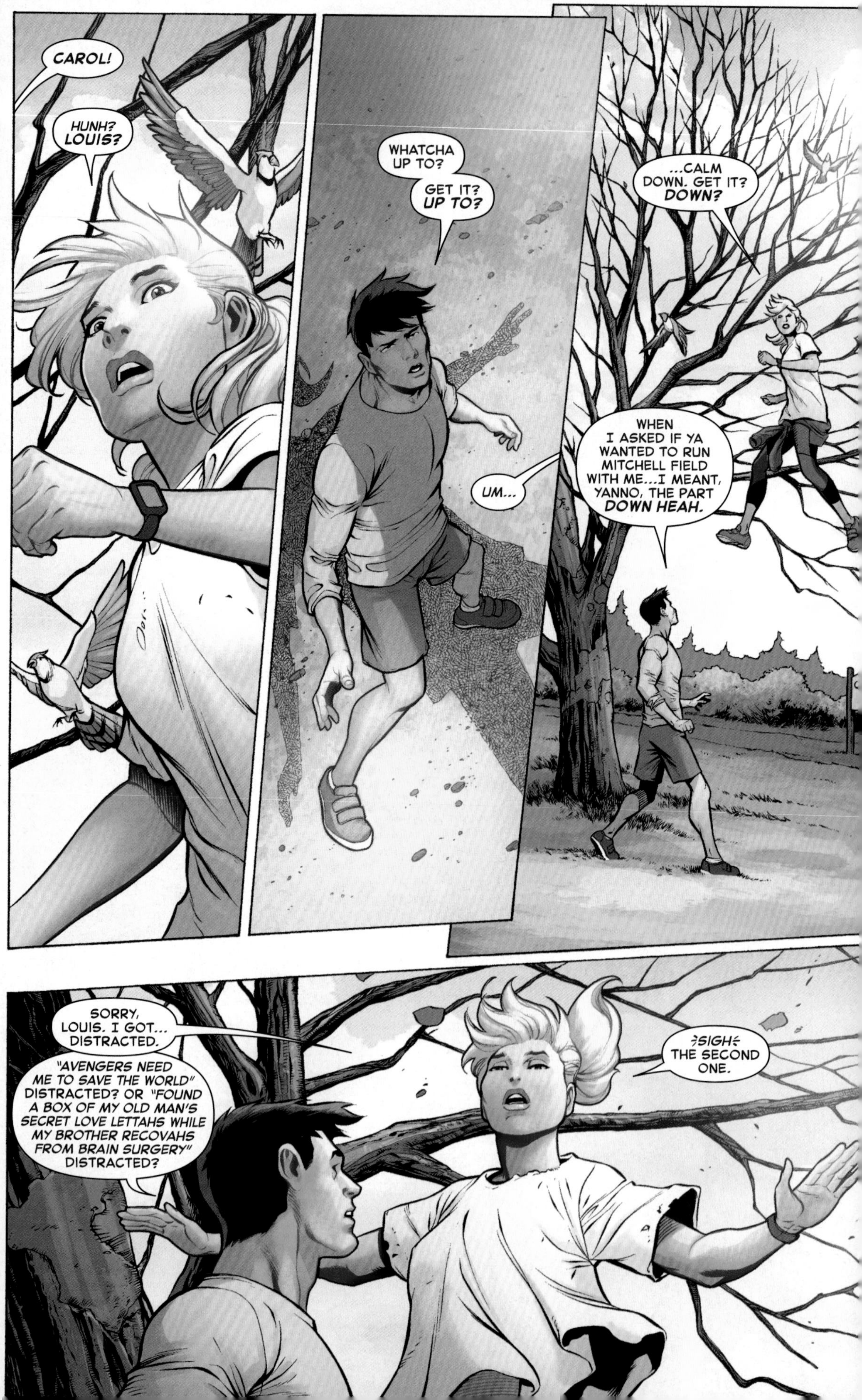

CAROL!
HUNH? LOUIS?
WHATCHA UP TO?
GET IT? UP TO?
...CALM DOWN. GET IT? DOWN?
UM...
WHEN I ASKED IF YA WANTED TO RUN MITCHELL FIELD WITH ME...I MEANT, YANNO, THE PART DOWN HEAH.
SORRY, LOUIS. I GOT... DISTRACTED.
"AVENGERS NEED ME TO SAVE THE WORLD" DISTRACTED? OR "FOUND A BOX OF MY OLD MAN'S SECRET LOVE LETTAHS WHILE MY BROTHER RECOVAHS FROM BRAIN SURGERY" DISTRACTED?
SIGH THE SECOND ONE.

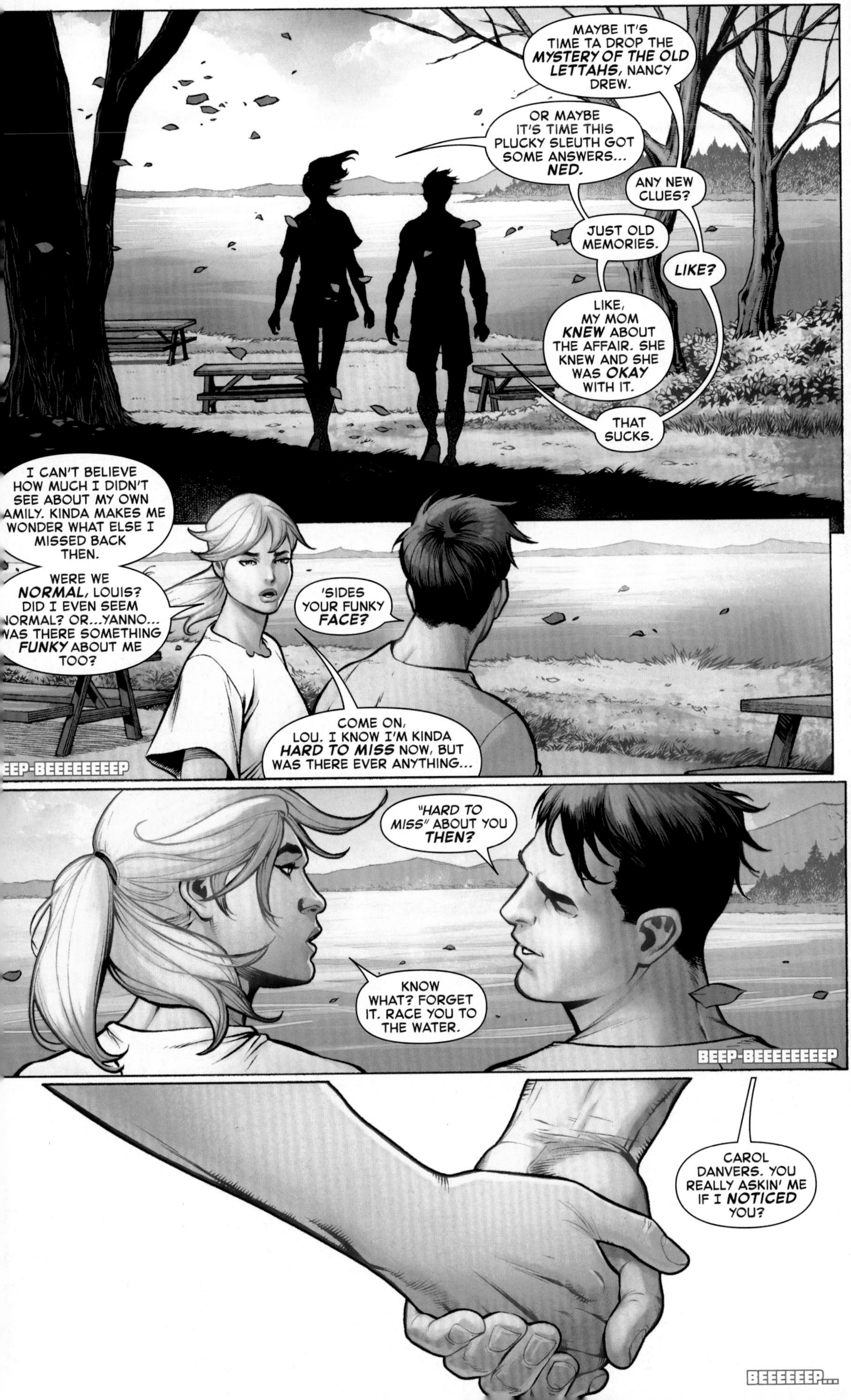
MAYBE IT'S TIME TA DROP THE MYSTERY OF THE OLD LETTAHS, NANCY DREW.
OR MAYBE IT'S TIME THIS PLUCKY SLEUTH GOT SOME ANSWERS... NED.
ANY NEW CLUES?
JUST OLD MEMORIES.
LIKE?
LIKE, MY MOM KNEW ABOUT THE AFFAIR. SHE KNEW AND SHE WAS OKAY WITH IT.
THAT SUCKS.
I CAN'T BELIEVE HOW MUCH I DIDN'T SEE ABOUT MY OWN AMILY. KINDA MAKES ME WONDER WHAT ELSE I MISSED BACK THEN.
WERE WE NORMAL, LOUIS? DID I EVEN SEEM NORMAL? OR...YANNO... WAS THERE SOMETHING FUNKY ABOUT ME TOO?
'SIDES YOUR FUNKY FACE?
COME ON, LOU. I KNOW I'M KINDA HARD TO MISS NOW, BUT WAS THERE EVER ANYTHING...
EEP-BEEEEEEEEP
"HARD TO MISS" ABOUT YOU THEN?
KNOW WHAT? FORGET IT. RACE YOU TO THE WATER.
BEEP-BEEEEEEEEP
CAROL DANVERS. YOU REALLY ASKIN' ME IF I NOTICED YOU?
BEEEEEEP...

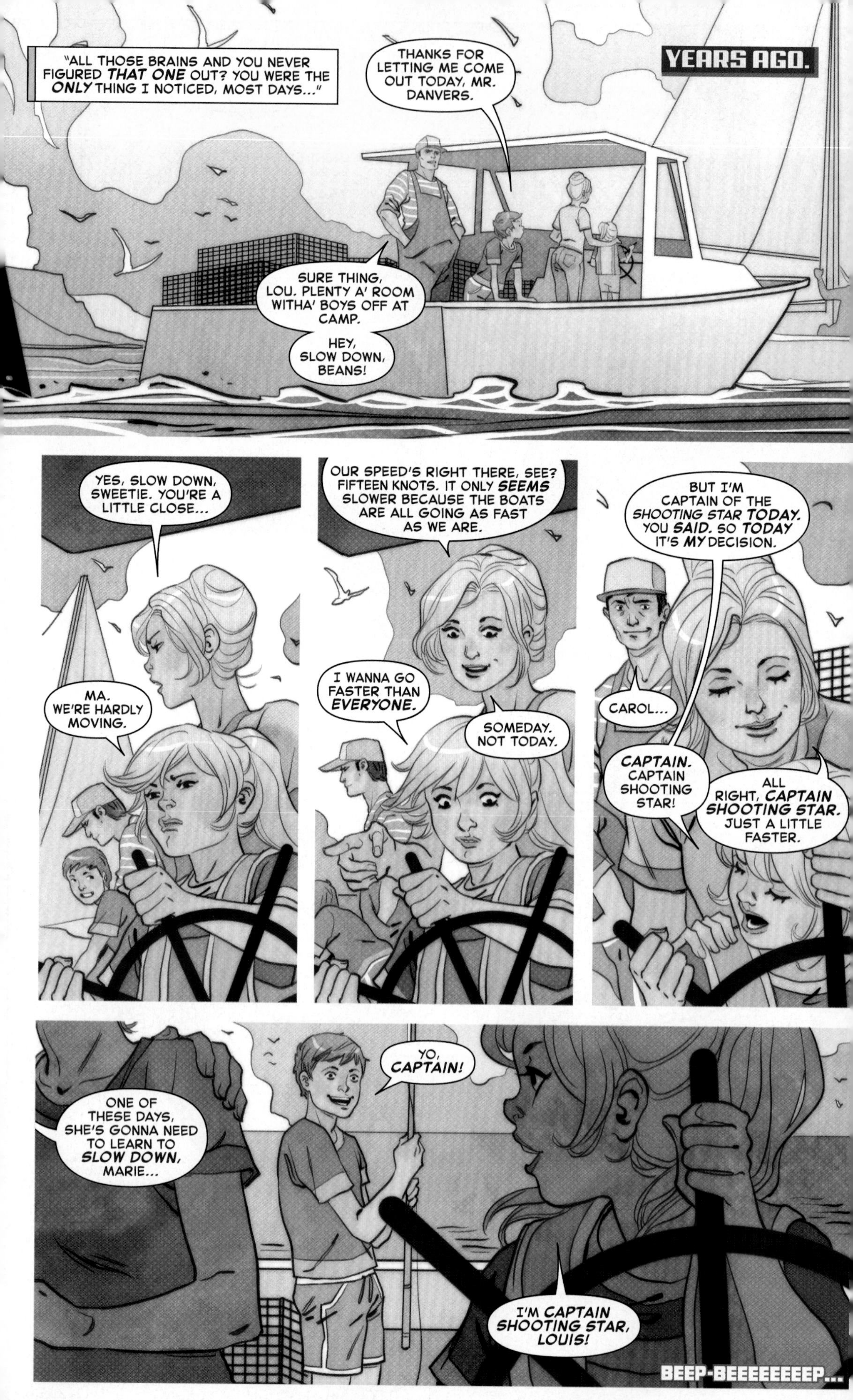
"ALL THOSE BRAINS AND YOU NEVER FIGURED THAT ONE OUT? YOU WERE THE ONLY THING I NOTICED, MOST DAYS..."
THANKS FOR LETTING ME COME OUT TODAY, MR. DANVERS.
YEARS AGO.
SURE THING, LOU. PLENTY A' ROOM WITHA' BOYS OFF AT CAMP.
HEY, SLOW DOWN, BEANS!
YES, SLOW DOWN, SWEETIE. YOU'RE A LITTLE CLOSE...
MA. WE'RE HARDLY MOVING.
OUR SPEED'S RIGHT THERE, SEE? FIFTEEN KNOTS. IT ONLY SEEMS SLOWER BECAUSE THE BOATS ARE ALL GOING AS FAST AS WE ARE.
I WANNA GO FASTER THAN EVERYONE.
SOMEDAY. NOT TODAY.
BUT I'M CAPTAIN OF THE SHOOTING STAR TODAY. YOU SAID. SO TODAY IT'S MY DECISION.
CAROL...
CAPTAIN. CAPTAIN SHOOTING STAR!
ALL RIGHT, CAPTAIN SHOOTING STAR. JUST A LITTLE FASTER.
YO, CAPTAIN!
ONE OF THESE DAYS, SHE'S GONNA NEED TO LEARN TO SLOW DOWN, MARIE...
I'M CAPTAIN SHOOTING STAR, LOUIS!
BEEP-BEEEEEEEEP...

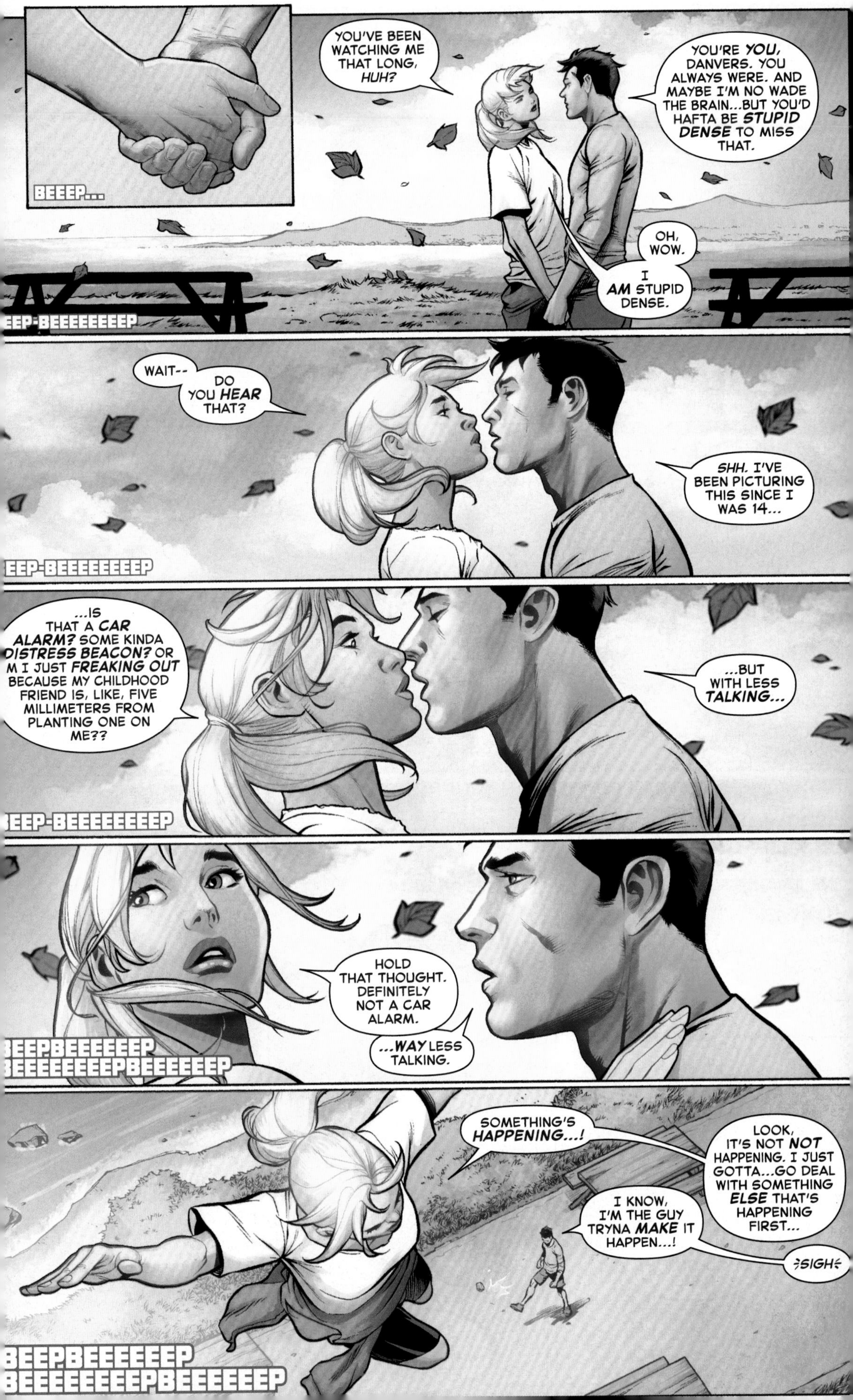
BEEEP...
YOU'VE BEEN WATCHING ME THAT LONG, HUH?
YOU'RE YOU, DANVERS. YOU ALWAYS WERE. AND MAYBE I'M NO WADE THE BRAIN...BUT YOU'D HAFTA BE STUPID DENSE TO MISS THAT.
OH, WOW.
I AM STUPID DENSE.
EEP-BEEEEEEEEP
WAIT--
DO YOU HEAR THAT?
SHH. I'VE BEEN PICTURING THIS SINCE I WAS 14...
EEP-BEEEEEEEEP
...IS THAT A CAR ALARM? SOME KINDA DISTRESS BEACON? OR M I JUST FREAKING OUT BECAUSE MY CHILDHOOD FRIEND IS, LIKE, FIVE MILLIMETERS FROM PLANTING ONE ON ME??
...BUT WITH LESS TALKING...
EEP-BEEEEEEEEP
HOLD THAT THOUGHT. DEFINITELY NOT A CAR ALARM.
...WAY LESS TALKING.
EEPBEEEEEEEP
EEEEEEEEPBEEEEEEP
SOMETHING'S HAPPENING...!
LOOK, IT'S NOT NOT HAPPENING. I JUST GOTTA...GO DEAL WITH SOMETHING ELSE THAT'S HAPPENING FIRST...
I KNOW, I'M THE GUY TRYNA MAKE IT HAPPEN...!
SIGH
BEEPBEEEEEEEP
BEEEEEEEEPBEEEEEEEP

BEEPBEEEEEEP BEEEEEEEP BEEEEEEP

THAT *SOUND*...RIPPING THROUGH MY HEAD... WHY CAN'T ANYONE ELSE *HEAR* IT?

BEEPBEEEEEEPBEEEEEEEEPBEEEEEEP

IT'S SO *LOUD* NOW... ALMOST TOO MUCH TO BEAR...

WHATCHA DOIN', BEANS?

...THINK IT'S COMING FROM THE GARAGE...

WHAT IS IT? BEANS? YOU OKAY?

STAY THERE, JOE!

BEEPBEEEEEEP BEEEEEEEP BEEEEEEP

MA? YOU HEAR IT TOO?

IT'S THIS OLD THING. IT SHOULDN'T *BE* HERE!

BEEPBEEEEEEP BEEEEEEEP

THAT'S WHAT'S MAKING THIS RACKET? I THINK IT WAS POPS'-- I FOUND IT IN THE CLOSET, WITH HIS LETTERS.

IT WASN'T *HIS.* I DON'T EVEN KNOW WHY HE KEPT IT...THIS PIECE OF JUNK...

THEN... WHOSE WAS IT?

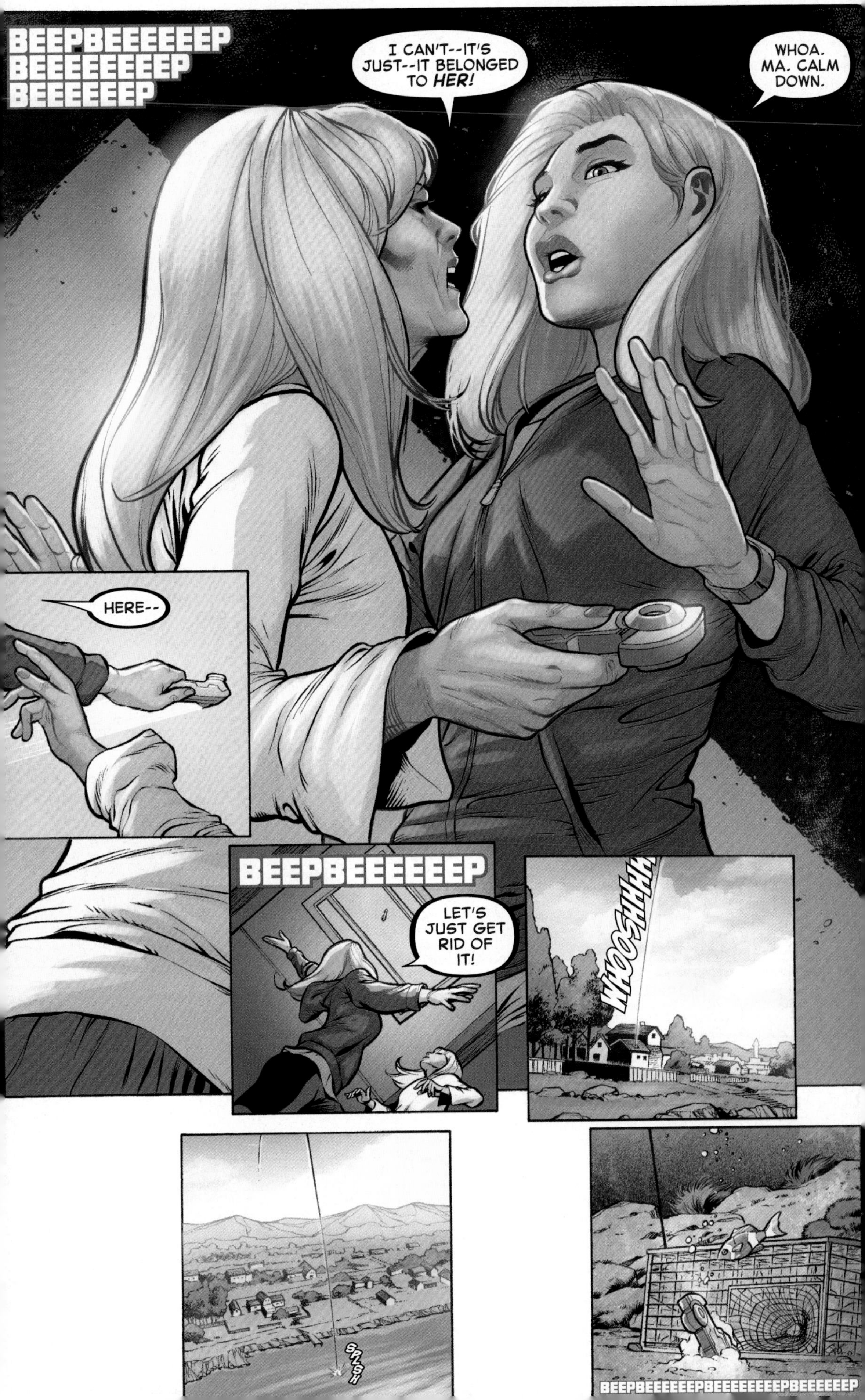
BEEPBEEEEEEP
BEEEEEEEEP
BEEEEEEP
I CAN'T--IT'S JUST--IT BELONGED TO *HER!*
WHOA. MA. CALM DOWN.
HERE--
BEEPBEEEEEEP
LET'S JUST GET RID OF IT!
WHOOSHHHH
SPLSH
BEEPBEEEEEEPBEEEEEEEEPBEEEEEEP

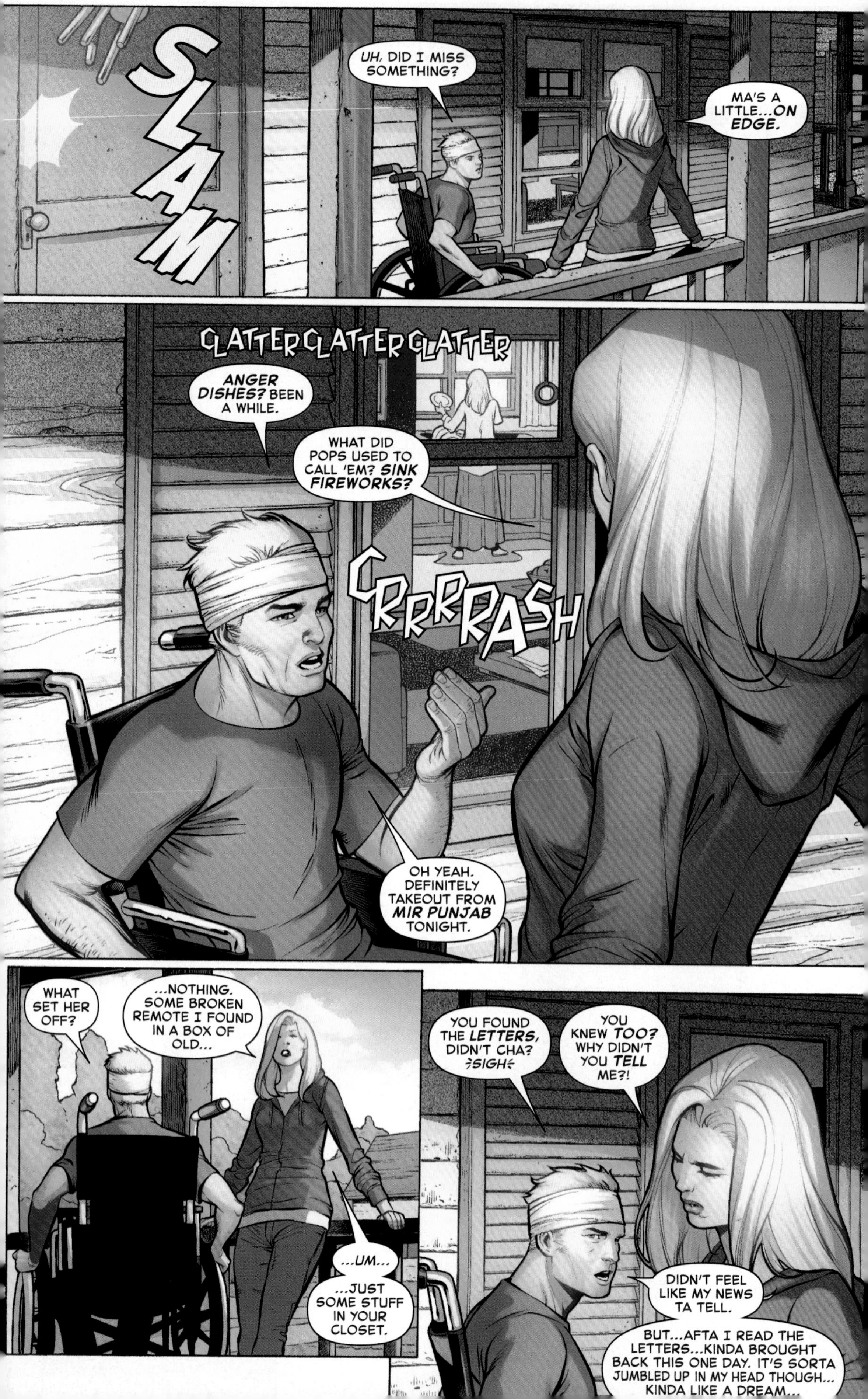
SLAM
UH, DID I MISS SOMETHING?
MA'S A LITTLE...ON EDGE.
CLATTER CLATTER CLATTER
ANGER DISHES? BEEN A WHILE.
WHAT DID POPS USED TO CALL 'EM? SINK FIREWORKS?
CRRRRASH
OH YEAH. DEFINITELY TAKEOUT FROM MIR PUNJAB TONIGHT.
WHAT SET HER OFF?
...NOTHING. SOME BROKEN REMOTE I FOUND IN A BOX OF OLD...
...UM...
...JUST SOME STUFF IN YOUR CLOSET.
YOU FOUND THE LETTERS, DIDN'T CHA? *SIGH*
YOU KNEW TOO? WHY DIDN'T YOU TELL ME?!
DIDN'T FEEL LIKE MY NEWS TA TELL.
BUT...AFTA I READ THE LETTERS...KINDA BROUGHT BACK THIS ONE DAY. IT'S SORTA JUMBLED UP IN MY HEAD THOUGH... KINDA LIKE A DREAM...

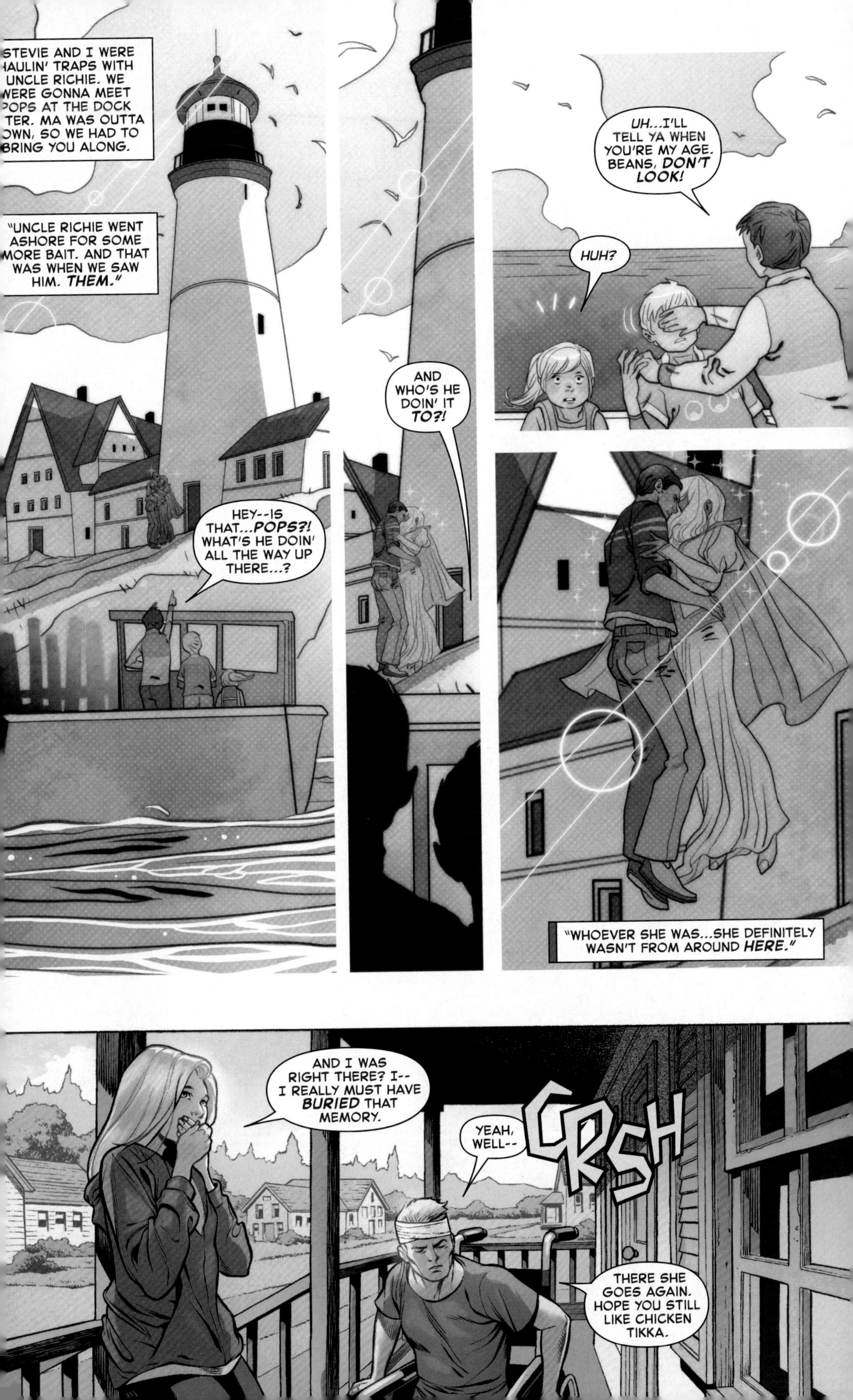
STEVIE AND I WERE HAULIN' TRAPS WITH UNCLE RICHIE. WE WERE GONNA MEET POPS AT THE DOCK LATER. MA WAS OUTTA TOWN, SO WE HAD TO BRING YOU ALONG.
"UNCLE RICHIE WENT ASHORE FOR SOME MORE BAIT. AND THAT WAS WHEN WE SAW HIM. THEM."
HEY--IS THAT...POPS?! WHAT'S HE DOIN' ALL THE WAY UP THERE...?
AND WHO'S HE DOIN' IT TO?!
UH...I'LL TELL YA WHEN YOU'RE MY AGE. BEANS, DON'T LOOK!
HUH?
"WHOEVER SHE WAS...SHE DEFINITELY WASN'T FROM AROUND HERE."
AND I WAS RIGHT THERE? I-- I REALLY MUST HAVE BURIED THAT MEMORY.
YEAH, WELL--
CRSH
THERE SHE GOES AGAIN. HOPE YOU STILL LIKE CHICKEN TIKKA.

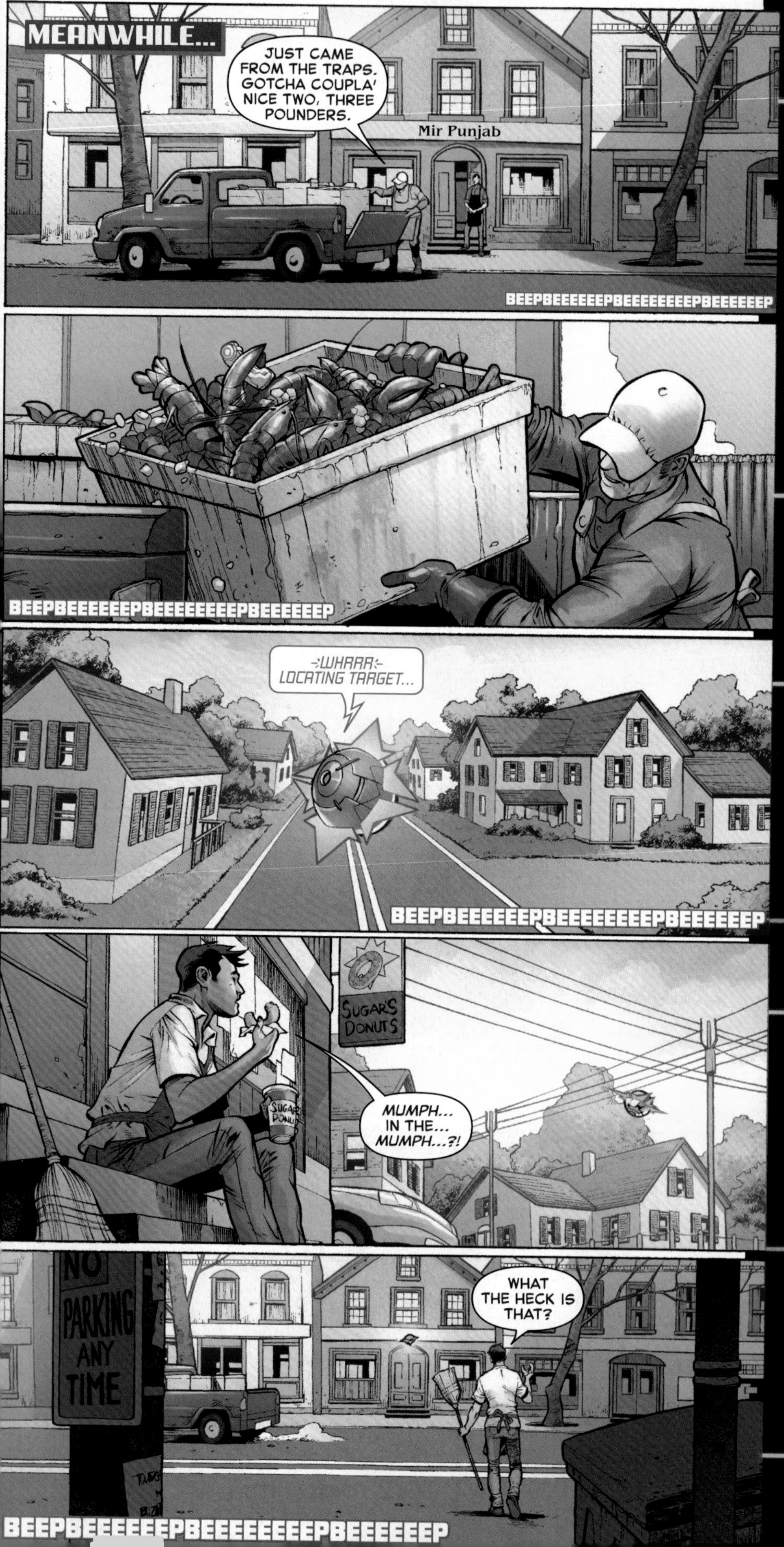

MEANWHILE...
JUST CAME FROM THE TRAPS. GOTCHA COUPLA' NICE TWO, THREE POUNDERS.
Mir Punjab
BEEPBEEEEEEPBEEEEEEEEPBEEEEEEP
BEEPBEEEEEEPBEEEEEEEEPBEEEEEEP
-WHRRR- LOCATING TARGET...
BEEPBEEEEEEEPBEEEEEEEEPBEEEEEEP
SUGAR'S DONUTS
MUMPH... IN THE... MUMPH...?!
NO PARKING ANY TIME
WHAT THE HECK IS THAT?
BEEPBEEEEEEEPBEEEEEEEEEPBEEEEEEEP

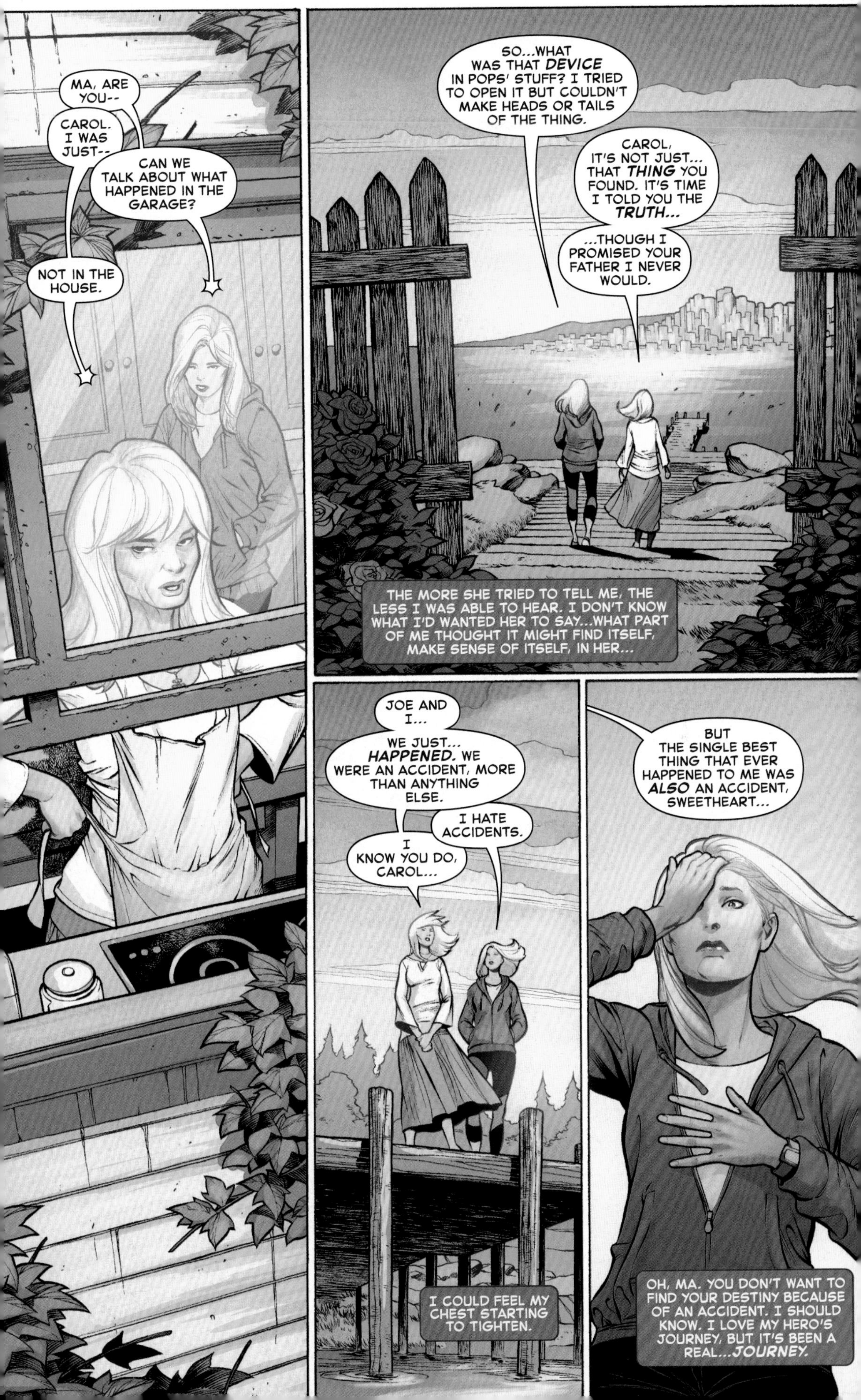
MA, ARE YOU--
CAROL. I WAS JUST--
CAN WE TALK ABOUT WHAT HAPPENED IN THE GARAGE?
NOT IN THE HOUSE.
SO...WHAT WAS THAT DEVICE IN POPS' STUFF? I TRIED TO OPEN IT BUT COULDN'T MAKE HEADS OR TAILS OF THE THING.
CAROL, IT'S NOT JUST... THAT THING YOU FOUND. IT'S TIME I TOLD YOU THE TRUTH...
...THOUGH I PROMISED YOUR FATHER I NEVER WOULD.
THE MORE SHE TRIED TO TELL ME, THE LESS I WAS ABLE TO HEAR. I DON'T KNOW WHAT I'D WANTED HER TO SAY...WHAT PART OF ME THOUGHT IT MIGHT FIND ITSELF, MAKE SENSE OF ITSELF, IN HER...
JOE AND I...
WE JUST... HAPPENED. WE WERE AN ACCIDENT, MORE THAN ANYTHING ELSE.
I HATE ACCIDENTS.
I KNOW YOU DO, CAROL...
I COULD FEEL MY CHEST STARTING TO TIGHTEN.
BUT THE SINGLE BEST THING THAT EVER HAPPENED TO ME WAS ALSO AN ACCIDENT, SWEETHEART...
OH, MA. YOU DON'T WANT TO FIND YOUR DESTINY BECAUSE OF AN ACCIDENT. I SHOULD KNOW. I LOVE MY HERO'S JOURNEY, BUT IT'S BEEN A REAL...JOURNEY.

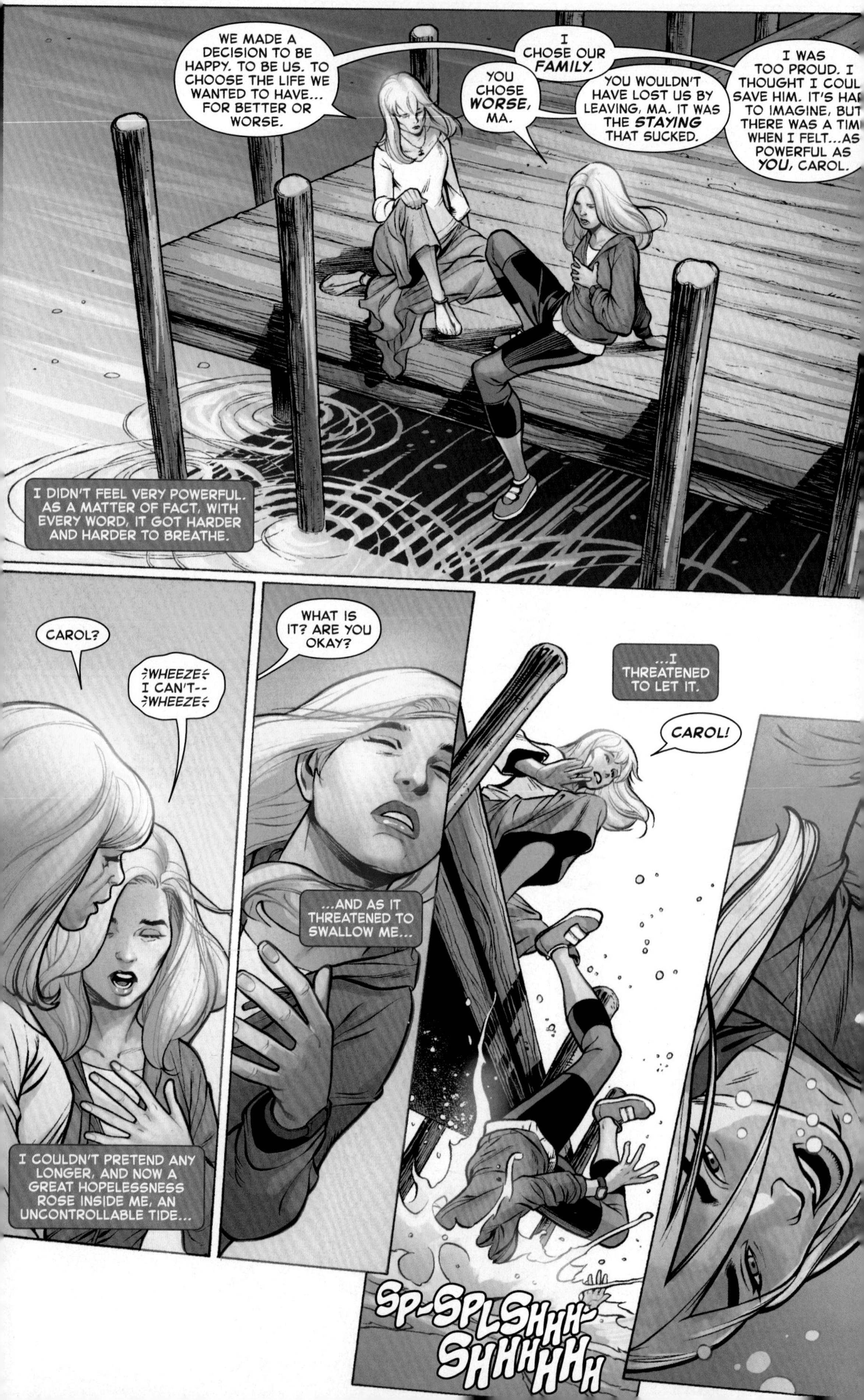

WE MADE A DECISION TO BE HAPPY. TO BE US. TO CHOOSE THE LIFE WE WANTED TO HAVE... FOR BETTER OR WORSE.
I CHOSE OUR *FAMILY.*
YOU CHOSE *WORSE,* MA.
YOU WOULDN'T HAVE LOST US BY LEAVING, MA. IT WAS THE *STAYING* THAT SUCKED.
I WAS TOO PROUD. I THOUGHT I COUL SAVE HIM. IT'S HA TO IMAGINE, BUT THERE WAS A TIM WHEN I FELT...AS POWERFUL AS *YOU,* CAROL.
I DIDN'T FEEL VERY POWERFUL. AS A MATTER OF FACT, WITH EVERY WORD, IT GOT HARDER AND HARDER TO BREATHE.
CAROL?
WHEEZE I CAN'T-- WHEEZE
I COULDN'T PRETEND ANY LONGER, AND NOW A GREAT HOPELESSNESS ROSE INSIDE ME, AN UNCONTROLLABLE TIDE...
WHAT IS IT? ARE YOU OKAY?
...AND AS IT THREATENED TO SWALLOW ME...
...I THREATENED TO LET IT.
CAROL!
SP-SPLSHHH-SHHHHHH

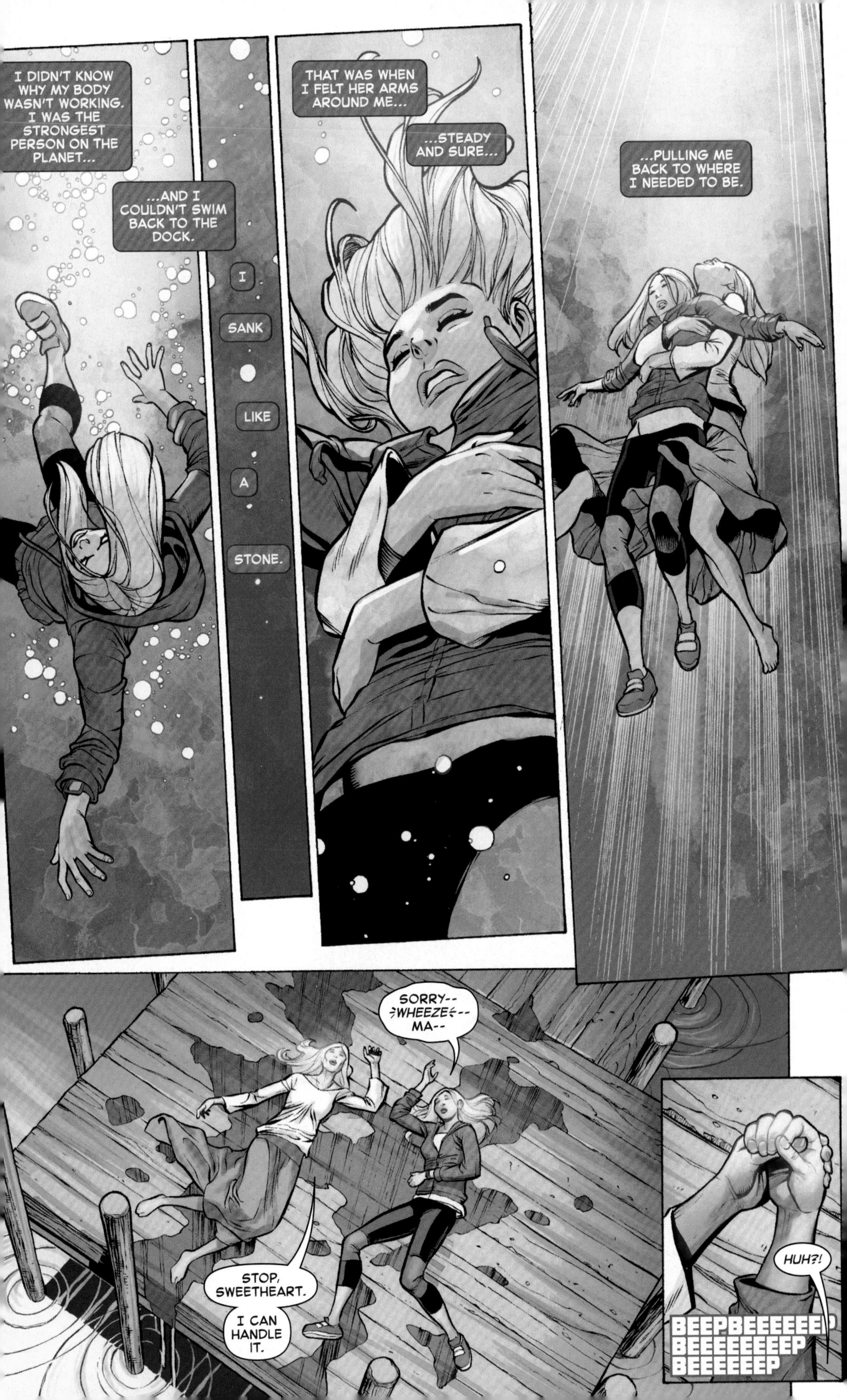
I DIDN'T KNOW WHY MY BODY WASN'T WORKING. I WAS THE STRONGEST PERSON ON THE PLANET...
...AND I COULDN'T SWIM BACK TO THE DOCK.
I
SANK
LIKE
A
STONE.
THAT WAS WHEN I FELT HER ARMS AROUND ME...
...STEADY AND SURE...
...PULLING ME BACK TO WHERE I NEEDED TO BE.
SORRY-- ≈WHEEZE≈-- MA--
STOP, SWEETHEART.
I CAN HANDLE IT.
HUH?!
BEEPBEEEEEEP BEEEEEEEEP BEEEEEEP

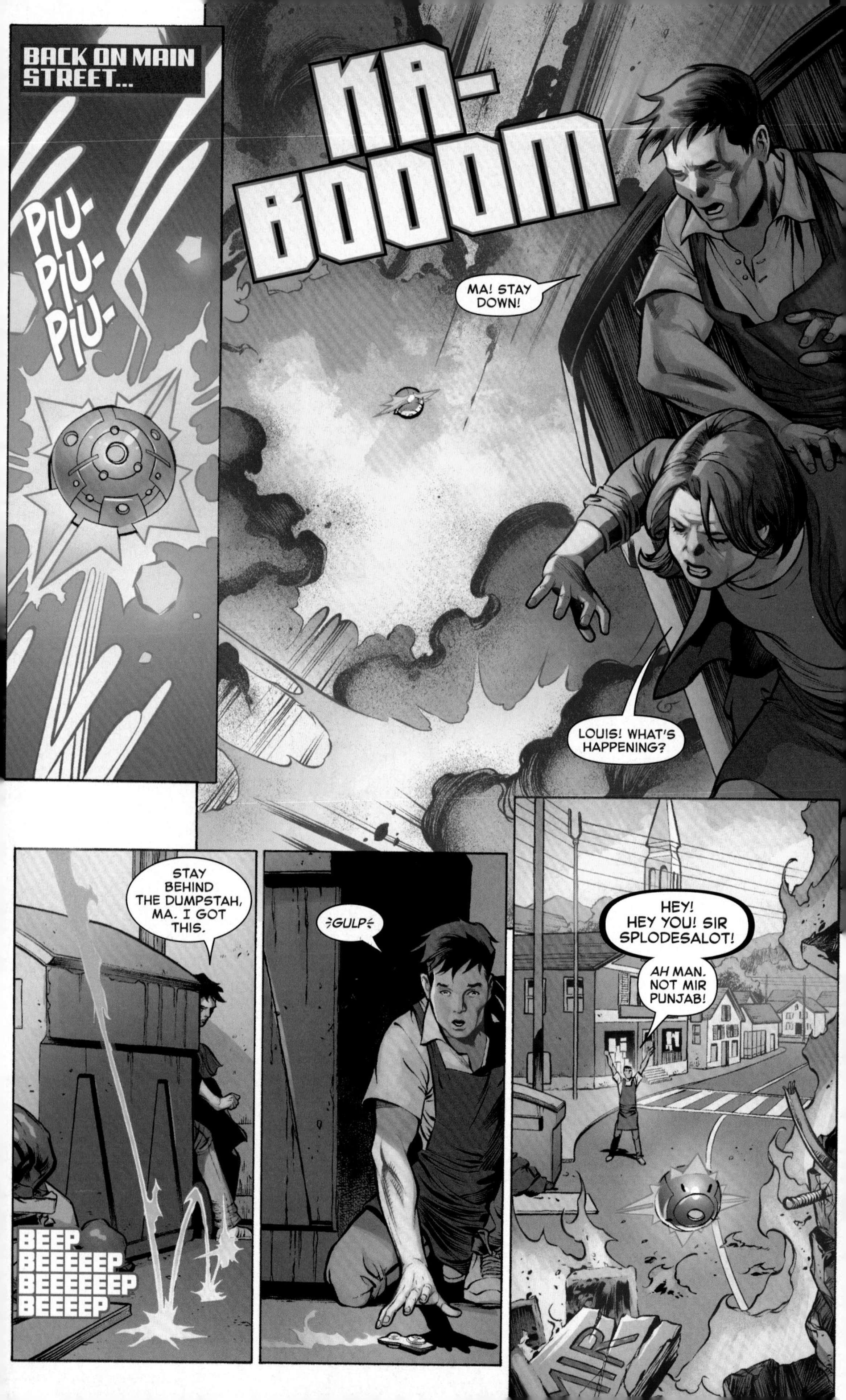

BACK ON MAIN STREET...
PIU-PIU-PIU-
KA-BOOOM
MA! STAY DOWN!
LOUIS! WHAT'S HAPPENING?
STAY BEHIND THE DUMPSTAH, MA. I GOT THIS.
BEEP BEEEEEP BEEEEEEP BEEEEP
GULP
HEY! HEY YOU! SIR SPLODESALOT!
AH MAN. NOT MIR PUNJAB!

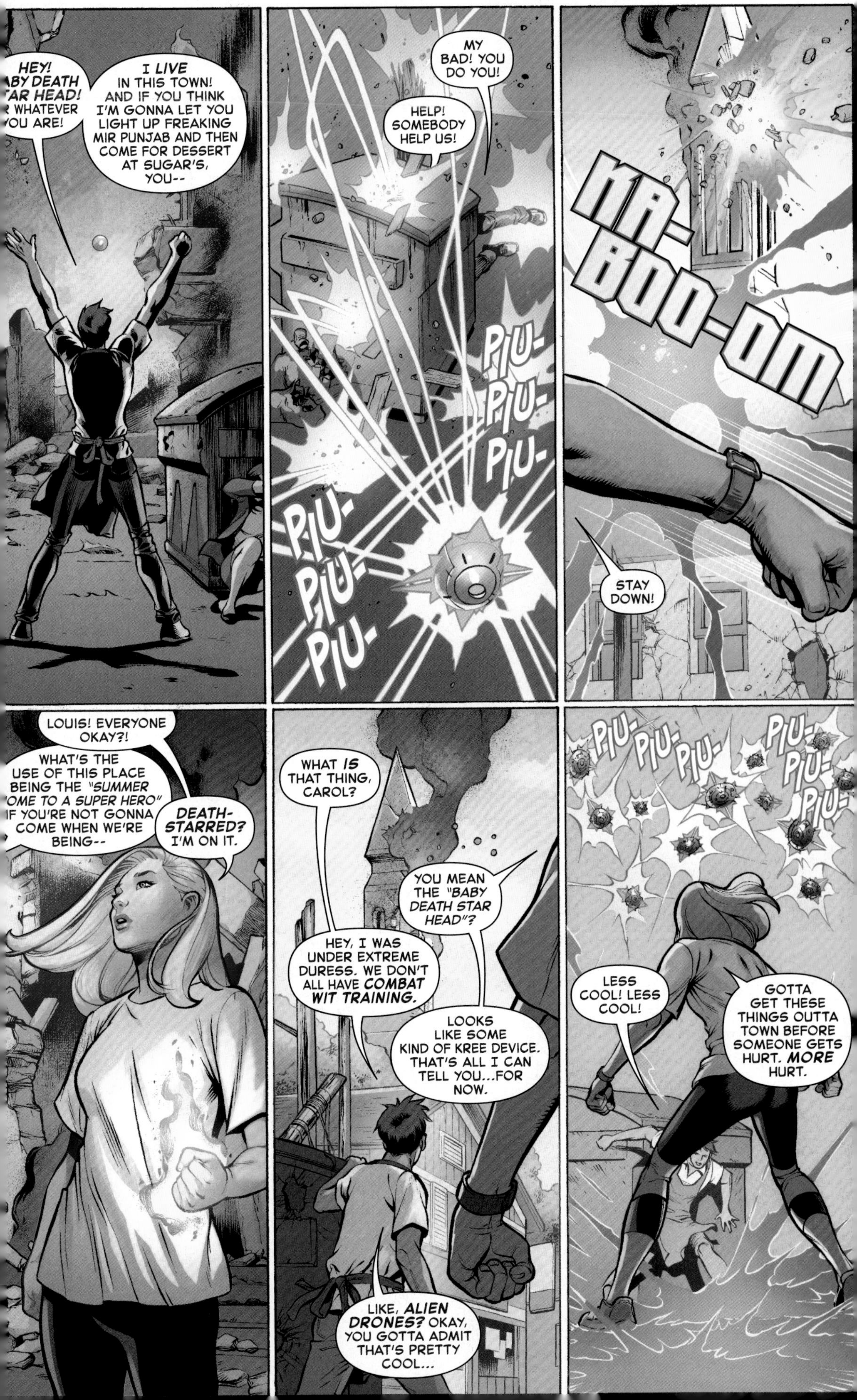

HEY! ...ABY DEATH ...TAR HEAD! ...R WHATEVER ...YOU ARE!
I LIVE IN THIS TOWN! AND IF YOU THINK I'M GONNA LET YOU LIGHT UP FREAKING MIR PUNJAB AND THEN COME FOR DESSERT AT SUGAR'S, YOU--
MY BAD! YOU DO YOU!
HELP! SOMEBODY HELP US!
PIU-PIU-PIU-
PIU-PIU-PIU-
KA-BOO-OM
STAY DOWN!
LOUIS! EVERYONE OKAY?!
WHAT'S THE USE OF THIS PLACE BEING THE "SUMMER ...OME TO A SUPER HERO" ...IF YOU'RE NOT GONNA COME WHEN WE'RE BEING--
DEATH-STARRED? I'M ON IT.
WHAT IS THAT THING, CAROL?
YOU MEAN THE "BABY DEATH STAR HEAD"?
HEY, I WAS UNDER EXTREME DURESS. WE DON'T ALL HAVE COMBAT WIT TRAINING.
LOOKS LIKE SOME KIND OF KREE DEVICE. THAT'S ALL I CAN TELL YOU...FOR NOW.
LIKE, ALIEN DRONES? OKAY, YOU GOTTA ADMIT THAT'S PRETTY COOL...
PIU-PIU-PIU-
PIU-PIU-PIU-
LESS COOL! LESS COOL!
GOTTA GET THESE THINGS OUTTA TOWN BEFORE SOMEONE GETS HURT. MORE HURT.

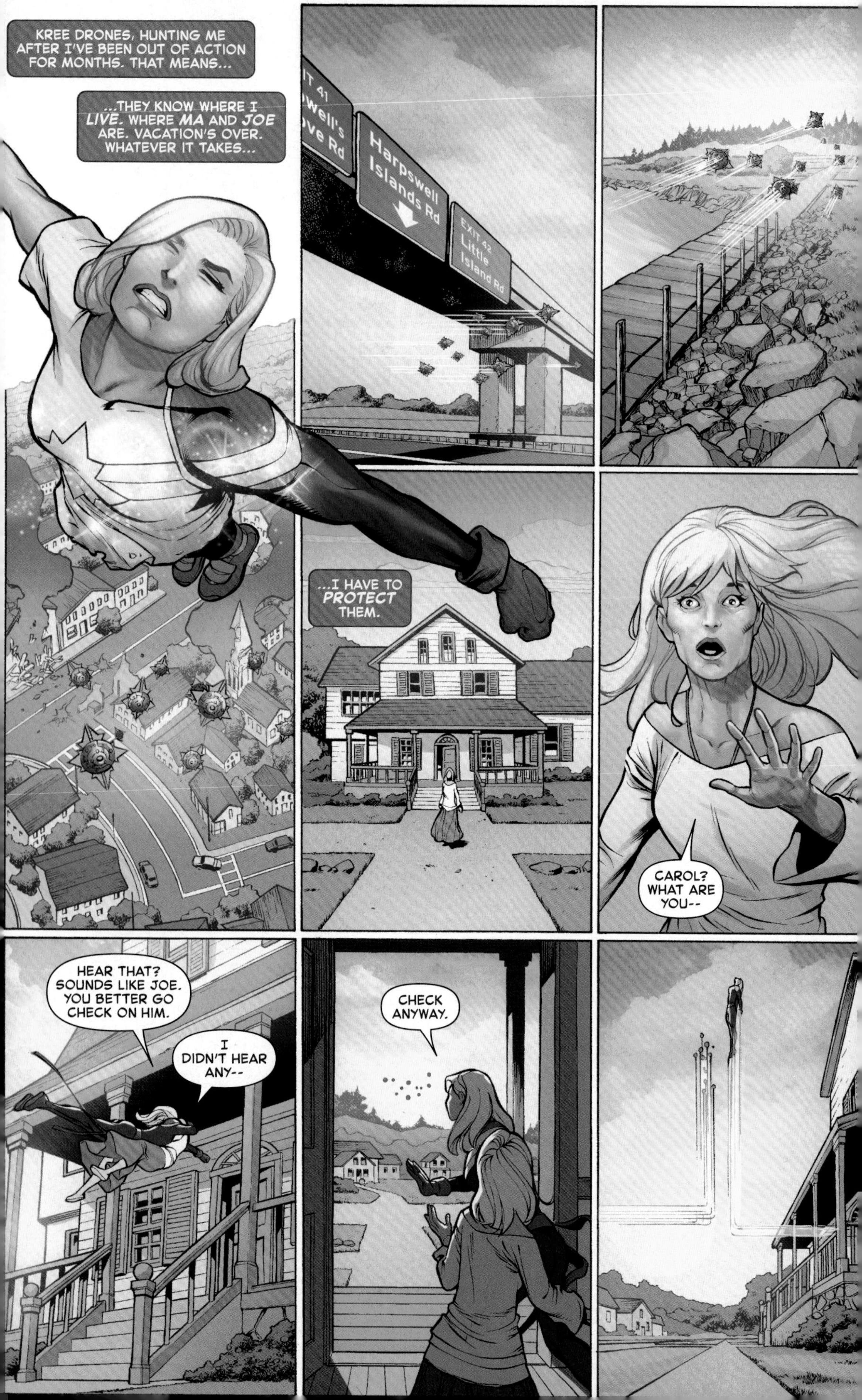
KREE DRONES, HUNTING ME AFTER I'VE BEEN OUT OF ACTION FOR MONTHS. THAT MEANS...
...THEY KNOW WHERE I *LIVE*. WHERE *MA* AND *JOE* ARE. VACATION'S OVER. WHATEVER IT TAKES...
EXIT 41
Harpswell Islands Rd
EXIT 42 Little Island Rd
...I HAVE TO *PROTECT* THEM.
CAROL? WHAT ARE YOU--
HEAR THAT? SOUNDS LIKE JOE. YOU BETTER GO CHECK ON HIM.
I DIDN'T HEAR ANY--
CHECK ANYWAY.

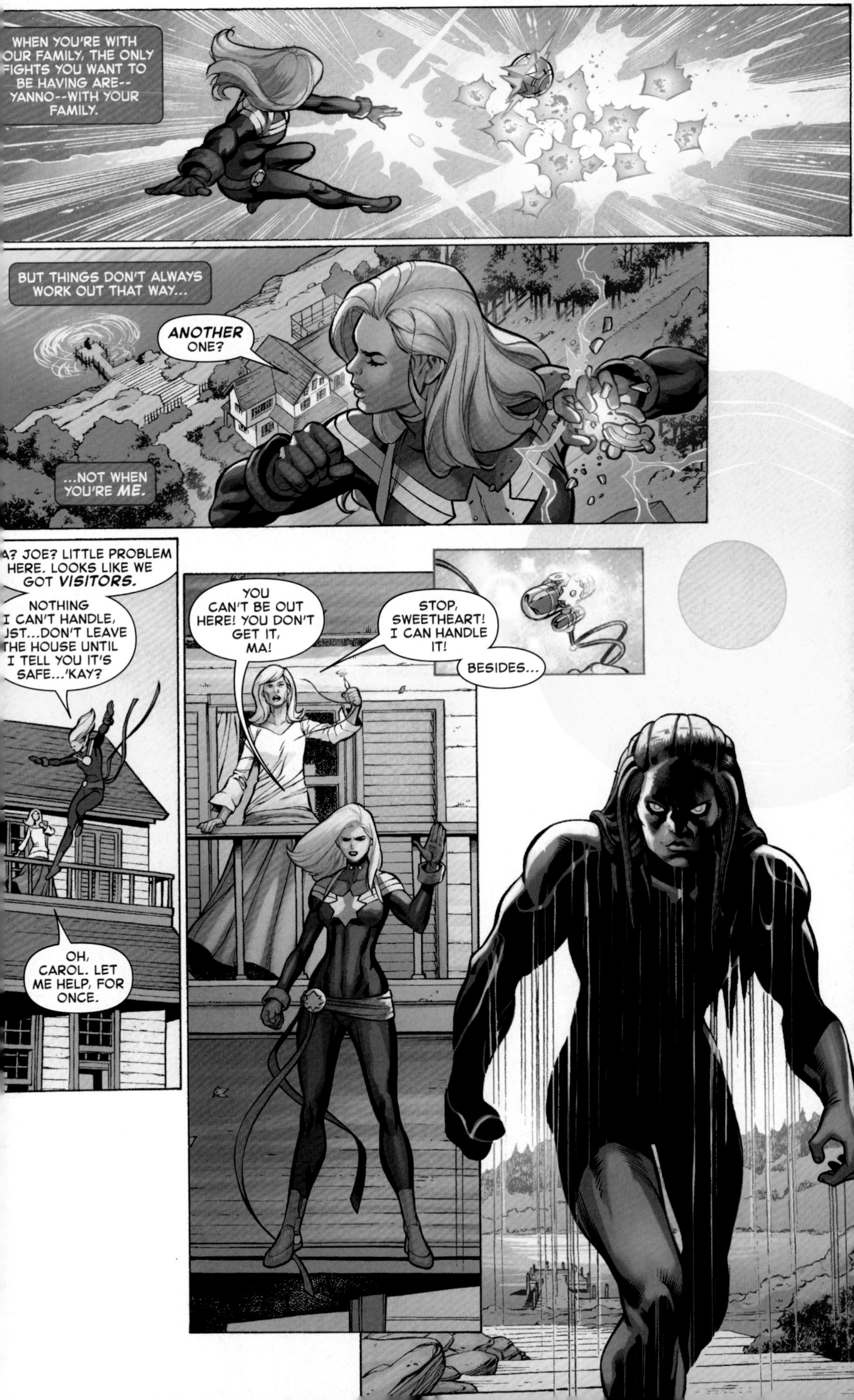
WHEN YOU'RE WITH OUR FAMILY, THE ONLY FIGHTS YOU WANT TO BE HAVING ARE--YANNO--WITH YOUR FAMILY.
BUT THINGS DON'T ALWAYS WORK OUT THAT WAY...
ANOTHER ONE?
...NOT WHEN YOU'RE ME.
A? JOE? LITTLE PROBLEM HERE. LOOKS LIKE WE GOT VISITORS.
NOTHING I CAN'T HANDLE, JST...DON'T LEAVE THE HOUSE UNTIL I TELL YOU IT'S SAFE...'KAY?
OH, CAROL. LET ME HELP, FOR ONCE.
YOU CAN'T BE OUT HERE! YOU DON'T GET IT, MA!
STOP, SWEETHEART! I CAN HANDLE IT!
BESIDES...

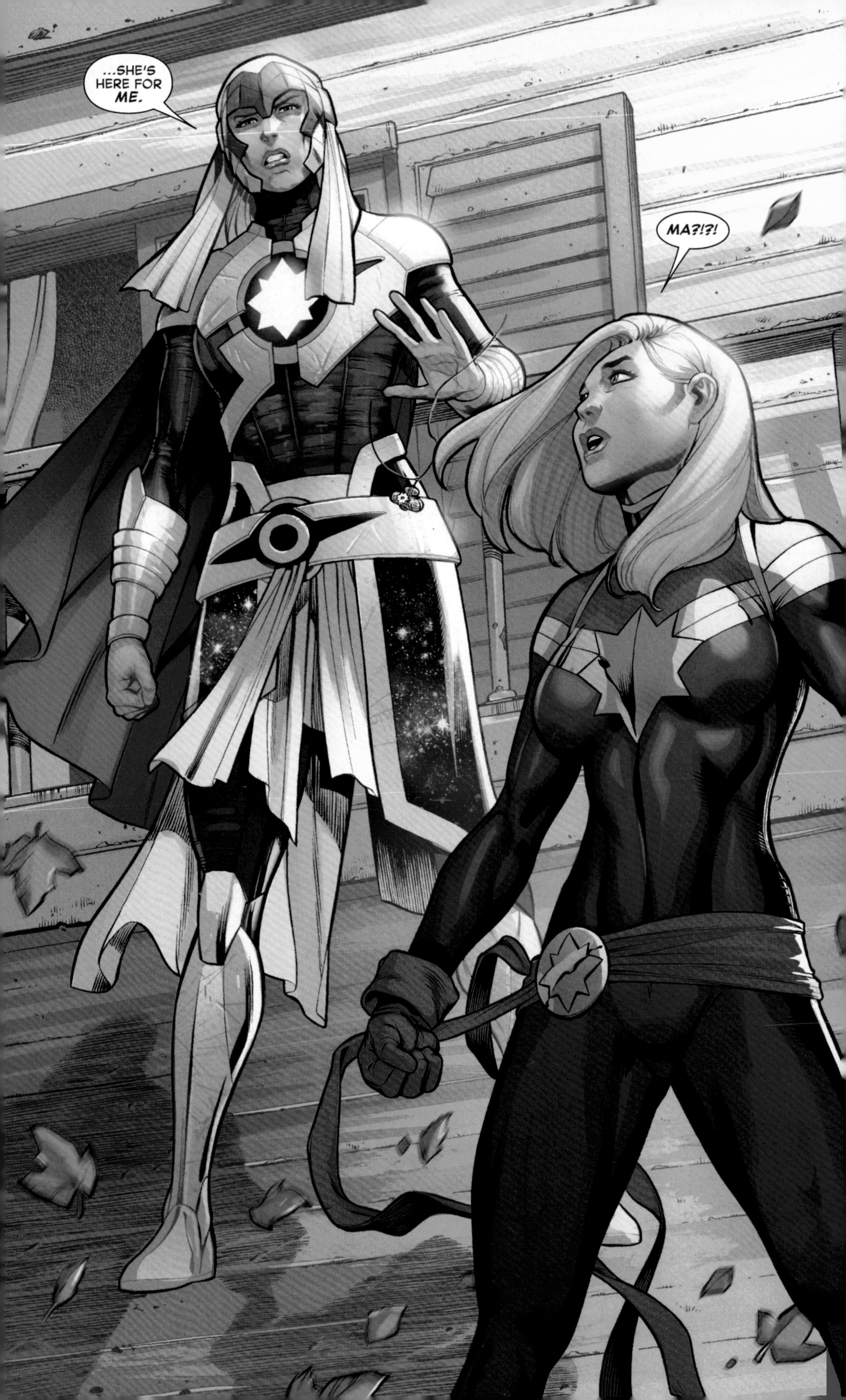
...SHE'S HERE FOR ME.
MA?!?!

PART 4: CHALLENGED

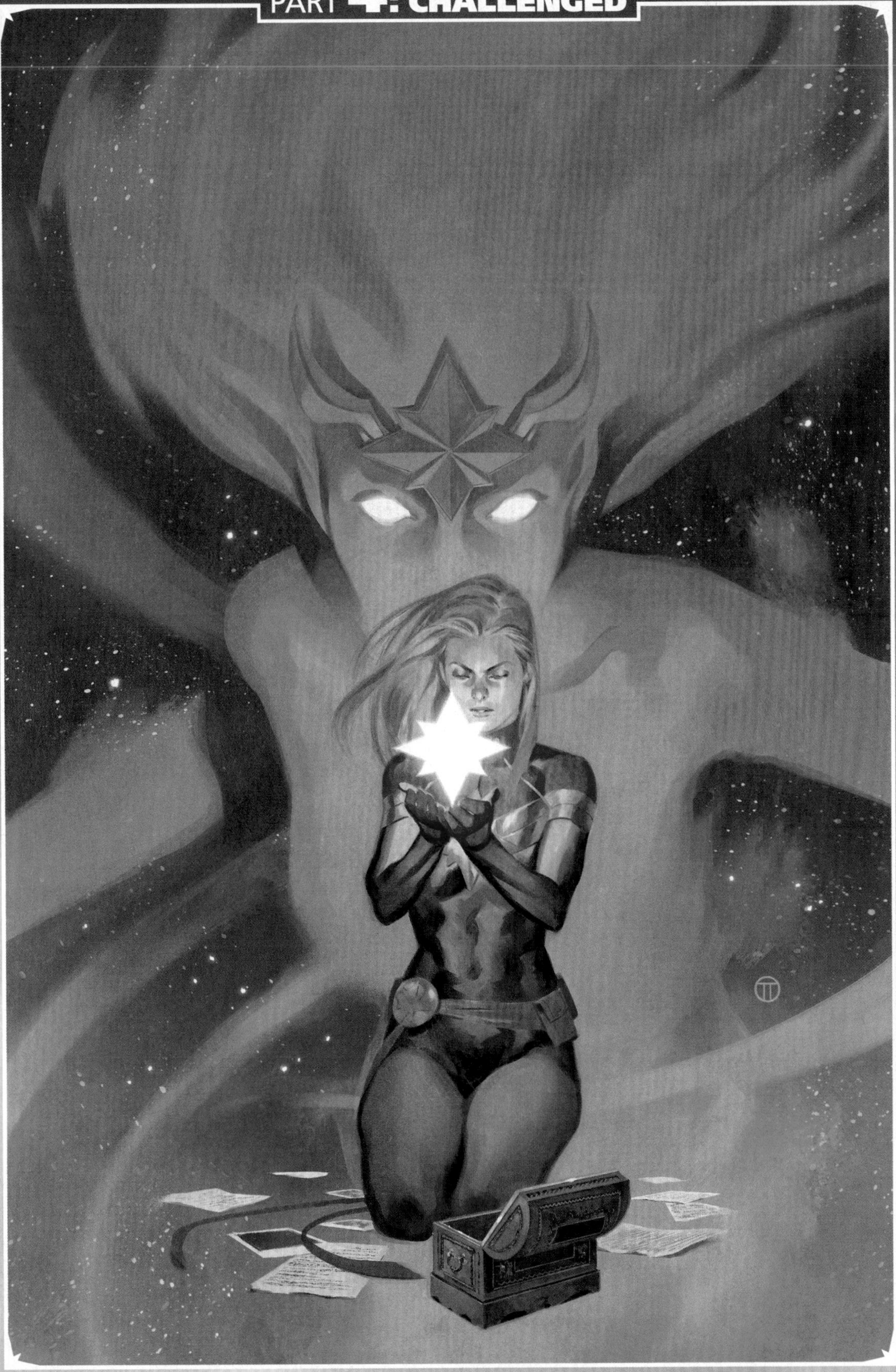

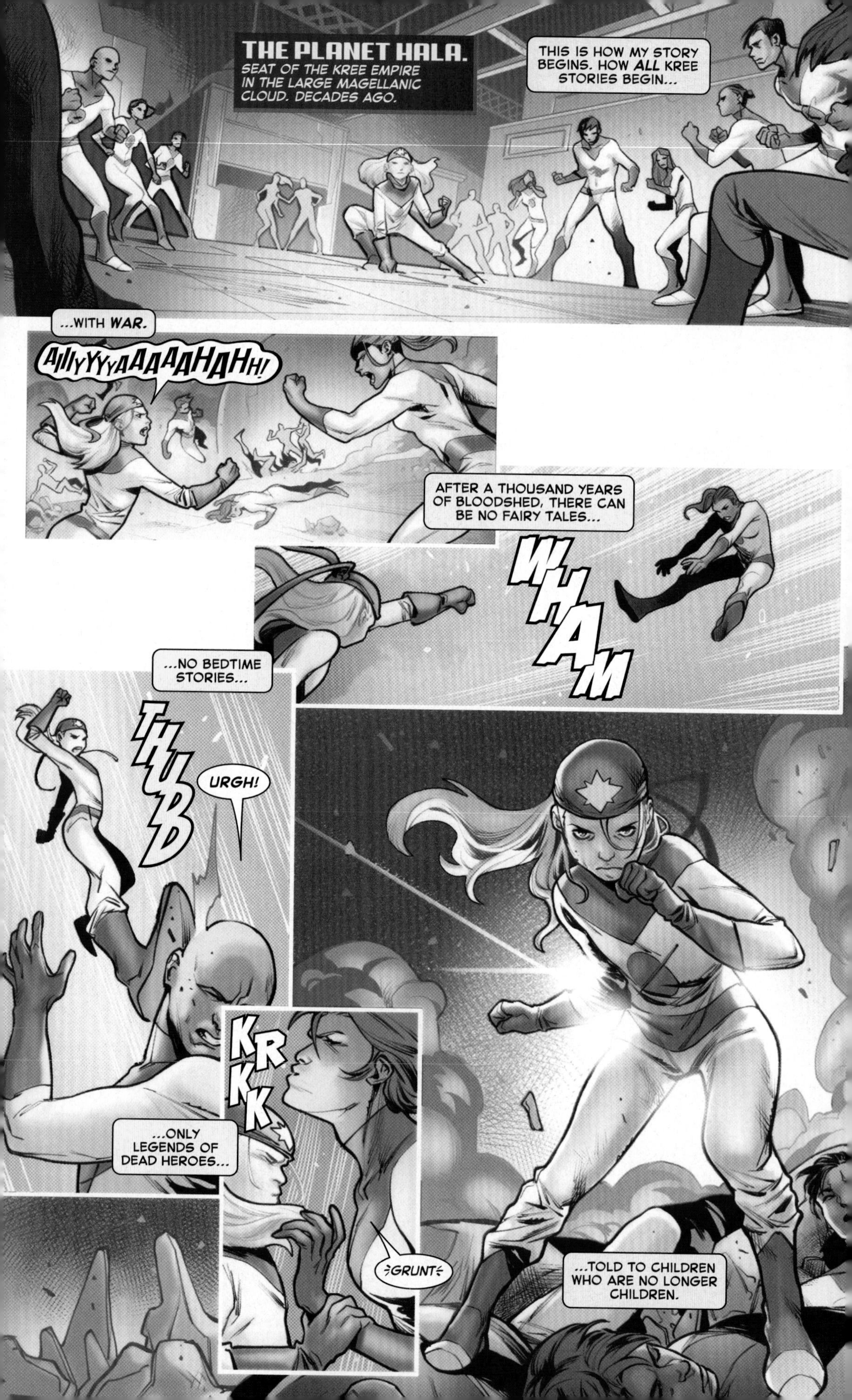
THE PLANET HALA.
SEAT OF THE KREE EMPIRE IN THE LARGE MAGELLANIC CLOUD. DECADES AGO.
THIS IS HOW MY STORY BEGINS. HOW ALL KREE STORIES BEGIN...
...WITH WAR.
AIIIYYYYAAAAAAHAHH!
AFTER A THOUSAND YEARS OF BLOODSHED, THERE CAN BE NO FAIRY TALES...
WHAM
...NO BEDTIME STORIES...
THUD
URGH!
KRKK
...ONLY LEGENDS OF DEAD HEROES...
GRUNT
...TOLD TO CHILDREN WHO ARE NO LONGER CHILDREN.

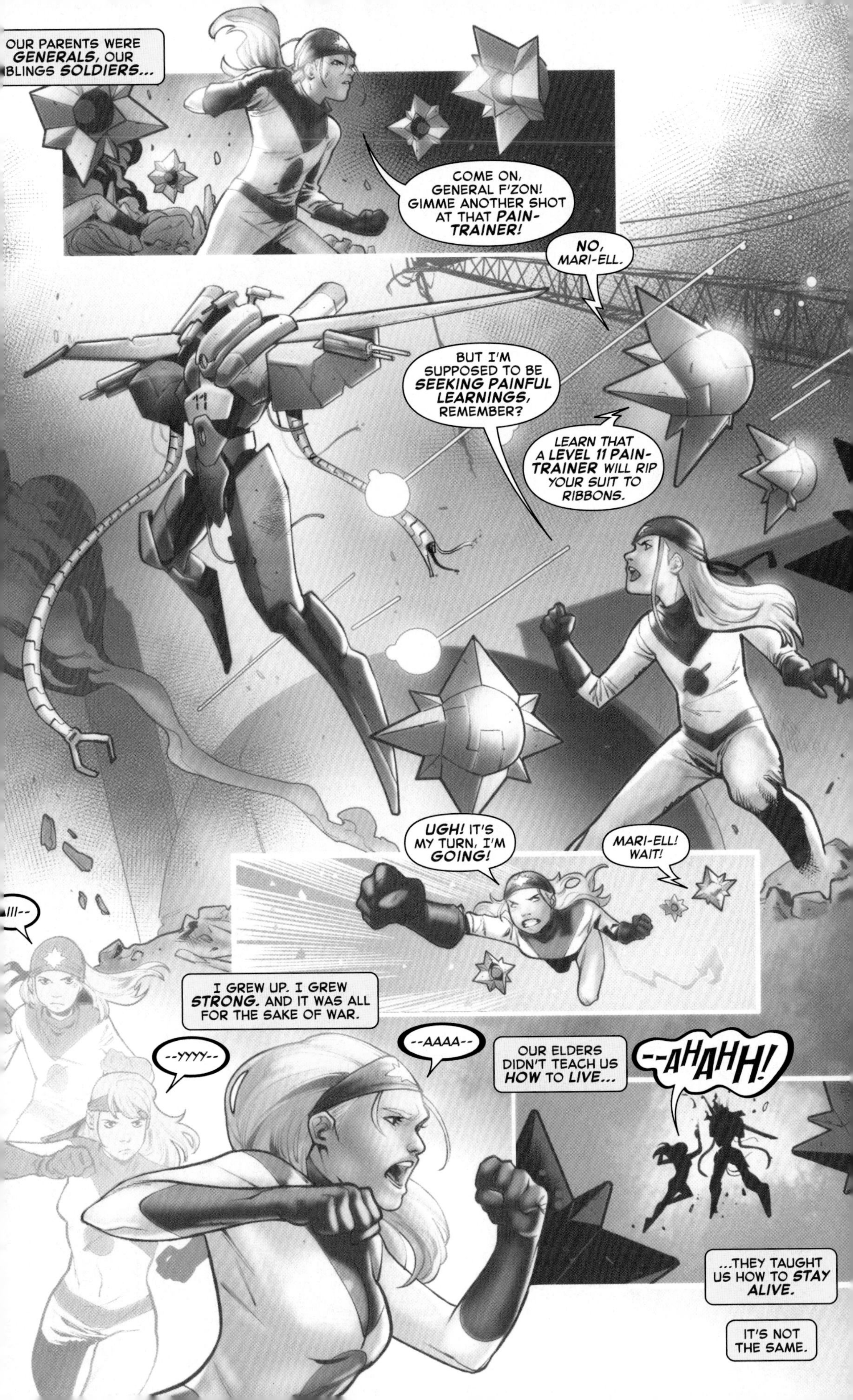

OUR PARENTS WERE GENERALS, OUR SIBLINGS SOLDIERS...
COME ON, GENERAL F'ZON! GIMME ANOTHER SHOT AT THAT PAIN-TRAINER!
NO, MARI-ELL.
BUT I'M SUPPOSED TO BE SEEKING PAINFUL LEARNINGS, REMEMBER?
LEARN THAT A LEVEL 11 PAIN-TRAINER WILL RIP YOUR SUIT TO RIBBONS.
UGH! IT'S MY TURN, I'M GOING!
MARI-ELL! WAIT!
III--
I GREW UP. I GREW STRONG. AND IT WAS ALL FOR THE SAKE OF WAR.
--YYYY--
--AAAA--
OUR ELDERS DIDN'T TEACH US HOW TO LIVE...
--AHAHH!
...THEY TAUGHT US HOW TO STAY ALIVE.
IT'S NOT THE SAME.

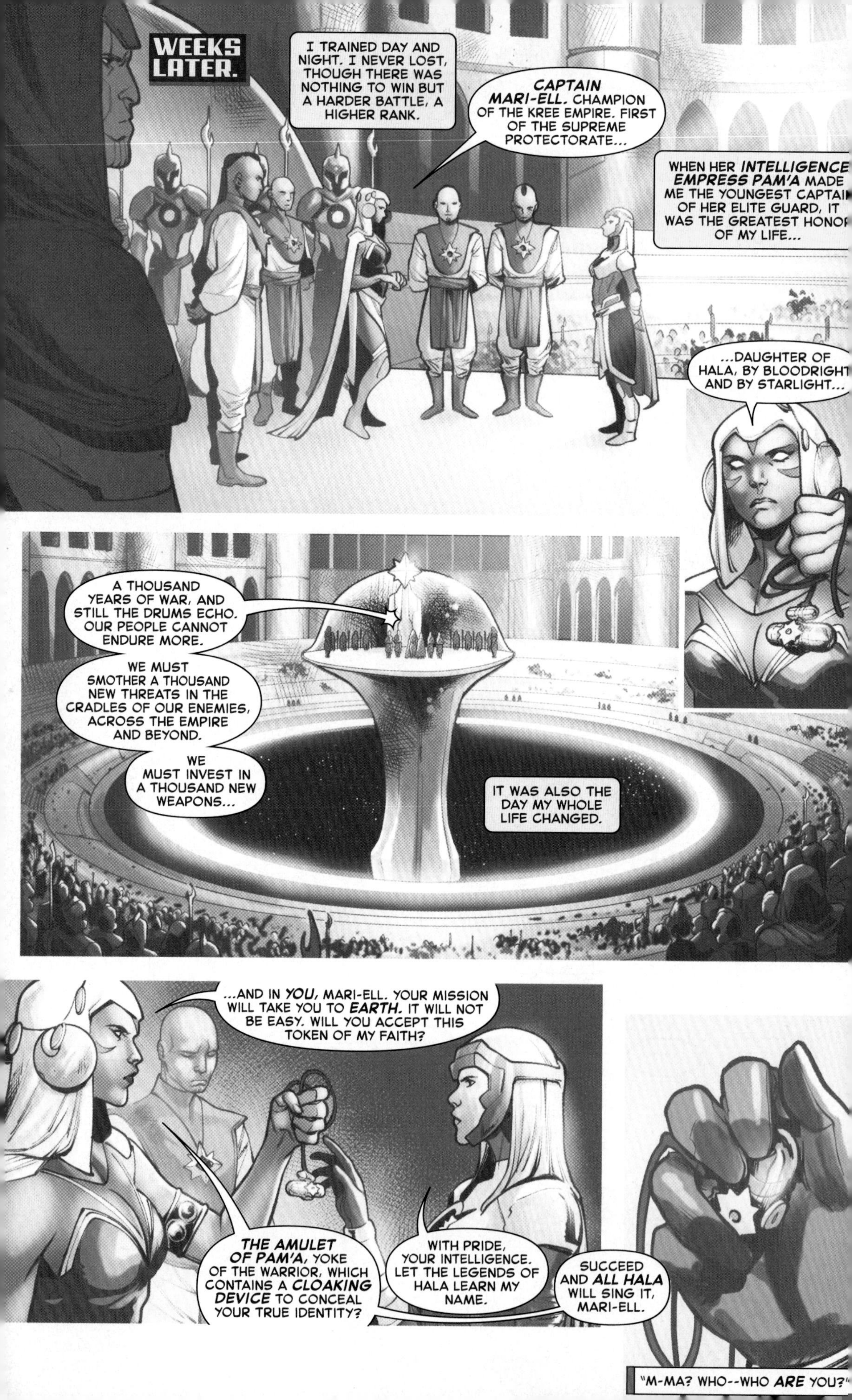
WEEKS LATER.
I TRAINED DAY AND NIGHT. I NEVER LOST, THOUGH THERE WAS NOTHING TO WIN BUT A HARDER BATTLE, A HIGHER RANK.
CAPTAIN MARI-ELL. CHAMPION OF THE KREE EMPIRE. FIRST OF THE SUPREME PROTECTORATE...
WHEN HER INTELLIGENCE EMPRESS PAM'A MADE ME THE YOUNGEST CAPTAI OF HER ELITE GUARD, IT WAS THE GREATEST HONOR OF MY LIFE...
...DAUGHTER OF HALA, BY BLOODRIGHT AND BY STARLIGHT...
A THOUSAND YEARS OF WAR, AND STILL THE DRUMS ECHO. OUR PEOPLE CANNOT ENDURE MORE.
WE MUST SMOTHER A THOUSAND NEW THREATS IN THE CRADLES OF OUR ENEMIES, ACROSS THE EMPIRE AND BEYOND.
WE MUST INVEST IN A THOUSAND NEW WEAPONS...
IT WAS ALSO THE DAY MY WHOLE LIFE CHANGED.
...AND IN YOU, MARI-ELL. YOUR MISSION WILL TAKE YOU TO EARTH. IT WILL NOT BE EASY. WILL YOU ACCEPT THIS TOKEN OF MY FAITH?
THE AMULET OF PAM'A, YOKE OF THE WARRIOR, WHICH CONTAINS A CLOAKING DEVICE TO CONCEAL YOUR TRUE IDENTITY?
WITH PRIDE, YOUR INTELLIGENCE. LET THE LEGENDS OF HALA LEARN MY NAME.
SUCCEED AND ALL HALA WILL SING IT, MARI-ELL.
"M-MA? WHO--WHO ARE YOU?"

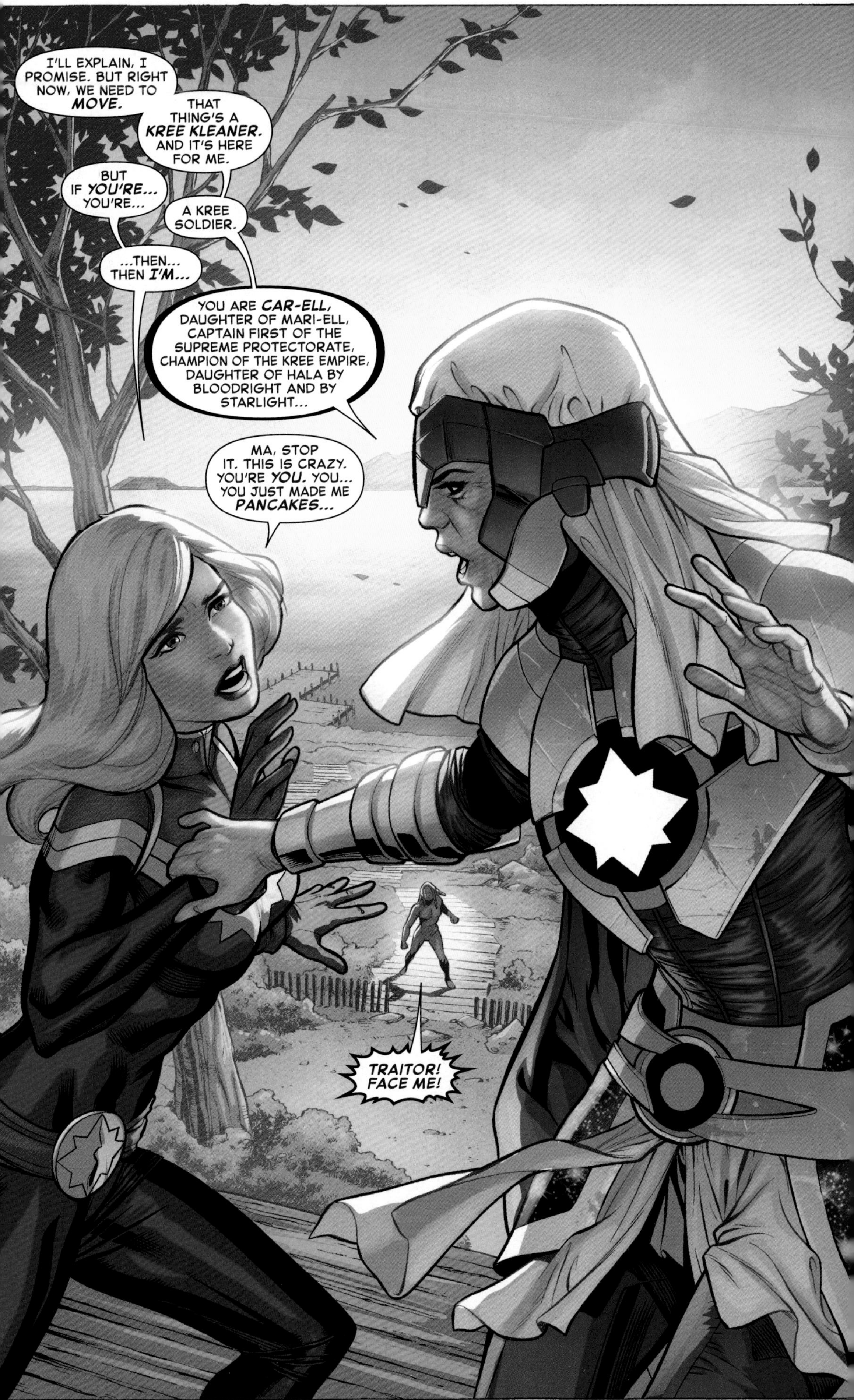
I'LL EXPLAIN, I PROMISE. BUT RIGHT NOW, WE NEED TO MOVE.
THAT THING'S A KREE KLEANER. AND IT'S HERE FOR ME.
BUT IF YOU'RE... YOU'RE...
A KREE SOLDIER.
...THEN... THEN I'M...
YOU ARE CAR-ELL, DAUGHTER OF MARI-ELL, CAPTAIN FIRST OF THE SUPREME PROTECTORATE, CHAMPION OF THE KREE EMPIRE, DAUGHTER OF HALA BY BLOODRIGHT AND BY STARLIGHT...
MA, STOP IT. THIS IS CRAZY. YOU'RE YOU. YOU... YOU JUST MADE ME PANCAKES...
TRAITOR! FACE ME!

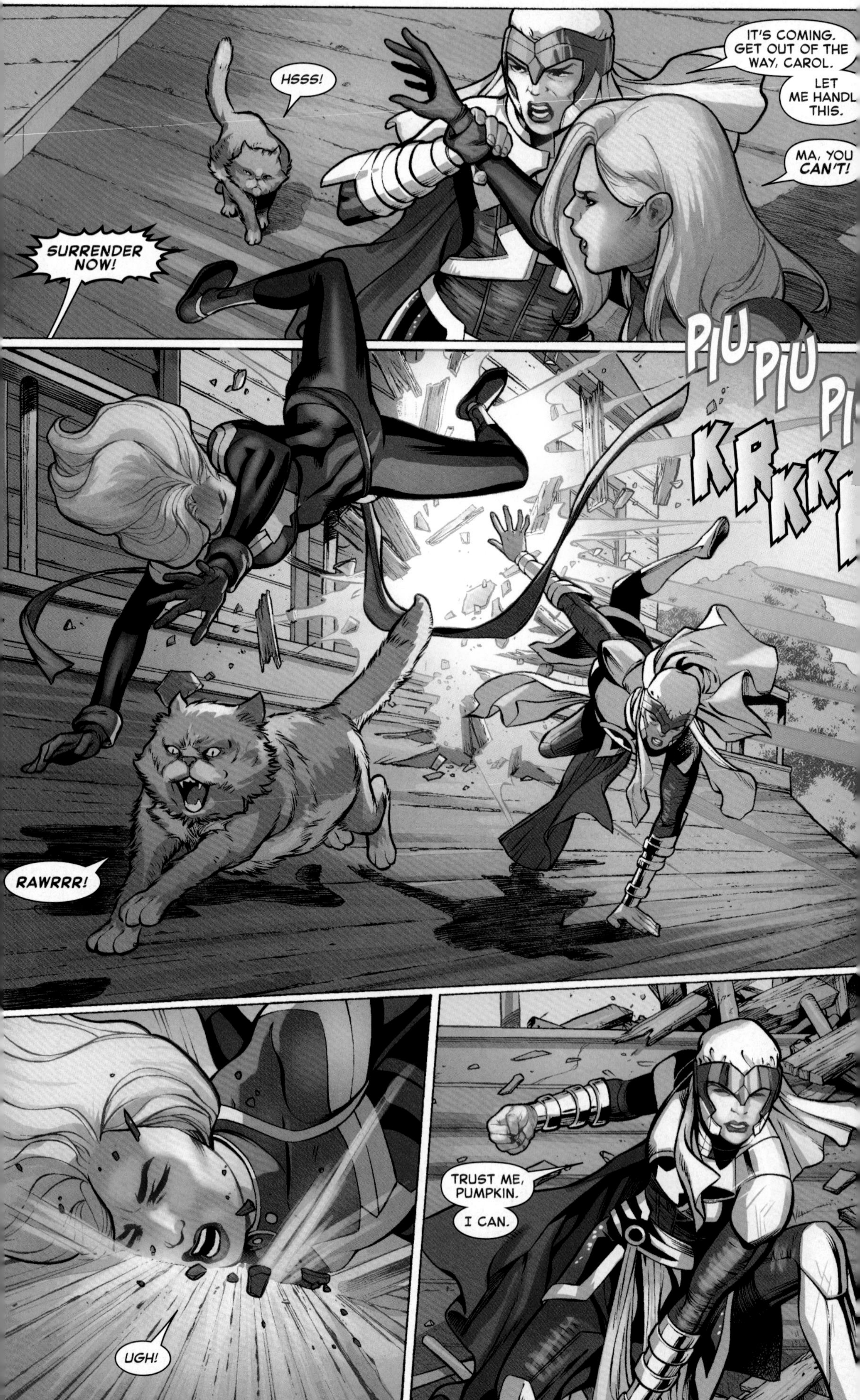
HSSS!
IT'S COMING. GET OUT OF THE WAY, CAROL.
LET ME HANDL THIS.
MA, YOU CAN'T!
SURRENDER NOW!
PIU PIU PI
KRKKK
RAWRRR!
UGH!
TRUST ME, PUMPKIN.
I CAN.

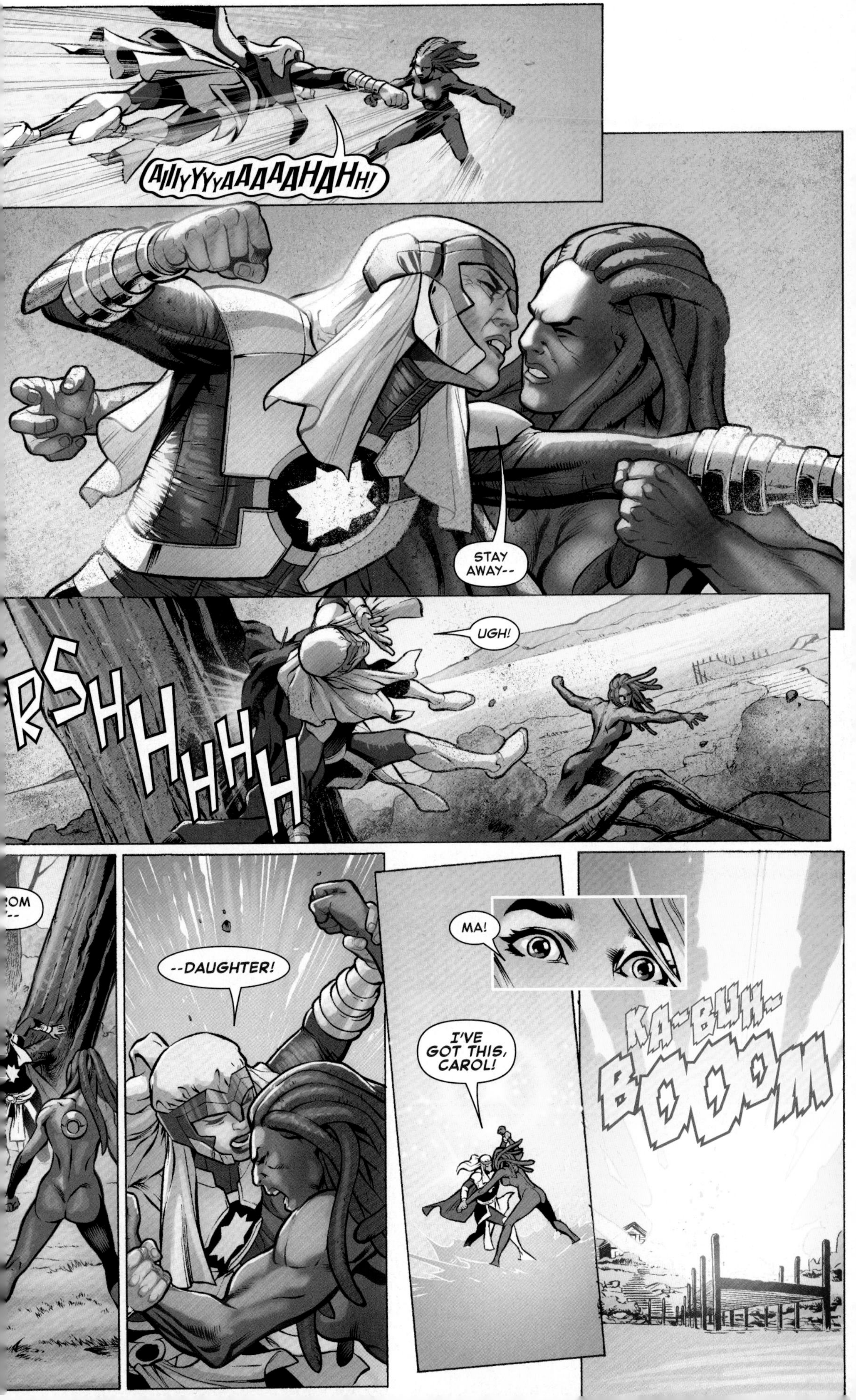
AIIIYYYYAAAAAAHAHH!
STAY AWAY--
UGH!
RSHHHHHH
--DAUGHTER!
MA!
I'VE GOT THIS, CAROL!
KA-BUH-BOOOM

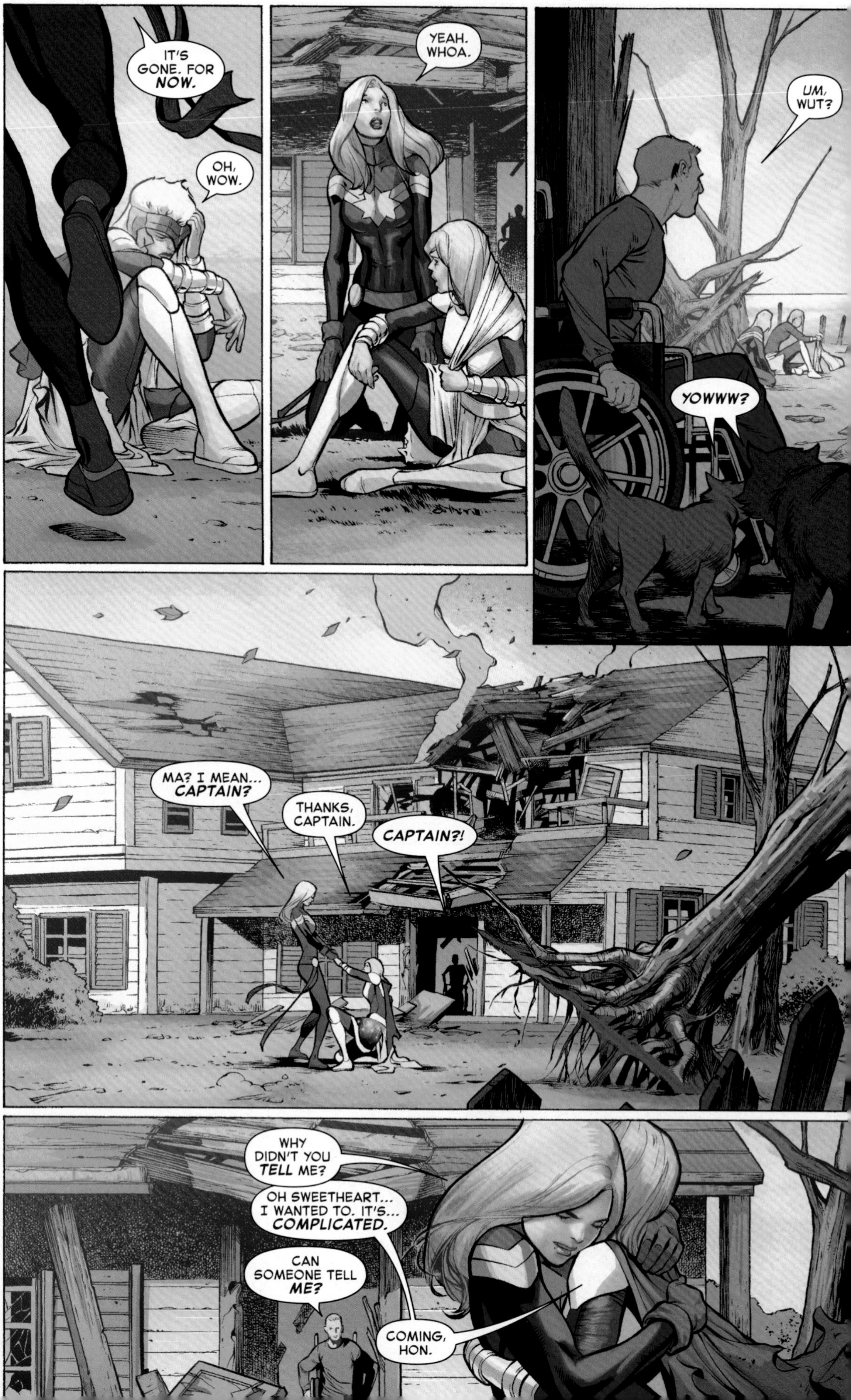
IT'S GONE. FOR NOW.
OH, WOW.
YEAH. WHOA.
UM, WUT?
YOWWW?
MA? I MEAN... CAPTAIN?
THANKS, CAPTAIN.
CAPTAIN?!
WHY DIDN'T YOU TELL ME?
OH SWEETHEART... I WANTED TO. IT'S... COMPLICATED.
CAN SOMEONE TELL ME?
COMING, HON.

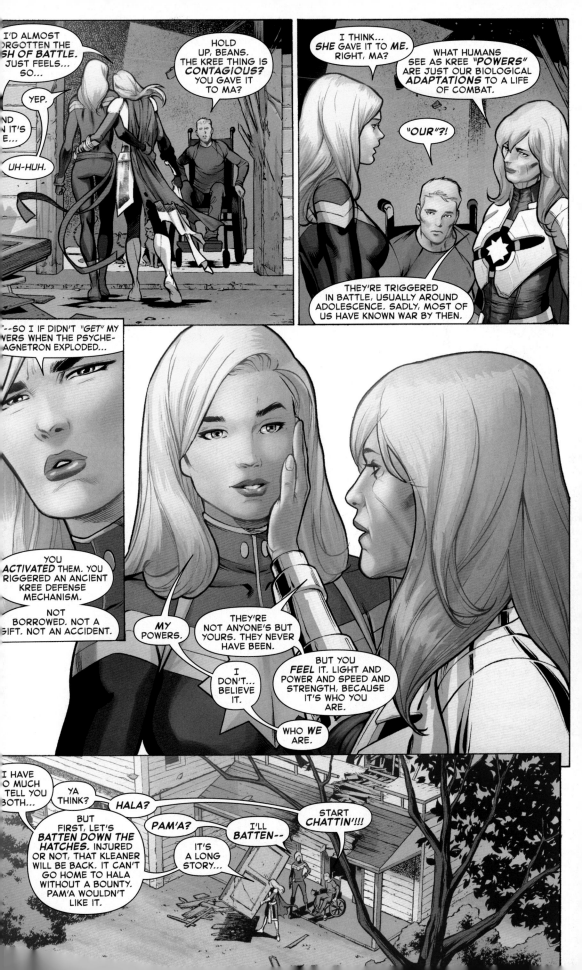

I'D ALMOST FORGOTTEN THE RUSH OF BATTLE. JUST FEELS... SO...

YEP.

AND IT'S LIKE...

UH-HUH.

HOLD UP, BEANS. THE KREE THING IS *CONTAGIOUS?* YOU GAVE IT TO MA?

I THINK... *SHE* GAVE IT TO *ME.* RIGHT, MA?

WHAT HUMANS SEE AS KREE *"POWERS"* ARE JUST OUR BIOLOGICAL *ADAPTATIONS* TO A LIFE OF COMBAT.

"OUR"?!

THEY'RE TRIGGERED IN BATTLE, USUALLY AROUND ADOLESCENCE. SADLY, MOST OF US HAVE KNOWN WAR BY THEN.

"--SO IF I DIDN'T *"GET"* MY POWERS WHEN THE PSYCHE-MAGNETRON EXPLODED...

YOU *ACTIVATED* THEM. YOU TRIGGERED AN ANCIENT KREE DEFENSE MECHANISM.

NOT BORROWED. NOT A GIFT. NOT AN ACCIDENT.

MY POWERS.

THEY'RE NOT ANYONE'S BUT YOURS. THEY NEVER HAVE BEEN.

I DON'T... BELIEVE IT.

BUT YOU *FEEL* IT. LIGHT AND POWER AND SPEED AND STRENGTH, BECAUSE IT'S WHO YOU ARE.

WHO *WE* ARE.

I HAVE SO MUCH TO TELL YOU BOTH...

YA THINK?

HALA?

PAM'A?

I'LL *BATTEN*--

START *CHATTIN'!!!*

BUT FIRST, LET'S *BATTEN DOWN THE HATCHES.* INJURED OR NOT, THAT KLEANER WILL BE BACK. IT CAN'T GO HOME TO HALA WITHOUT A BOUNTY. PAM'A WOULDN'T LIKE IT.

IT'S A LONG STORY...

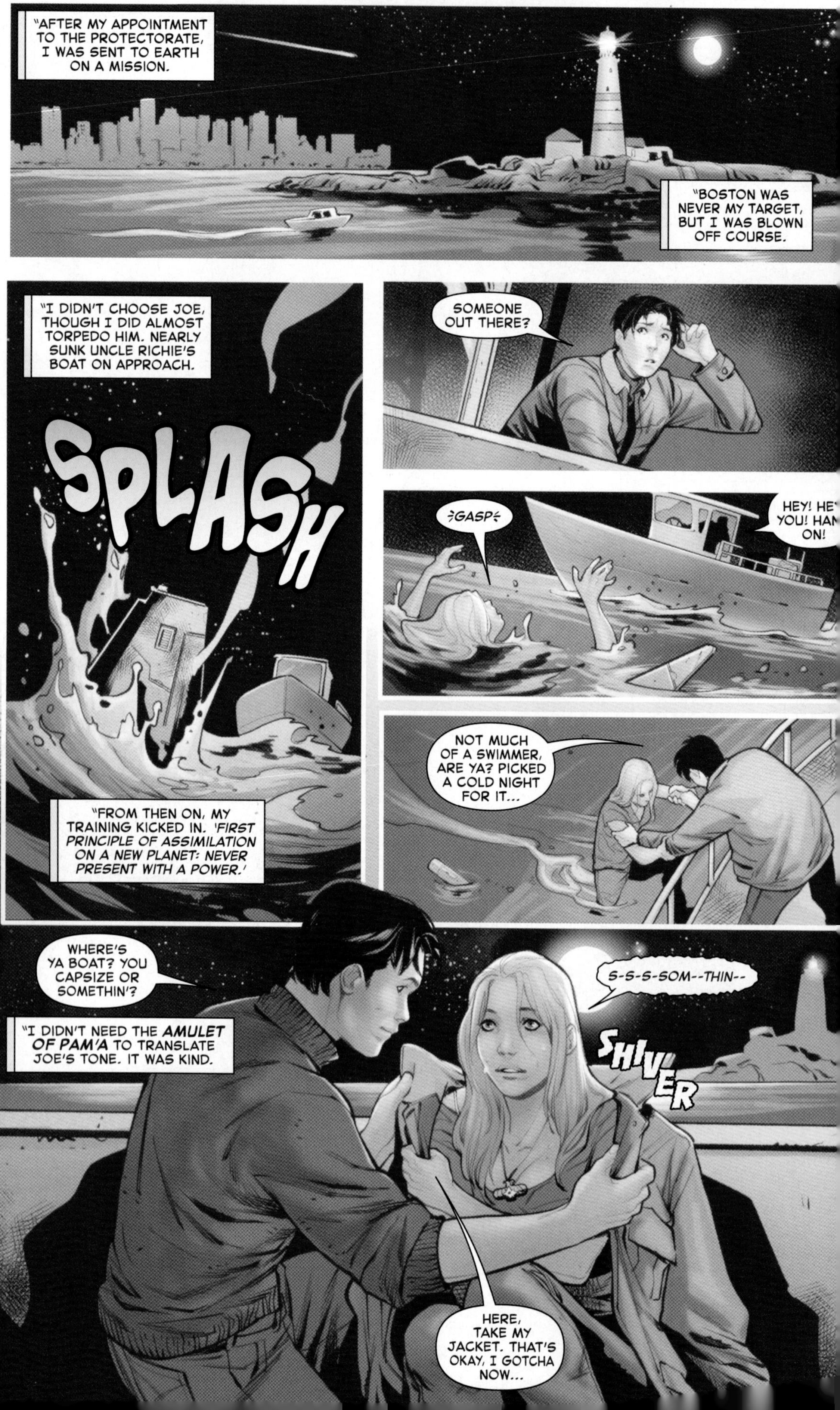
"AFTER MY APPOINTMENT TO THE PROTECTORATE, I WAS SENT TO EARTH ON A MISSION.
"BOSTON WAS NEVER MY TARGET, BUT I WAS BLOWN OFF COURSE.
"I DIDN'T CHOOSE JOE, THOUGH I DID ALMOST TORPEDO HIM. NEARLY SUNK UNCLE RICHIE'S BOAT ON APPROACH.
SPLASH
"FROM THEN ON, MY TRAINING KICKED IN. '*FIRST PRINCIPLE OF ASSIMILATION ON A NEW PLANET: NEVER PRESENT WITH A POWER.*'
SOMEONE OUT THERE?
GASP
HEY! HE YOU! HAN ON!
NOT MUCH OF A SWIMMER, ARE YA? PICKED A COLD NIGHT FOR IT...
WHERE'S YA BOAT? YOU CAPSIZE OR SOMETHIN'?
"I DIDN'T NEED THE *AMULET OF PAM'A* TO TRANSLATE JOE'S TONE. IT WAS KIND.
S-S-S-SOM--THIN'--
SHIVER
HERE, TAKE MY JACKET. THAT'S OKAY, I GOTCHA NOW...

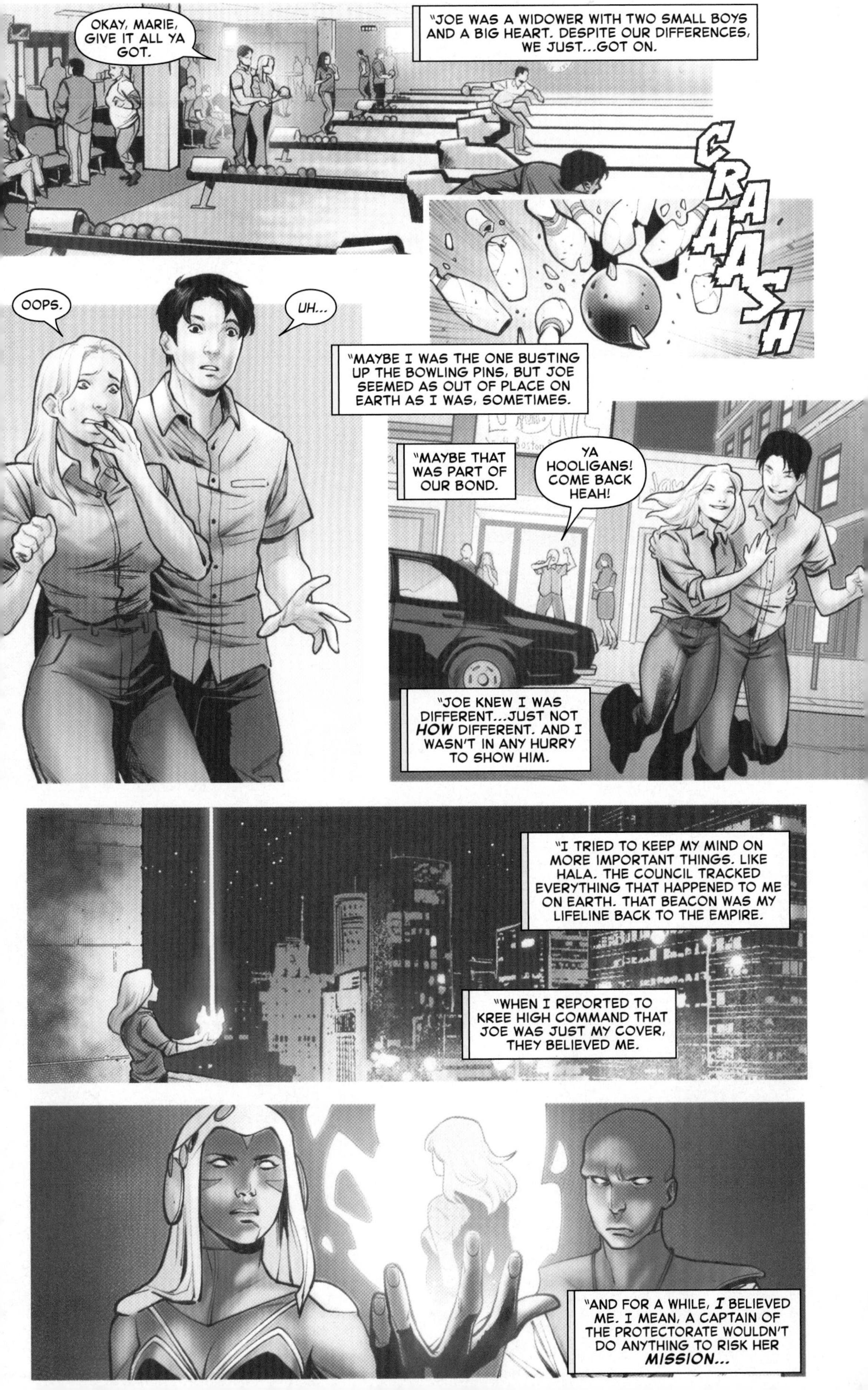
OKAY, MARIE, GIVE IT ALL YA GOT.
"JOE WAS A WIDOWER WITH TWO SMALL BOYS AND A BIG HEART. DESPITE OUR DIFFERENCES, WE JUST...GOT ON.
CRAAASH
OOPS.
UH...
"MAYBE I WAS THE ONE BUSTING UP THE BOWLING PINS, BUT JOE SEEMED AS OUT OF PLACE ON EARTH AS I WAS, SOMETIMES.
"MAYBE THAT WAS PART OF OUR BOND.
YA HOOLIGANS! COME BACK HEAH!
"JOE KNEW I WAS DIFFERENT...JUST NOT *HOW* DIFFERENT. AND I WASN'T IN ANY HURRY TO SHOW HIM.
"I TRIED TO KEEP MY MIND ON MORE IMPORTANT THINGS. LIKE HALA. THE COUNCIL TRACKED EVERYTHING THAT HAPPENED TO ME ON EARTH. THAT BEACON WAS MY LIFELINE BACK TO THE EMPIRE.
"WHEN I REPORTED TO KREE HIGH COMMAND THAT JOE WAS JUST MY COVER, THEY BELIEVED ME.
"AND FOR A WHILE, *I* BELIEVED ME. I MEAN, A CAPTAIN OF THE PROTECTORATE WOULDN'T DO ANYTHING TO RISK HER *MISSION*...

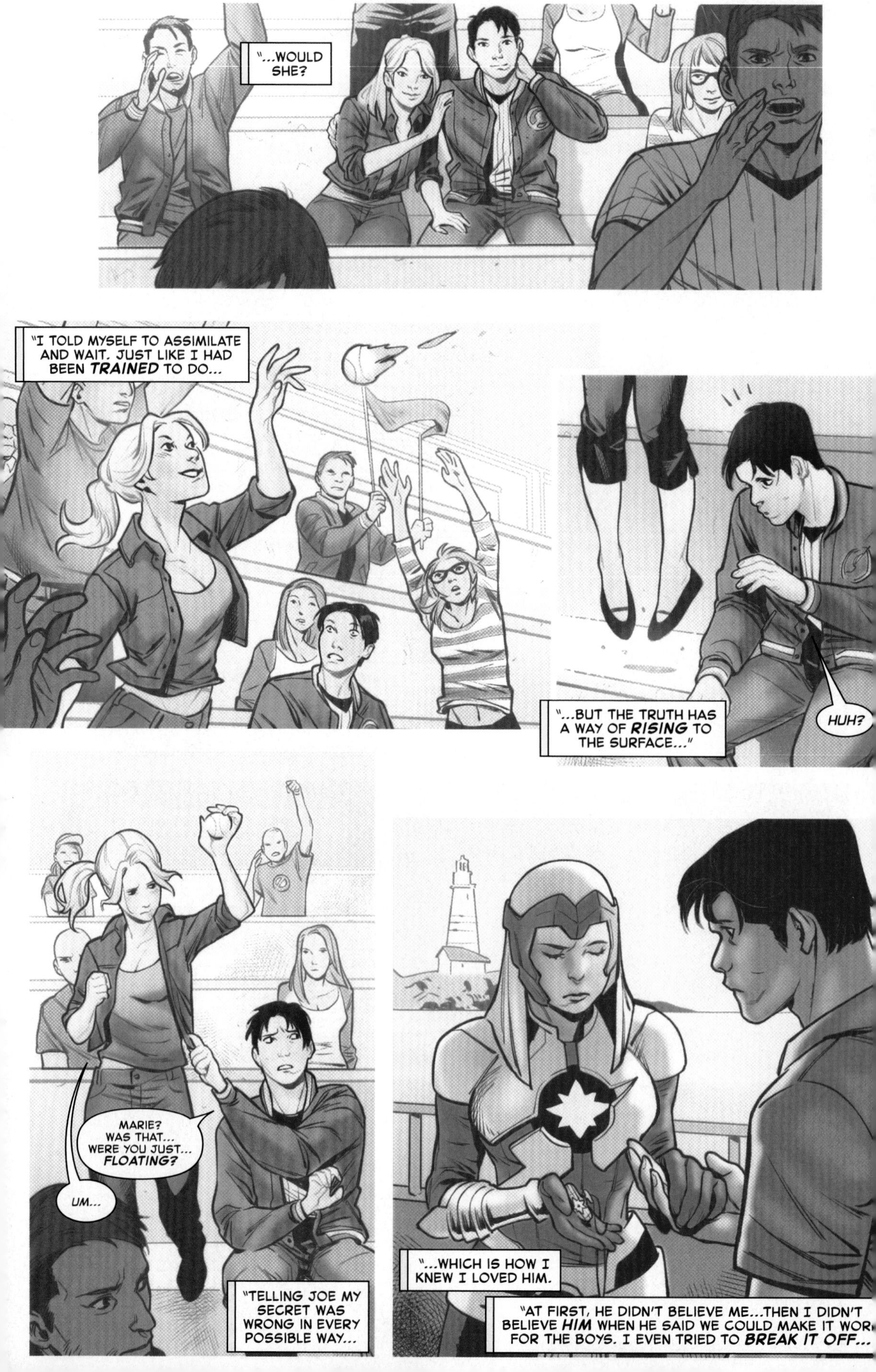
"...WOULD SHE?
"I TOLD MYSELF TO ASSIMILATE AND WAIT. JUST LIKE I HAD BEEN TRAINED TO DO...
"...BUT THE TRUTH HAS A WAY OF RISING TO THE SURFACE..."
HUH?
MARIE? WAS THAT... WERE YOU JUST... FLOATING?
UM...
"TELLING JOE MY SECRET WAS WRONG IN EVERY POSSIBLE WAY...
"...WHICH IS HOW I KNEW I LOVED HIM.
"AT FIRST, HE DIDN'T BELIEVE ME...THEN I DIDN'T BELIEVE HIM WHEN HE SAID WE COULD MAKE IT WOR
FOR THE BOYS. I EVEN TRIED TO BREAK IT OFF...

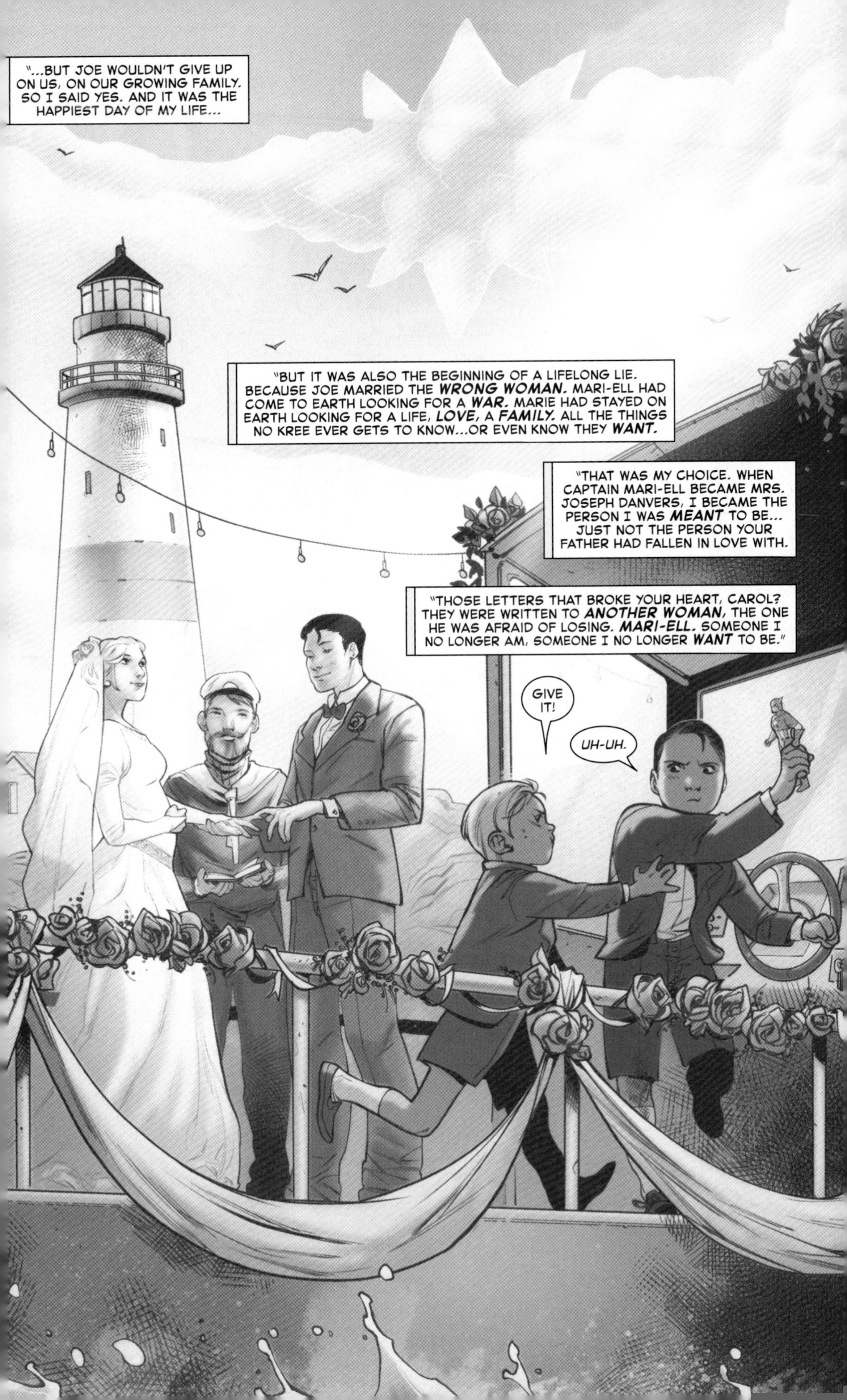
"...BUT JOE WOULDN'T GIVE UP ON US, ON OUR GROWING FAMILY. SO I SAID YES. AND IT WAS THE HAPPIEST DAY OF MY LIFE...
"BUT IT WAS ALSO THE BEGINNING OF A LIFELONG LIE. BECAUSE JOE MARRIED THE WRONG WOMAN. MARI-ELL HAD COME TO EARTH LOOKING FOR A WAR. MARIE HAD STAYED ON EARTH LOOKING FOR A LIFE, LOVE, A FAMILY. ALL THE THINGS NO KREE EVER GETS TO KNOW...OR EVEN KNOW THEY WANT.
"THAT WAS MY CHOICE. WHEN CAPTAIN MARI-ELL BECAME MRS. JOSEPH DANVERS, I BECAME THE PERSON I WAS MEANT TO BE... JUST NOT THE PERSON YOUR FATHER HAD FALLEN IN LOVE WITH.
"THOSE LETTERS THAT BROKE YOUR HEART, CAROL? THEY WERE WRITTEN TO ANOTHER WOMAN, THE ONE HE WAS AFRAID OF LOSING. MARI-ELL. SOMEONE I NO LONGER AM, SOMEONE I NO LONGER WANT TO BE."
GIVE IT!
UH-UH.

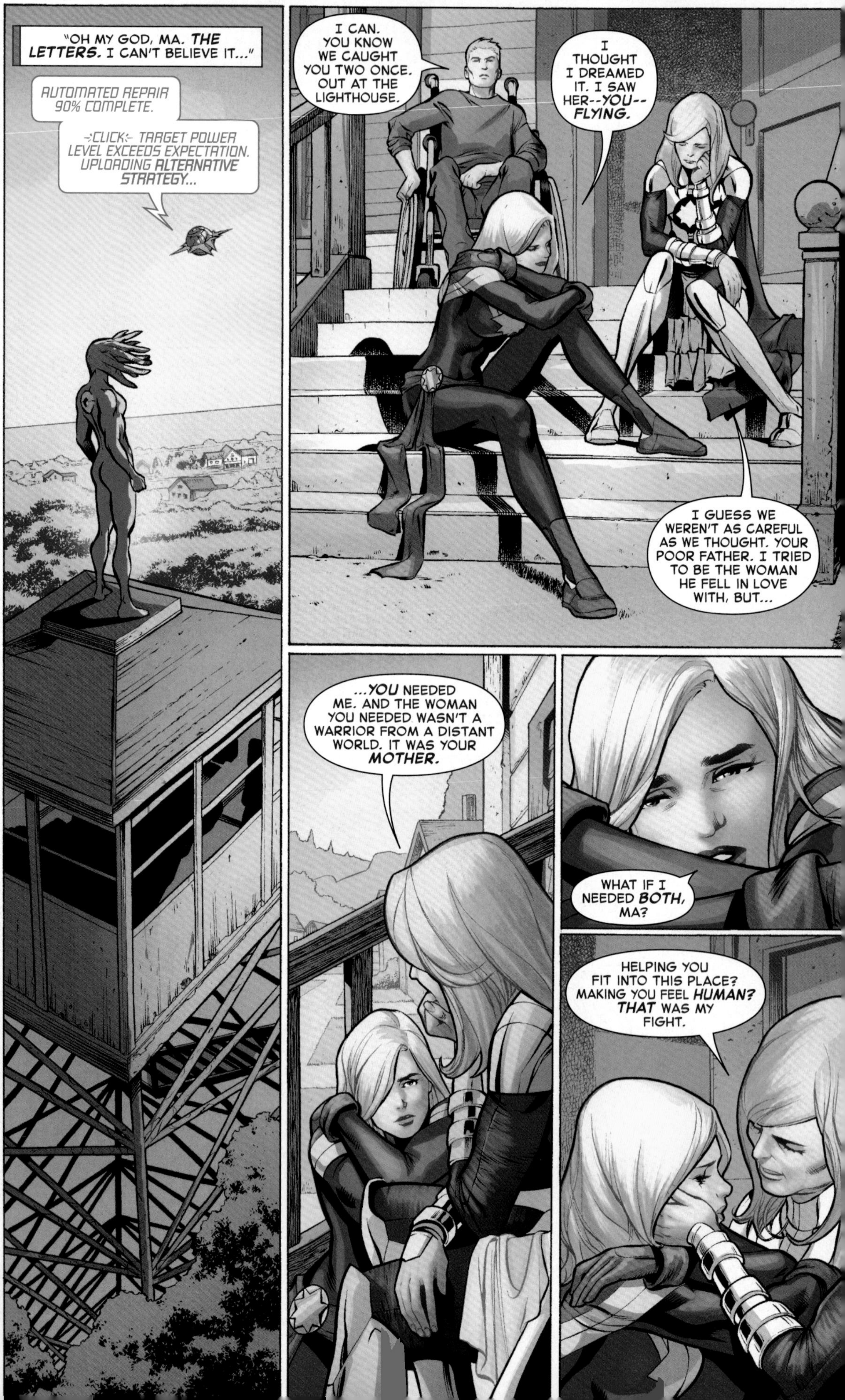
"OH MY GOD, MA. THE LETTERS. I CAN'T BELIEVE IT..."
AUTOMATED REPAIR 90% COMPLETE.
⇒CLICK⇐ TARGET POWER LEVEL EXCEEDS EXPECTATION. UPLOADING ALTERNATIVE STRATEGY...
I CAN. YOU KNOW WE CAUGHT YOU TWO ONCE. OUT AT THE LIGHTHOUSE.
I THOUGHT I DREAMED IT. I SAW HER--YOU--FLYING.
I GUESS WE WEREN'T AS CAREFUL AS WE THOUGHT. YOUR POOR FATHER. I TRIED TO BE THE WOMAN HE FELL IN LOVE WITH, BUT...
...YOU NEEDED ME. AND THE WOMAN YOU NEEDED WASN'T A WARRIOR FROM A DISTANT WORLD. IT WAS YOUR MOTHER.
WHAT IF I NEEDED BOTH, MA?
HELPING YOU FIT INTO THIS PLACE? MAKING YOU FEEL HUMAN? THAT WAS MY FIGHT.

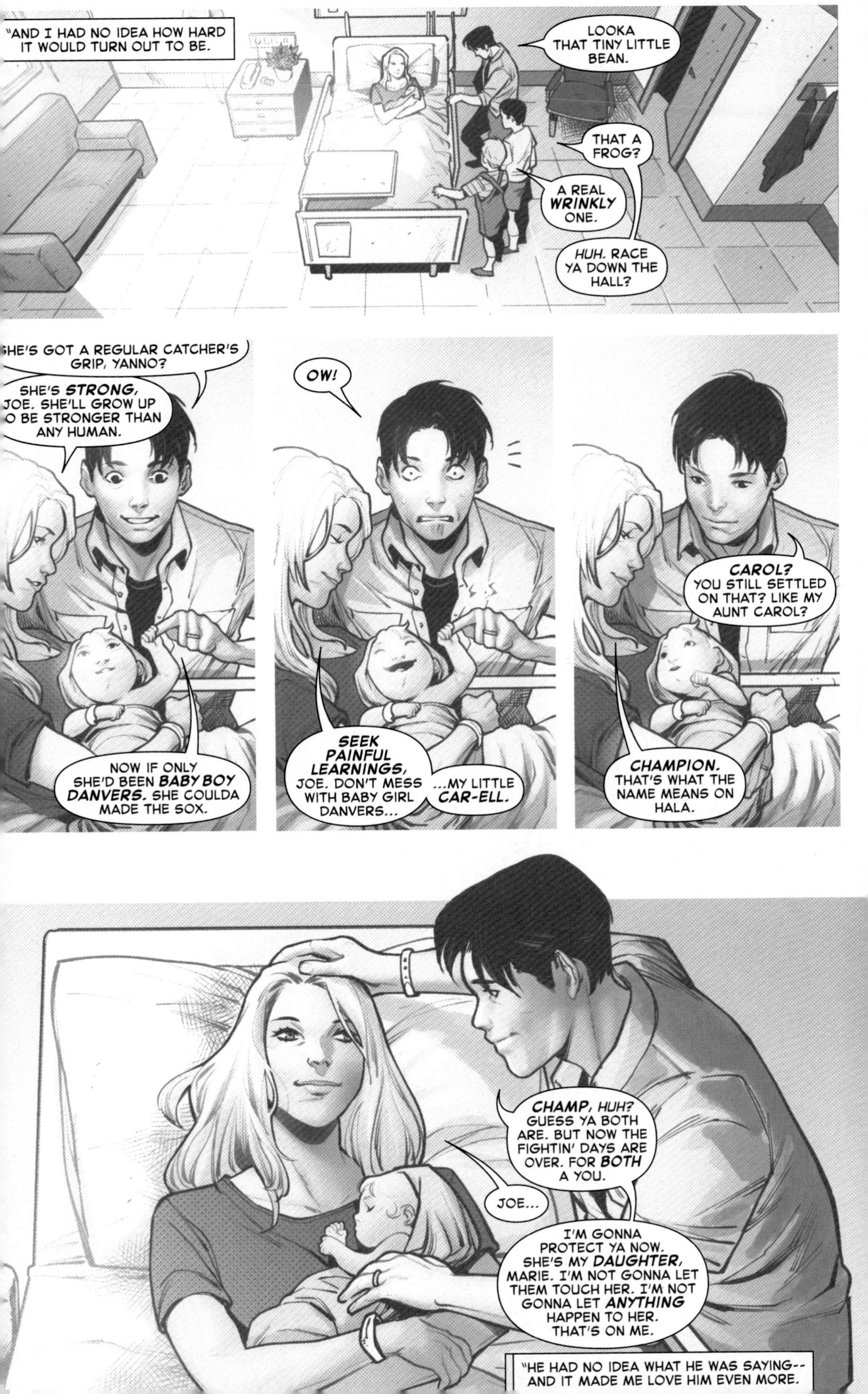
"AND I HAD NO IDEA HOW HARD IT WOULD TURN OUT TO BE.
LOOKA THAT TINY LITTLE BEAN.
THAT A FROG?
A REAL WRINKLY ONE.
HUH. RACE YA DOWN THE HALL?
SHE'S GOT A REGULAR CATCHER'S GRIP, YANNO?
SHE'S STRONG, JOE. SHE'LL GROW UP TO BE STRONGER THAN ANY HUMAN.
NOW IF ONLY SHE'D BEEN BABY BOY DANVERS. SHE COULDA MADE THE SOX.
OW!
SEEK PAINFUL LEARNINGS, JOE. DON'T MESS WITH BABY GIRL DANVERS...
...MY LITTLE CAR-ELL.
CAROL? YOU STILL SETTLED ON THAT? LIKE MY AUNT CAROL?
CHAMPION. THAT'S WHAT THE NAME MEANS ON HALA.
CHAMP, HUH? GUESS YA BOTH ARE. BUT NOW THE FIGHTIN' DAYS ARE OVER. FOR BOTH A YOU.
JOE...
I'M GONNA PROTECT YA NOW. SHE'S MY DAUGHTER, MARIE. I'M NOT GONNA LET THEM TOUCH HER. I'M NOT GONNA LET ANYTHING HAPPEN TO HER. THAT'S ON ME.
"HE HAD NO IDEA WHAT HE WAS SAYING-- AND IT MADE ME LOVE HIM EVEN MORE.

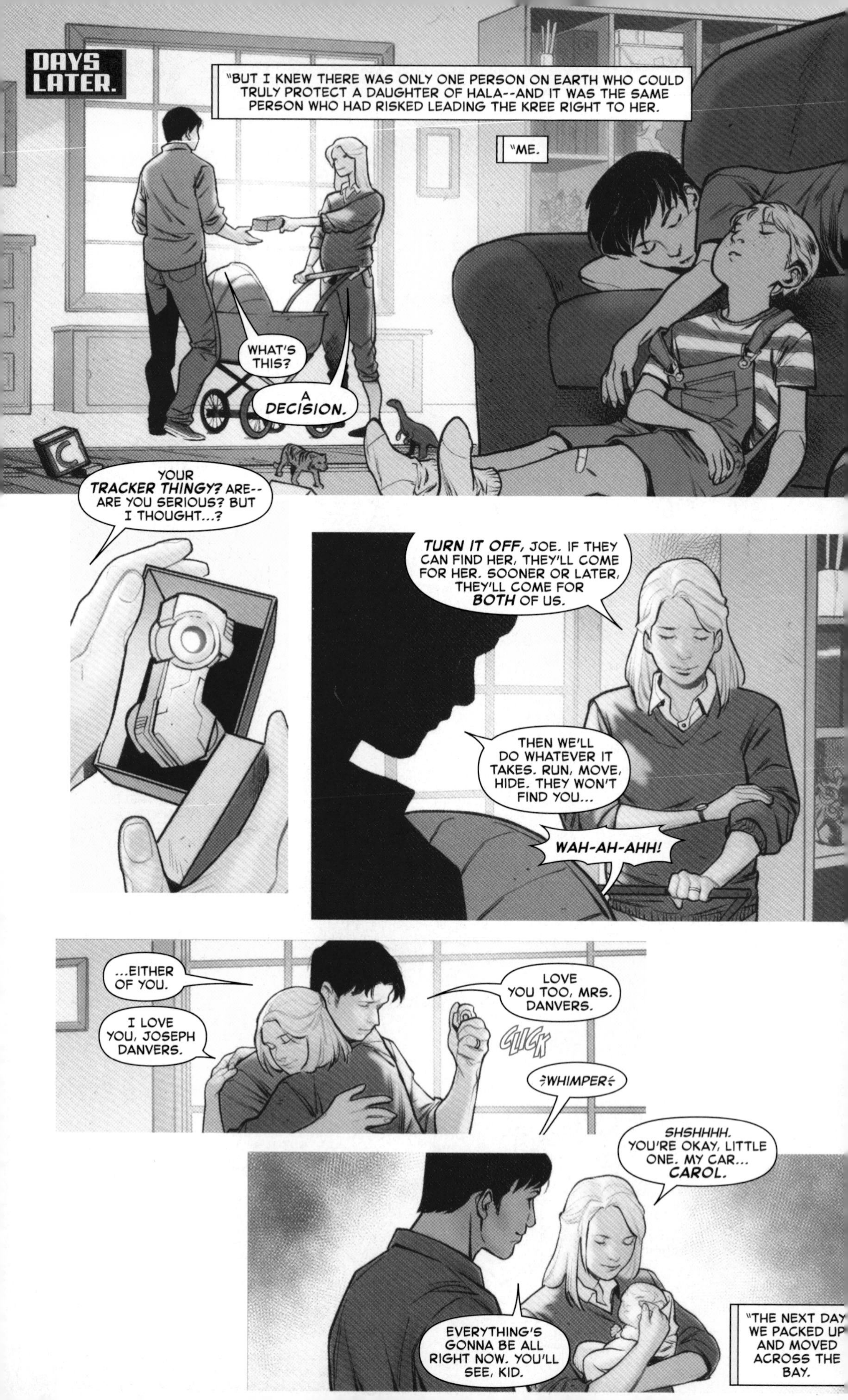
DAYS LATER.
"BUT I KNEW THERE WAS ONLY ONE PERSON ON EARTH WHO COULD TRULY PROTECT A DAUGHTER OF HALA--AND IT WAS THE SAME PERSON WHO HAD RISKED LEADING THE KREE RIGHT TO HER.
"ME.
WHAT'S THIS?
A DECISION.
YOUR TRACKER THINGY? ARE--ARE YOU SERIOUS? BUT I THOUGHT...?
TURN IT OFF, JOE. IF THEY CAN FIND HER, THEY'LL COME FOR HER. SOONER OR LATER, THEY'LL COME FOR BOTH OF US.
THEN WE'LL DO WHATEVER IT TAKES. RUN, MOVE, HIDE. THEY WON'T FIND YOU...
WAH-AH-AHH!
...EITHER OF YOU.
I LOVE YOU, JOSEPH DANVERS.
LOVE YOU TOO, MRS. DANVERS.
CLICK
WHIMPER
SHSHHHH. YOU'RE OKAY, LITTLE ONE. MY CAR... CAROL.
EVERYTHING'S GONNA BE ALL RIGHT NOW. YOU'LL SEE, KID.
"THE NEXT DAY WE PACKED UP AND MOVED ACROSS THE BAY.

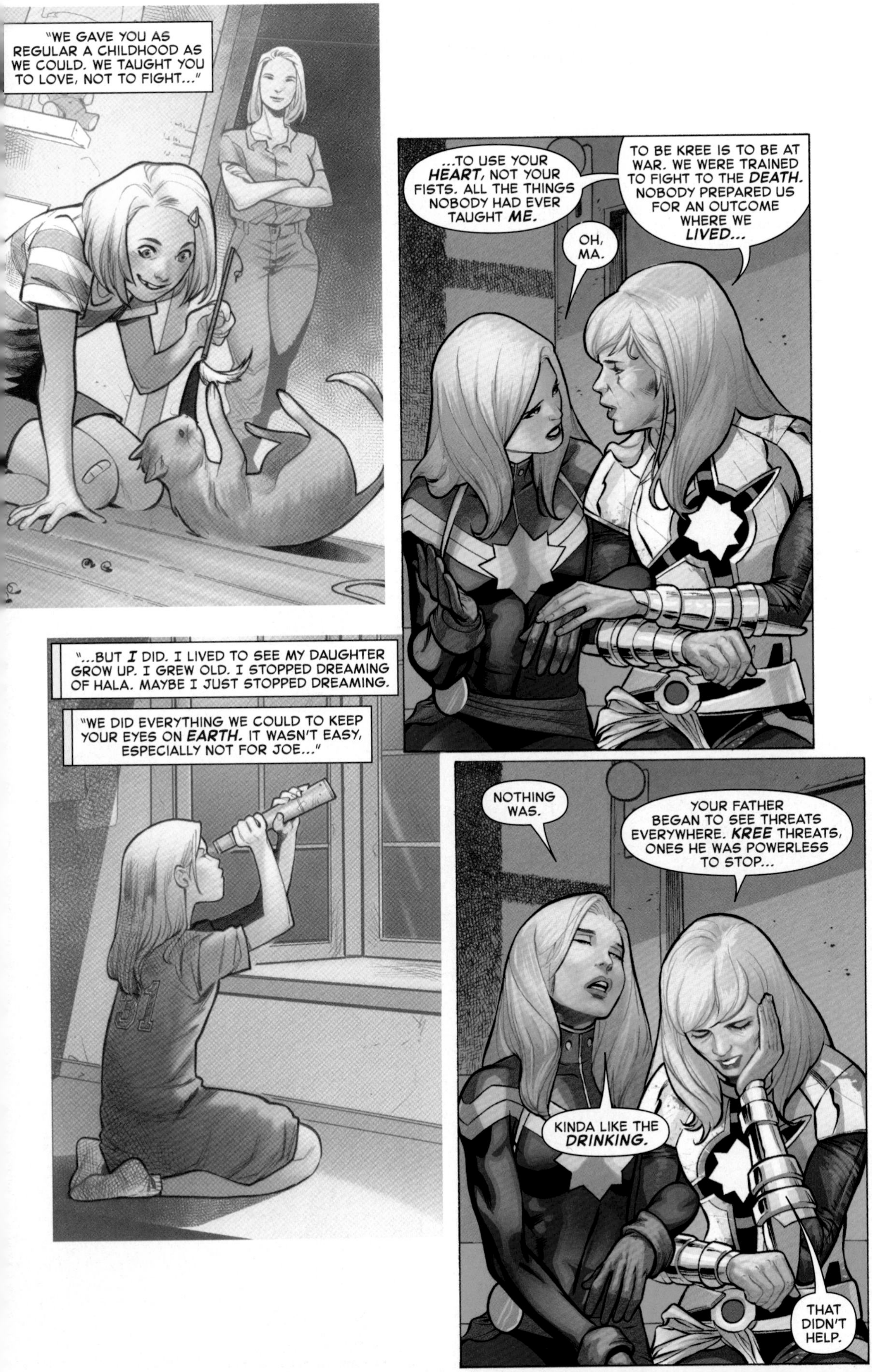
"WE GAVE YOU AS REGULAR A CHILDHOOD AS WE COULD. WE TAUGHT YOU TO LOVE, NOT TO FIGHT..."
...TO USE YOUR HEART, NOT YOUR FISTS. ALL THE THINGS NOBODY HAD EVER TAUGHT ME.
TO BE KREE IS TO BE AT WAR. WE WERE TRAINED TO FIGHT TO THE DEATH. NOBODY PREPARED US FOR AN OUTCOME WHERE WE LIVED...
OH, MA.
"...BUT I DID. I LIVED TO SEE MY DAUGHTER GROW UP. I GREW OLD. I STOPPED DREAMING OF HALA. MAYBE I JUST STOPPED DREAMING.
"WE DID EVERYTHING WE COULD TO KEEP YOUR EYES ON EARTH. IT WASN'T EASY, ESPECIALLY NOT FOR JOE..."
NOTHING WAS.
YOUR FATHER BEGAN TO SEE THREATS EVERYWHERE. KREE THREATS, ONES HE WAS POWERLESS TO STOP...
KINDA LIKE THE DRINKING.
THAT DIDN'T HELP.

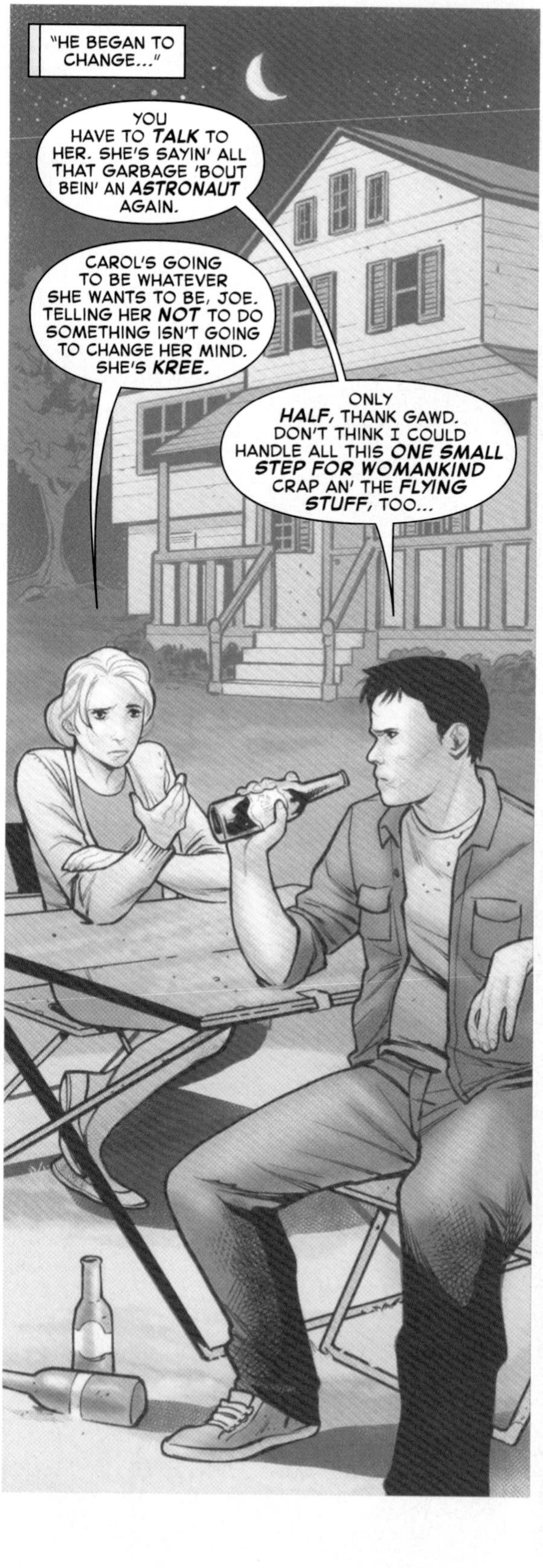
"HE BEGAN TO CHANGE..."
YOU HAVE TO TALK TO HER. SHE'S SAYIN' ALL THAT GARBAGE 'BOUT BEIN' AN ASTRONAUT AGAIN.
CAROL'S GOING TO BE WHATEVER SHE WANTS TO BE, JOE. TELLING HER NOT TO DO SOMETHING ISN'T GOING TO CHANGE HER MIND. SHE'S KREE.
ONLY HALF, THANK GAWD. DON'T THINK I COULD HANDLE ALL THIS ONE SMALL STEP FOR WOMANKIND CRAP AN' THE FLYING STUFF, TOO...

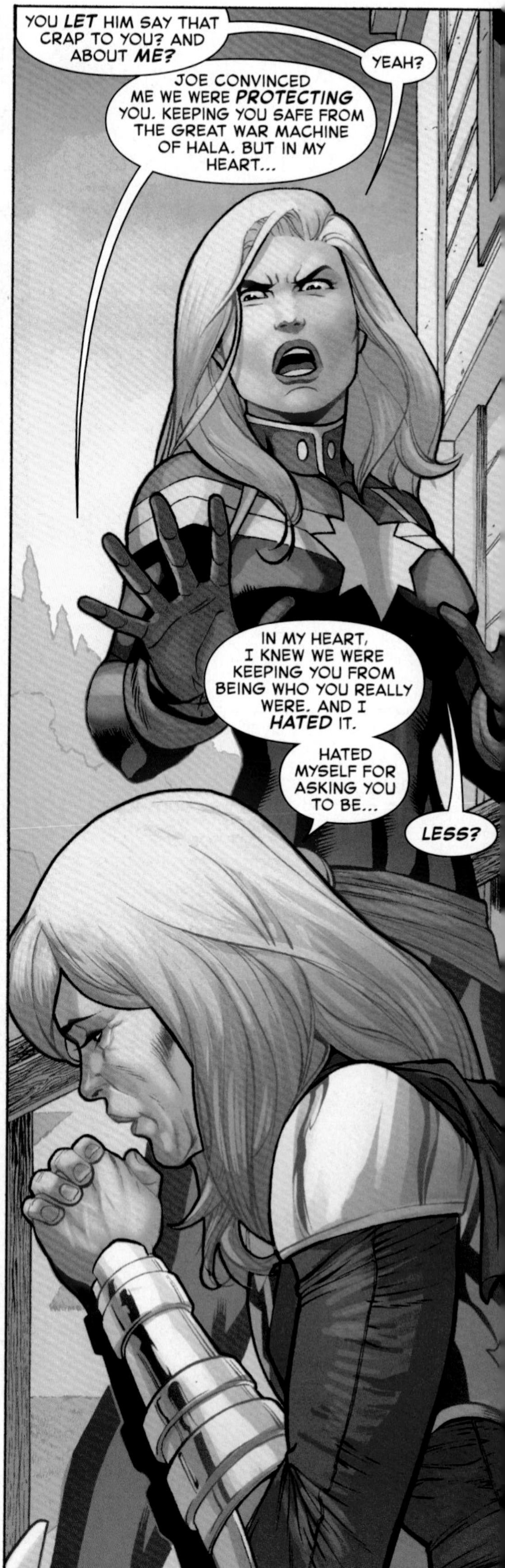
YOU LET HIM SAY THAT CRAP TO YOU? AND ABOUT ME?
JOE CONVINCED ME WE WERE PROTECTING YOU. KEEPING YOU SAFE FROM THE GREAT WAR MACHINE OF HALA. BUT IN MY HEART...
YEAH?
IN MY HEART, I KNEW WE WERE KEEPING YOU FROM BEING WHO YOU REALLY WERE. AND I HATED IT.
HATED MYSELF FOR ASKING YOU TO BE...
LESS?

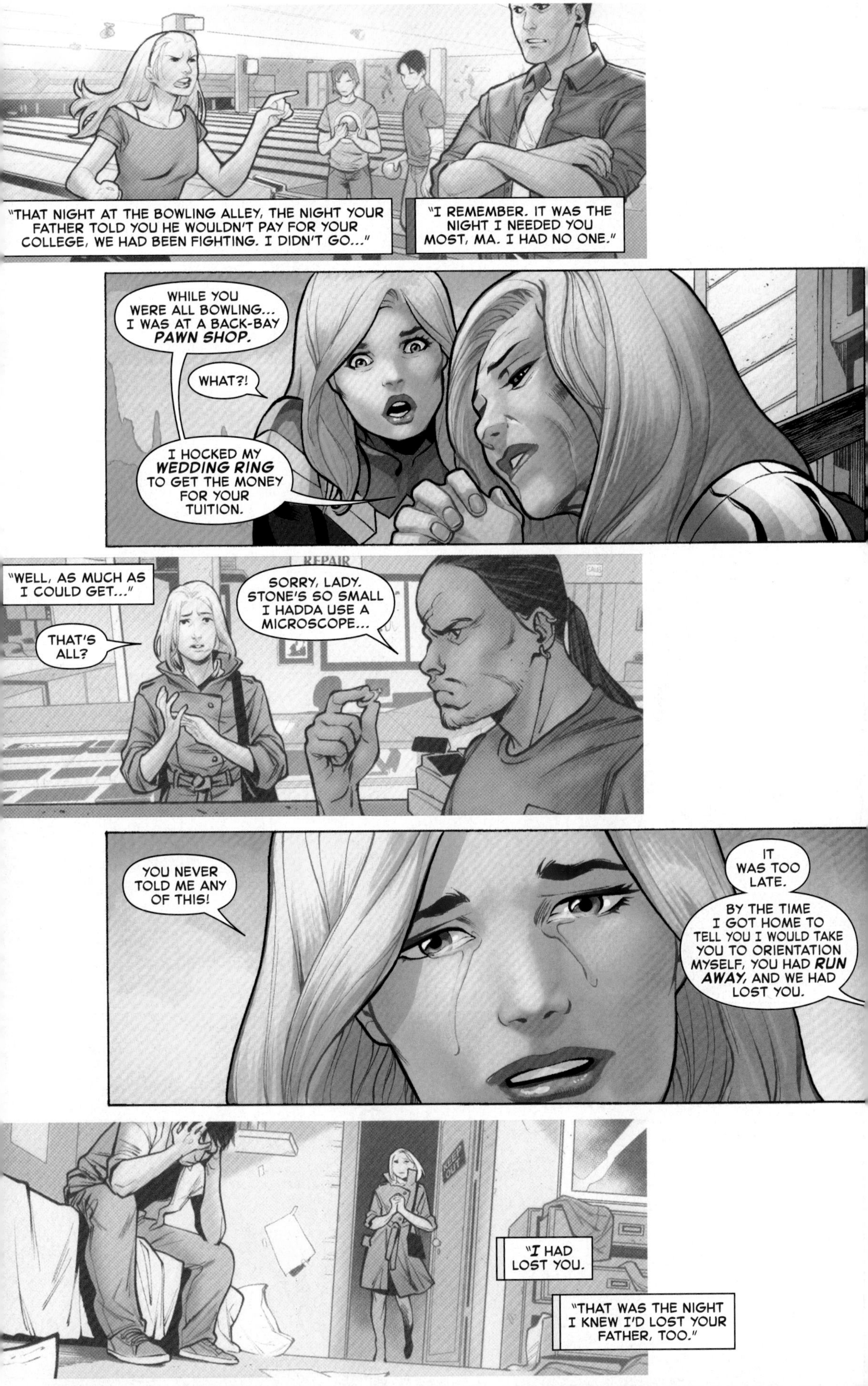
"THAT NIGHT AT THE BOWLING ALLEY, THE NIGHT YOUR FATHER TOLD YOU HE WOULDN'T PAY FOR YOUR COLLEGE, WE HAD BEEN FIGHTING. I DIDN'T GO..."
"I REMEMBER. IT WAS THE NIGHT I NEEDED YOU MOST, MA. I HAD NO ONE."
WHILE YOU WERE ALL BOWLING... I WAS AT A BACK-BAY PAWN SHOP.
WHAT?!
I HOCKED MY WEDDING RING TO GET THE MONEY FOR YOUR TUITION.
REPAIR
"WELL, AS MUCH AS I COULD GET..."
SORRY, LADY. STONE'S SO SMALL I HADDA USE A MICROSCOPE...
THAT'S ALL?
YOU NEVER TOLD ME ANY OF THIS!
IT WAS TOO LATE.
BY THE TIME I GOT HOME TO TELL YOU I WOULD TAKE YOU TO ORIENTATION MYSELF, YOU HAD RUN AWAY, AND WE HAD LOST YOU.
"I HAD LOST YOU.
"THAT WAS THE NIGHT I KNEW I'D LOST YOUR FATHER, TOO."

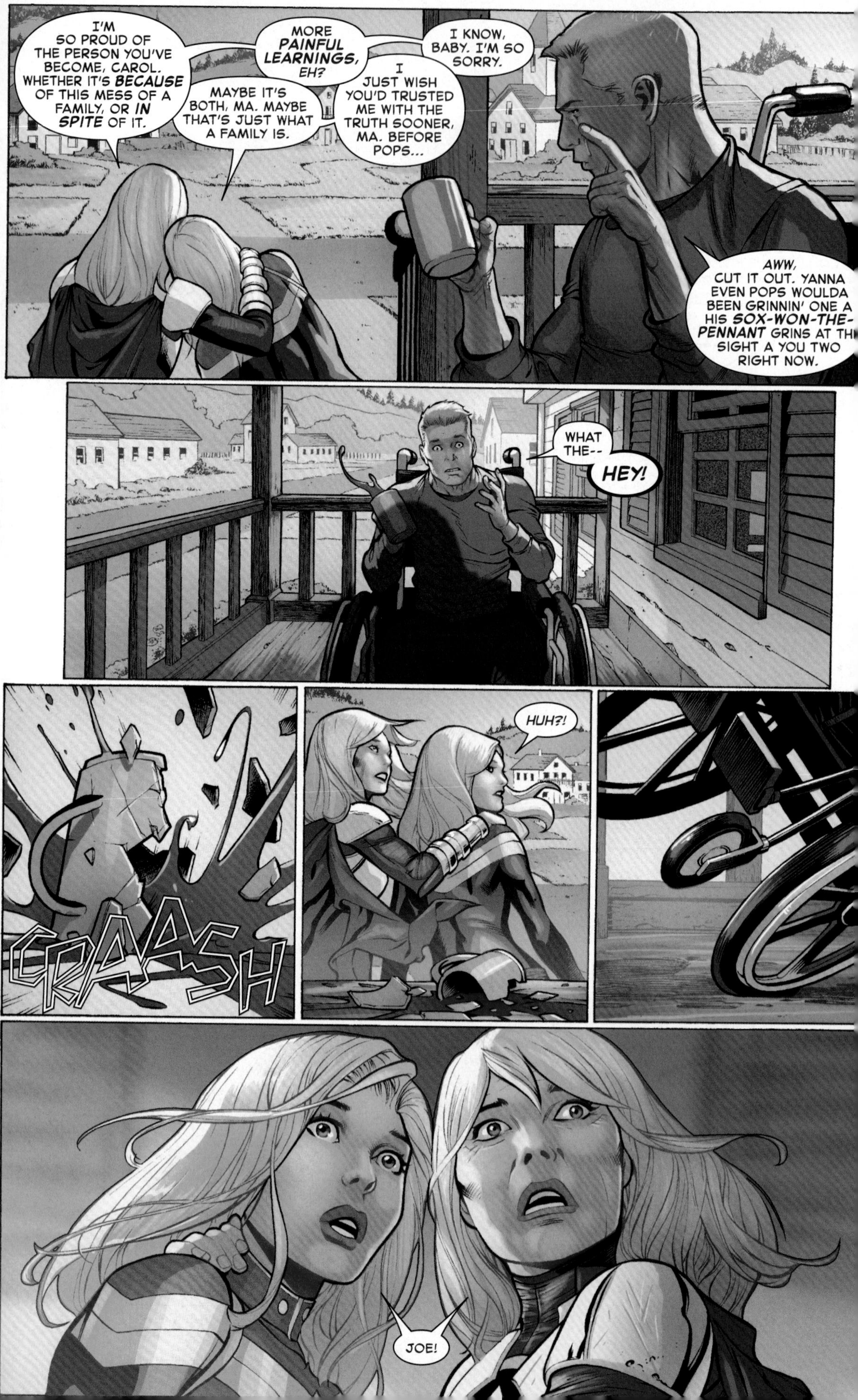
I'M SO PROUD OF THE PERSON YOU'VE BECOME, CAROL. WHETHER IT'S BECAUSE OF THIS MESS OF A FAMILY, OR IN SPITE OF IT.
MAYBE IT'S BOTH, MA. MAYBE THAT'S JUST WHAT A FAMILY IS.
MORE PAINFUL LEARNINGS, EH?
I JUST WISH YOU'D TRUSTED ME WITH THE TRUTH SOONER, MA. BEFORE POPS...
I KNOW, BABY. I'M SO SORRY.
AWW, CUT IT OUT. YANNA EVEN POPS WOULDA BEEN GRINNIN' ONE A HIS SOX-WON-THE-PENNANT GRINS AT TH SIGHT A YOU TWO RIGHT NOW.
WHAT THE--
HEY!
CRAAASH
HUH?!
JOE!

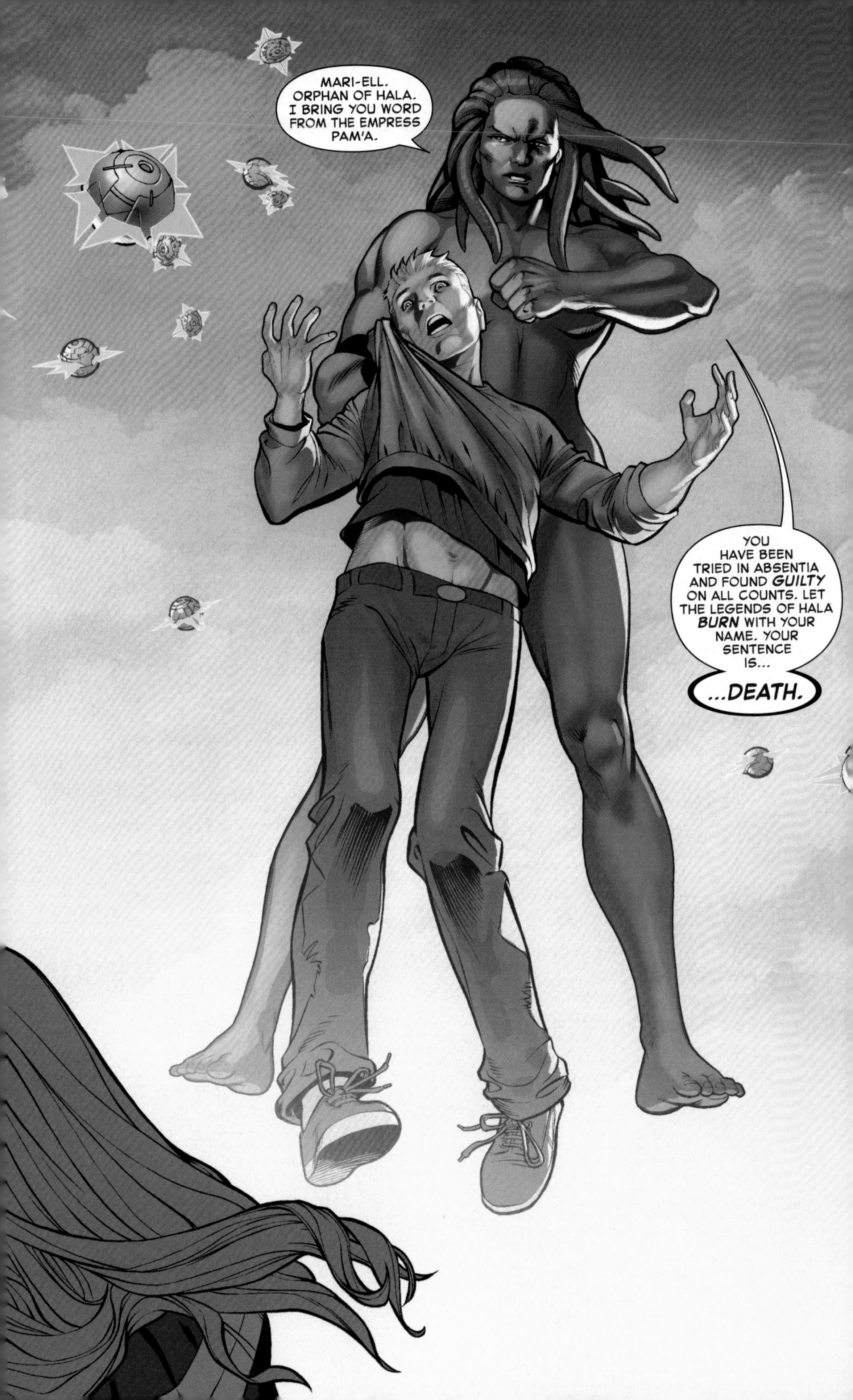
MARI-ELL. ORPHAN OF HALA. I BRING YOU WORD FROM THE EMPRESS PAM'A.
YOU HAVE BEEN TRIED IN ABSENTIA AND FOUND **GUILTY** ON ALL COUNTS. LET THE LEGENDS OF HALA **BURN** WITH YOUR NAME. YOUR SENTENCE IS...
...DEATH.

#1 VARIANT BY **JOE QUESADA** & **RICHARD ISANOVE**

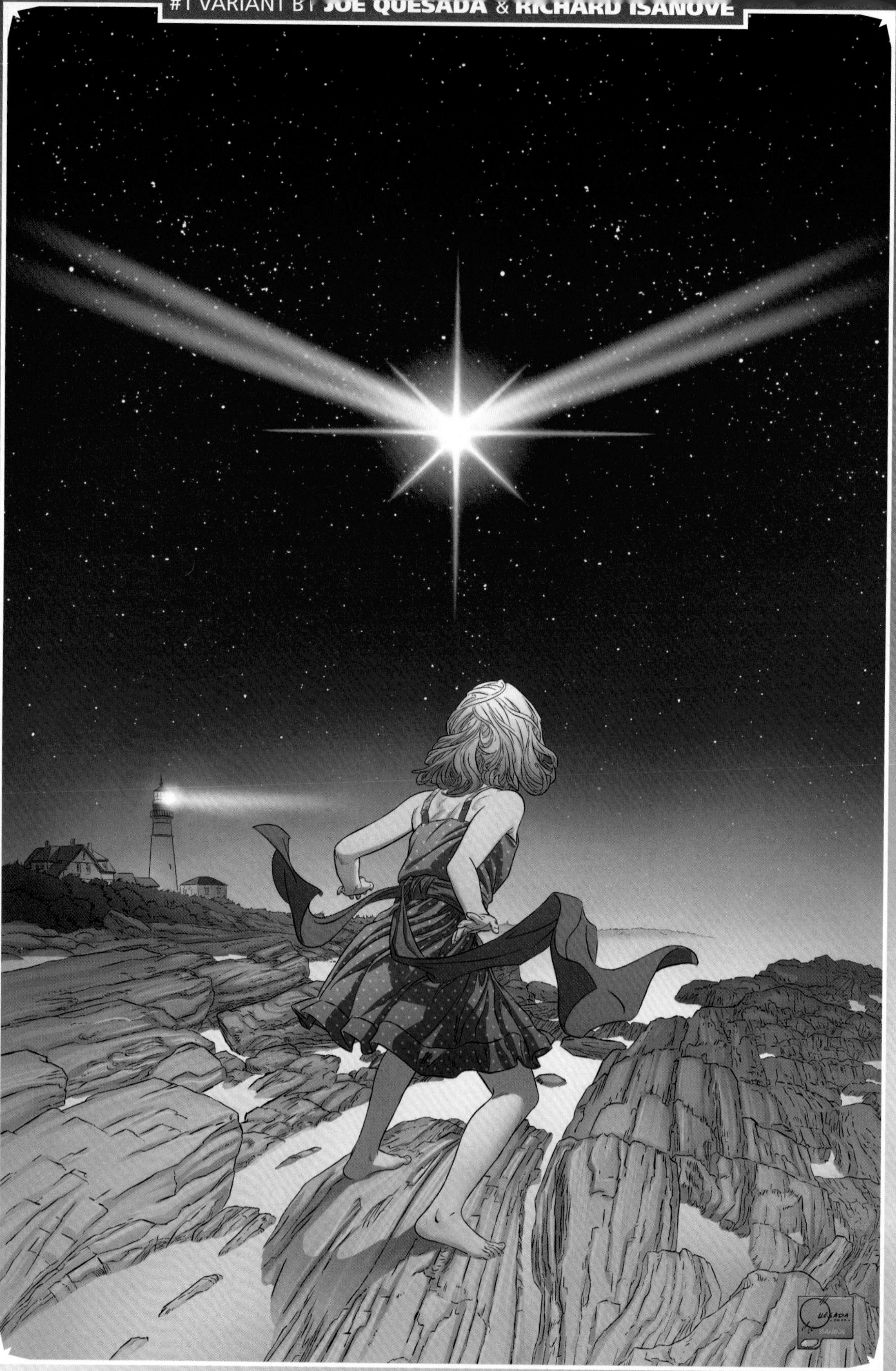

PART 5: CHAMPIONED

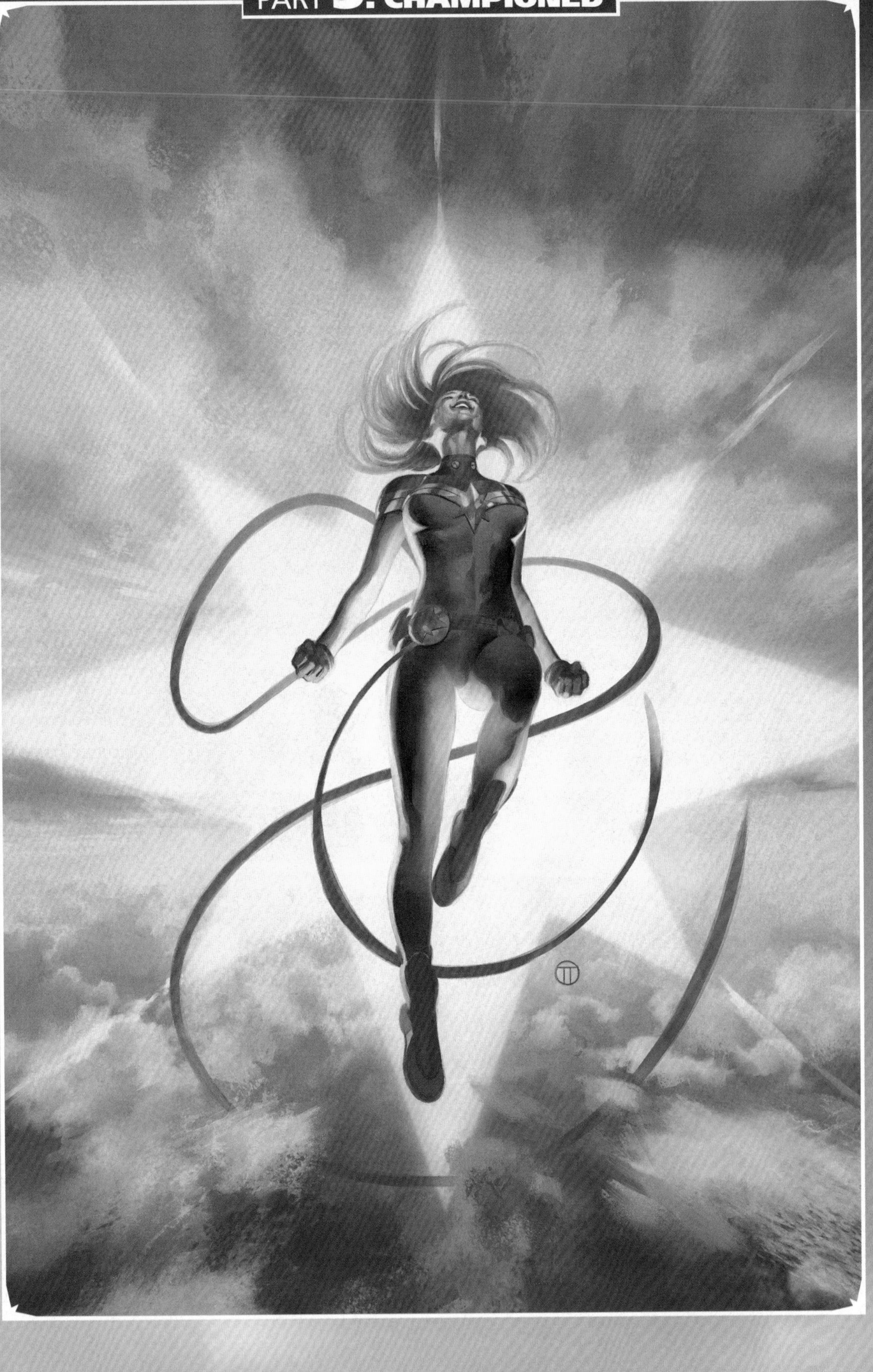

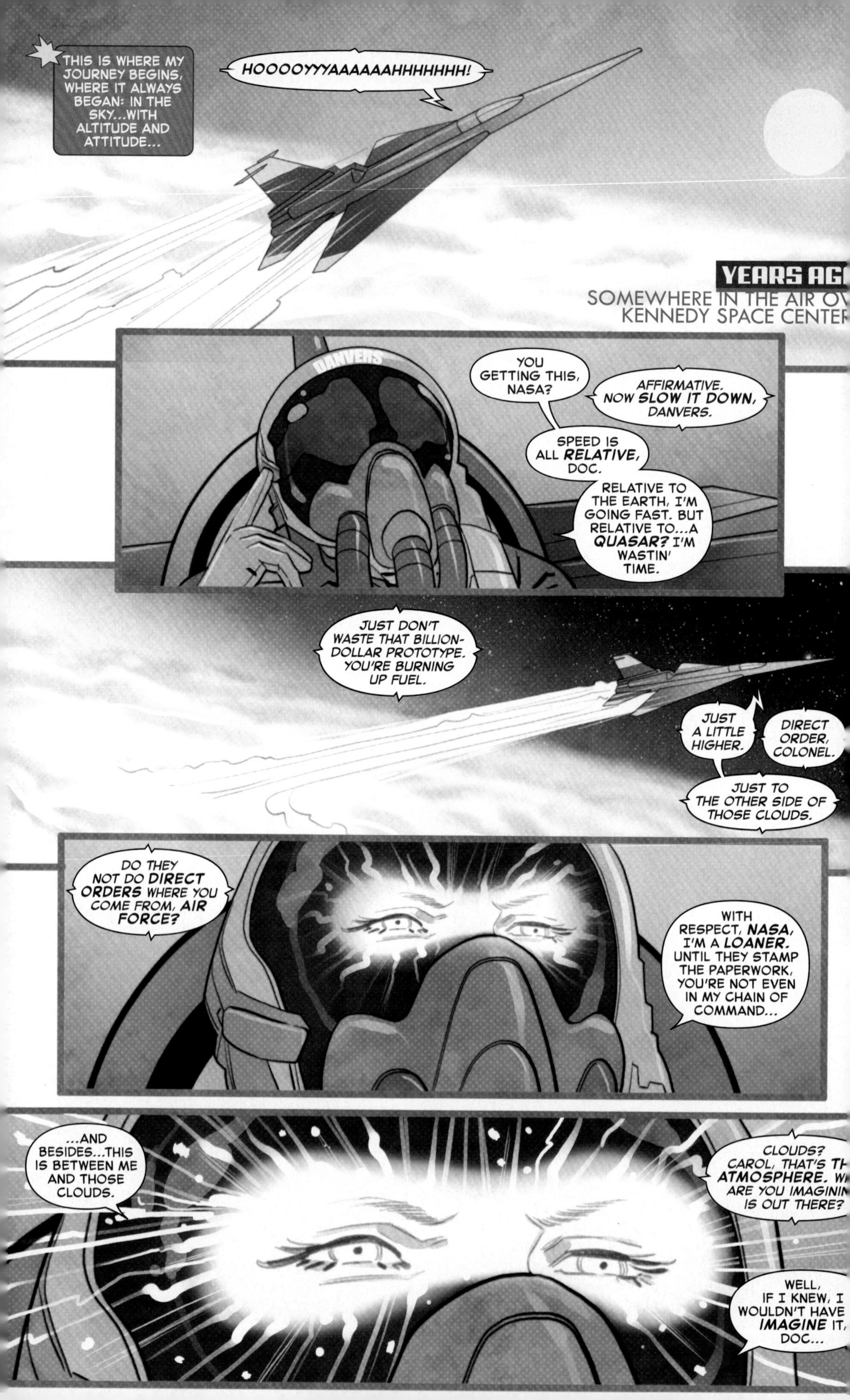
THIS IS WHERE MY JOURNEY BEGINS, WHERE IT ALWAYS BEGAN: IN THE SKY...WITH ALTITUDE AND ATTITUDE...
HOOOOYYYAAAAAAHHHHHHH!
YEARS AG
SOMEWHERE IN THE AIR OV
KENNEDY SPACE CENTE
DANVERS
YOU GETTING THIS, NASA?
AFFIRMATIVE. NOW SLOW IT DOWN, DANVERS.
SPEED IS ALL RELATIVE, DOC.
RELATIVE TO THE EARTH, I'M GOING FAST. BUT RELATIVE TO...A QUASAR? I'M WASTIN' TIME.
JUST DON'T WASTE THAT BILLION-DOLLAR PROTOTYPE. YOU'RE BURNING UP FUEL.
JUST A LITTLE HIGHER.
DIRECT ORDER, COLONEL.
JUST TO THE OTHER SIDE OF THOSE CLOUDS.
DO THEY NOT DO DIRECT ORDERS WHERE YOU COME FROM, AIR FORCE?
WITH RESPECT, NASA, I'M A LOANER. UNTIL THEY STAMP THE PAPERWORK, YOU'RE NOT EVEN IN MY CHAIN OF COMMAND...
...AND BESIDES...THIS IS BETWEEN ME AND THOSE CLOUDS.
CLOUDS? CAROL, THAT'S TH ATMOSPHERE. W ARE YOU IMAGININ IS OUT THERE?
WELL, IF I KNEW, I WOULDN'T HAVE IMAGINE IT, DOC...

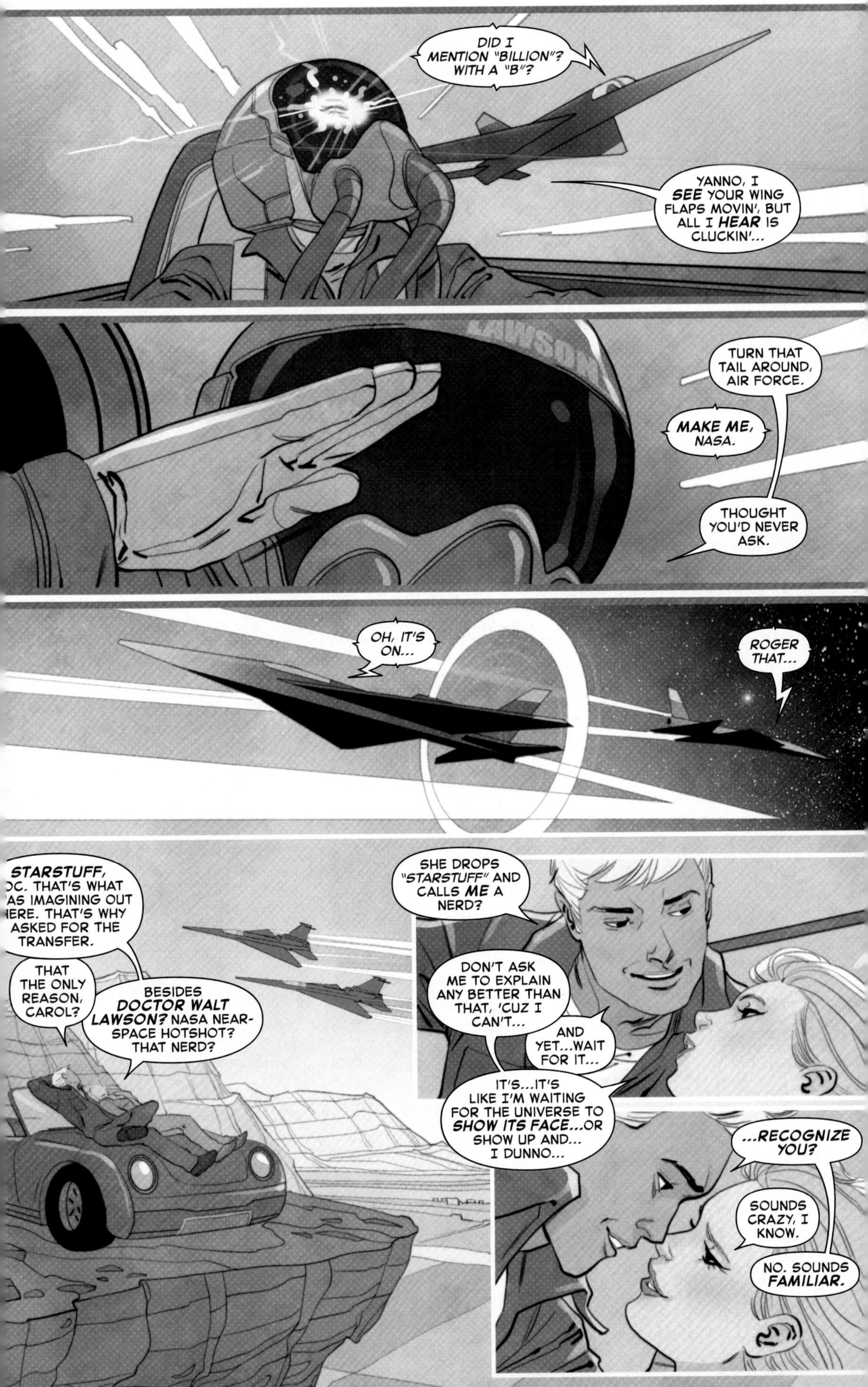
DID I MENTION "BILLION"? WITH A "B"?
YANNO, I SEE YOUR WING FLAPS MOVIN', BUT ALL I HEAR IS CLUCKIN'...
TURN THAT TAIL AROUND, AIR FORCE.
MAKE ME, NASA.
THOUGHT YOU'D NEVER ASK.
OH, IT'S ON...
ROGER THAT...
STARSTUFF, OC. THAT'S WHAT AS IMAGINING OUT ERE. THAT'S WHY ASKED FOR THE TRANSFER.
THAT THE ONLY REASON, CAROL?
BESIDES DOCTOR WALT LAWSON? NASA NEAR-SPACE HOTSHOT? THAT NERD?
SHE DROPS "STARSTUFF" AND CALLS ME A NERD?
DON'T ASK ME TO EXPLAIN ANY BETTER THAN THAT, 'CUZ I CAN'T...
AND YET...WAIT FOR IT...
IT'S...IT'S LIKE I'M WAITING FOR THE UNIVERSE TO SHOW ITS FACE...OR SHOW UP AND... I DUNNO...
...RECOGNIZE YOU?
SOUNDS CRAZY, I KNOW.
NO. SOUNDS FAMILIAR.

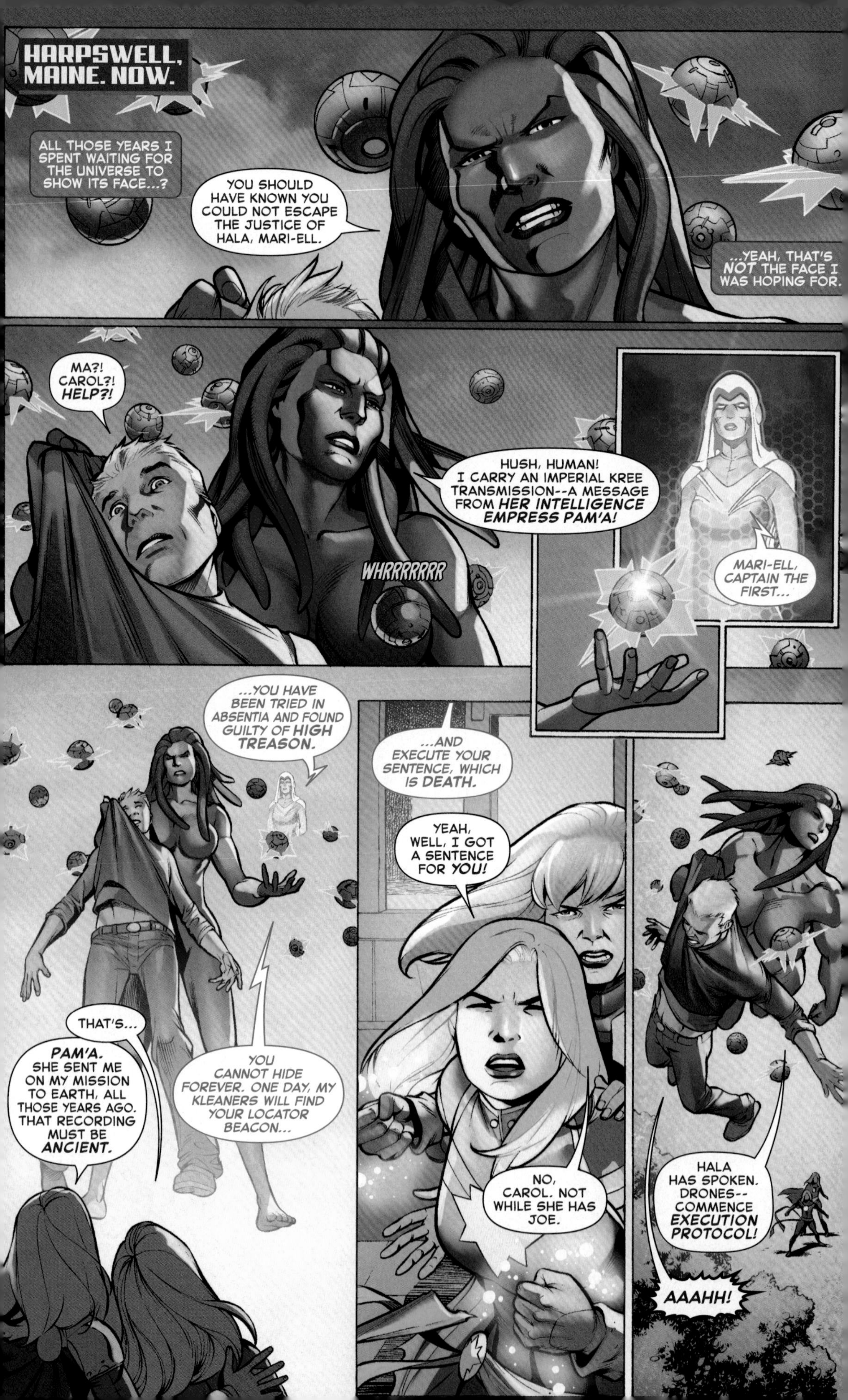

HARPSWELL, MAINE. NOW.
ALL THOSE YEARS I SPENT WAITING FOR THE UNIVERSE TO SHOW ITS FACE...?
YOU SHOULD HAVE KNOWN YOU COULD NOT ESCAPE THE JUSTICE OF HALA, MARI-ELL.
...YEAH, THAT'S NOT THE FACE I WAS HOPING FOR.
MA?! CAROL?! HELP?!
HUSH, HUMAN! I CARRY AN IMPERIAL KREE TRANSMISSION--A MESSAGE FROM HER INTELLIGENCE EMPRESS PAM'A!
WHRRRRRRR
MARI-ELL, CAPTAIN THE FIRST...
...YOU HAVE BEEN TRIED IN ABSENTIA AND FOUND GUILTY OF HIGH TREASON.
THAT'S...
PAM'A. SHE SENT ME ON MY MISSION TO EARTH, ALL THOSE YEARS AGO. THAT RECORDING MUST BE ANCIENT.
YOU CANNOT HIDE FOREVER. ONE DAY, MY KLEANERS WILL FIND YOUR LOCATOR BEACON...
...AND EXECUTE YOUR SENTENCE, WHICH IS DEATH.
YEAH, WELL, I GOT A SENTENCE FOR YOU!
NO, CAROL. NOT WHILE SHE HAS JOE.
HALA HAS SPOKEN. DRONES--COMMENCE EXECUTION PROTOCOL!
AAAHH!

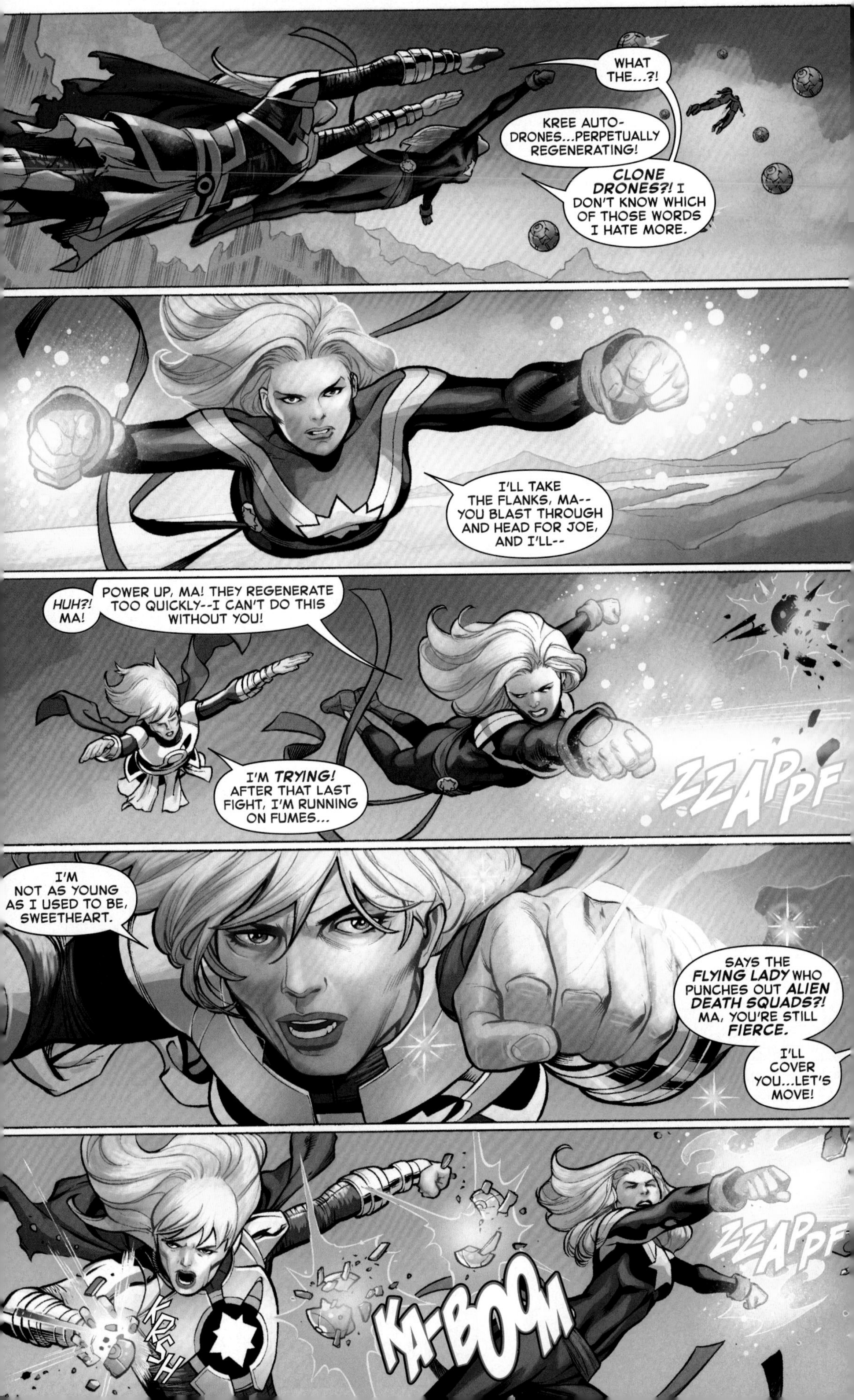
WHAT THE...?!
KREE AUTO-DRONES...PERPETUALLY REGENERATING!
CLONE DRONES?! I DON'T KNOW WHICH OF THOSE WORDS I HATE MORE.
I'LL TAKE THE FLANKS, MA-- YOU BLAST THROUGH AND HEAD FOR JOE, AND I'LL--
HUH?! MA!
POWER UP, MA! THEY REGENERATE TOO QUICKLY--I CAN'T DO THIS WITHOUT YOU!
I'M TRYING! AFTER THAT LAST FIGHT, I'M RUNNING ON FUMES...
ZZAPPF
I'M NOT AS YOUNG AS I USED TO BE, SWEETHEART.
SAYS THE FLYING LADY WHO PUNCHES OUT ALIEN DEATH SQUADS?! MA, YOU'RE STILL FIERCE.
I'LL COVER YOU...LET'S MOVE!
KRSH
KA-BOOM
ZZAPPF

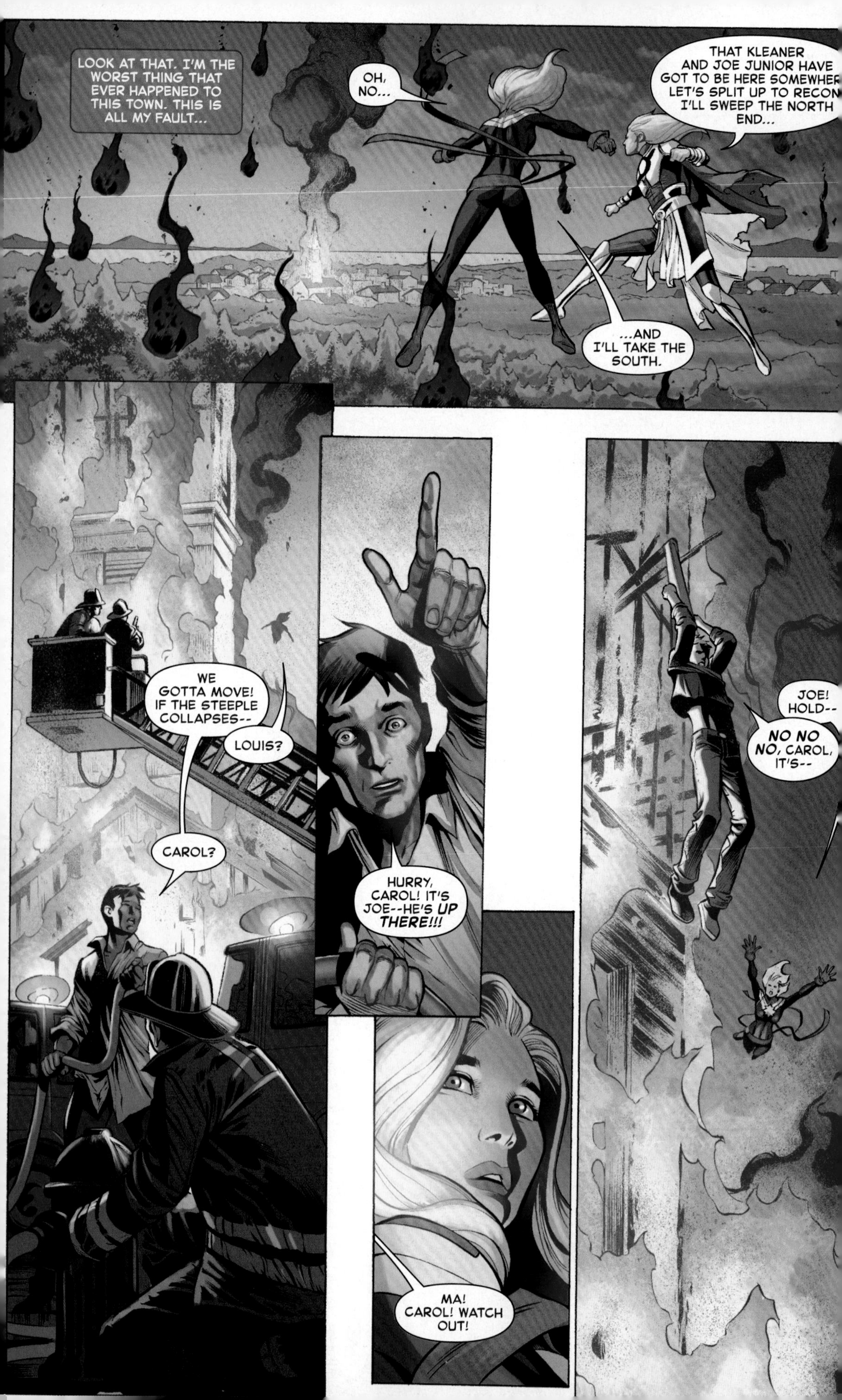

LOOK AT THAT. I'M THE WORST THING THAT EVER HAPPENED TO THIS TOWN. THIS IS ALL MY FAULT...
OH, NO...
THAT KLEANER AND JOE JUNIOR HAVE GOT TO BE HERE SOMEWHER LET'S SPLIT UP TO RECON I'LL SWEEP THE NORTH END...
...AND I'LL TAKE THE SOUTH.
WE GOTTA MOVE! IF THE STEEPLE COLLAPSES--
LOUIS?
CAROL?
HURRY, CAROL! IT'S JOE--HE'S UP THERE!!!
MA! CAROL! WATCH OUT!
JOE! HOLD--
NO NO NO, CAROL, IT'S--

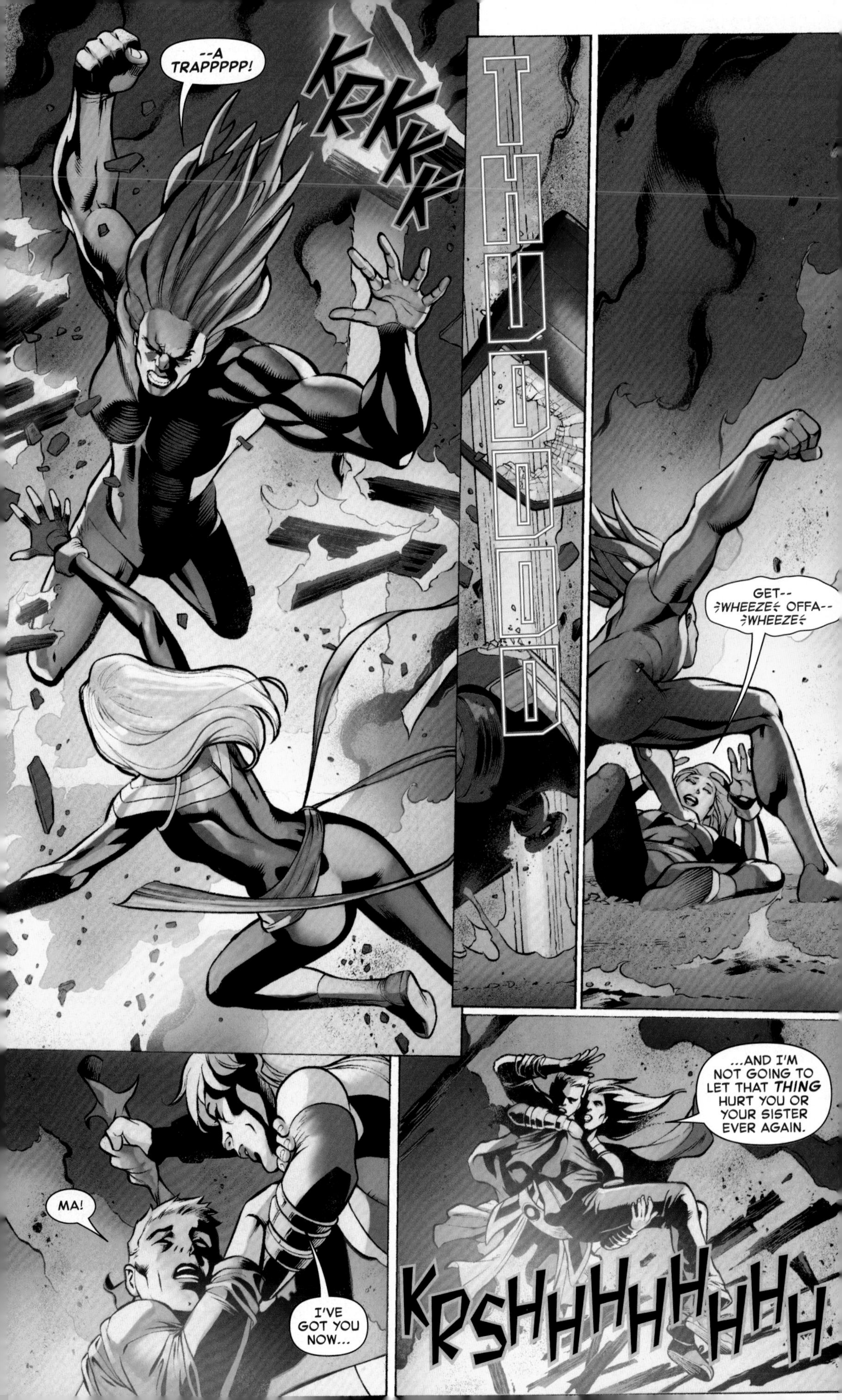
--A TRAPPPPP!
KRKKK
THUDDDDD
GET-- *WHEEZE* OFFA-- *WHEEZE*
MA!
I'VE GOT YOU NOW...
...AND I'M NOT GOING TO LET THAT THING HURT YOU OR YOUR SISTER EVER AGAIN.
KRSHHHHHHHH

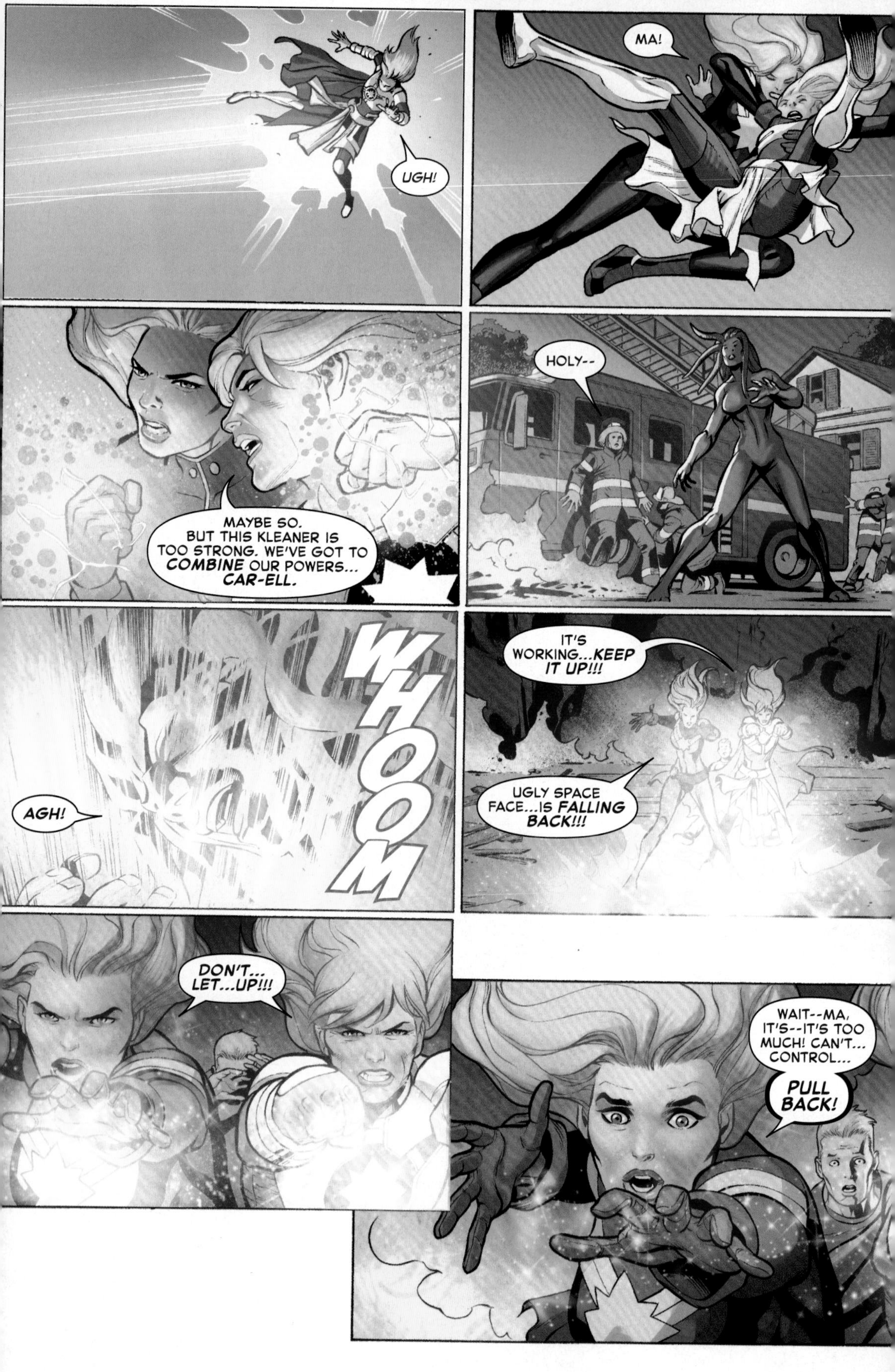
UGH!
MA!
MAYBE SO. BUT THIS KLEANER IS TOO STRONG. WE'VE GOT TO COMBINE OUR POWERS... CAR-ELL.
HOLY--
WHOOM
AGH!
IT'S WORKING...KEEP IT UP!!!
UGLY SPACE FACE...IS FALLING BACK!!!
DON'T... LET...UP!!!
WAIT--MA, IT'S--IT'S TOO MUCH! CAN'T... CONTROL...
PULL BACK!

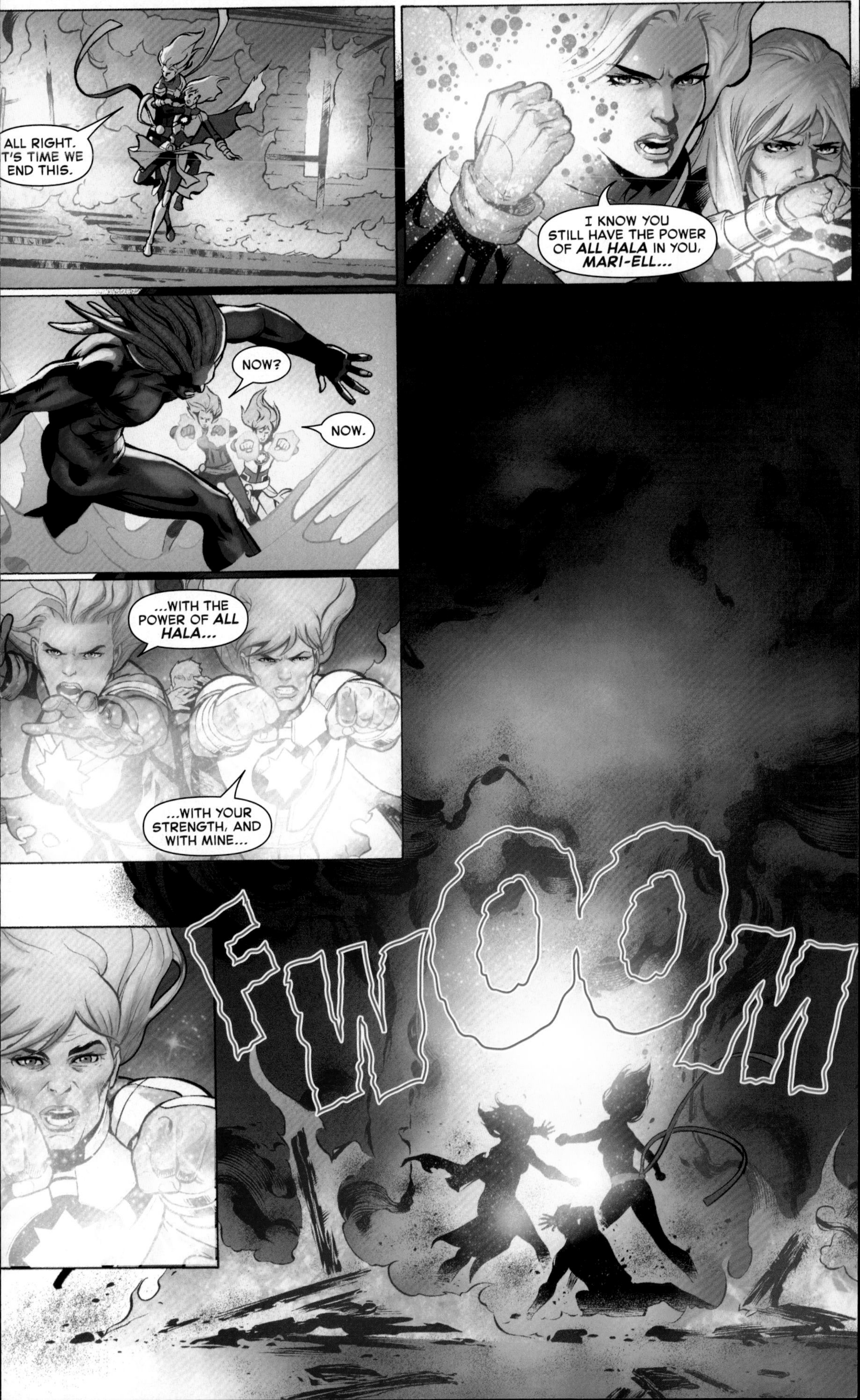
ALL RIGHT. IT'S TIME WE END THIS.
I KNOW YOU STILL HAVE THE POWER OF ALL HALA IN YOU, MARI-ELL...
NOW?
NOW.
...WITH THE POWER OF ALL HALA...
...WITH YOUR STRENGTH, AND WITH MINE...
FWOOM

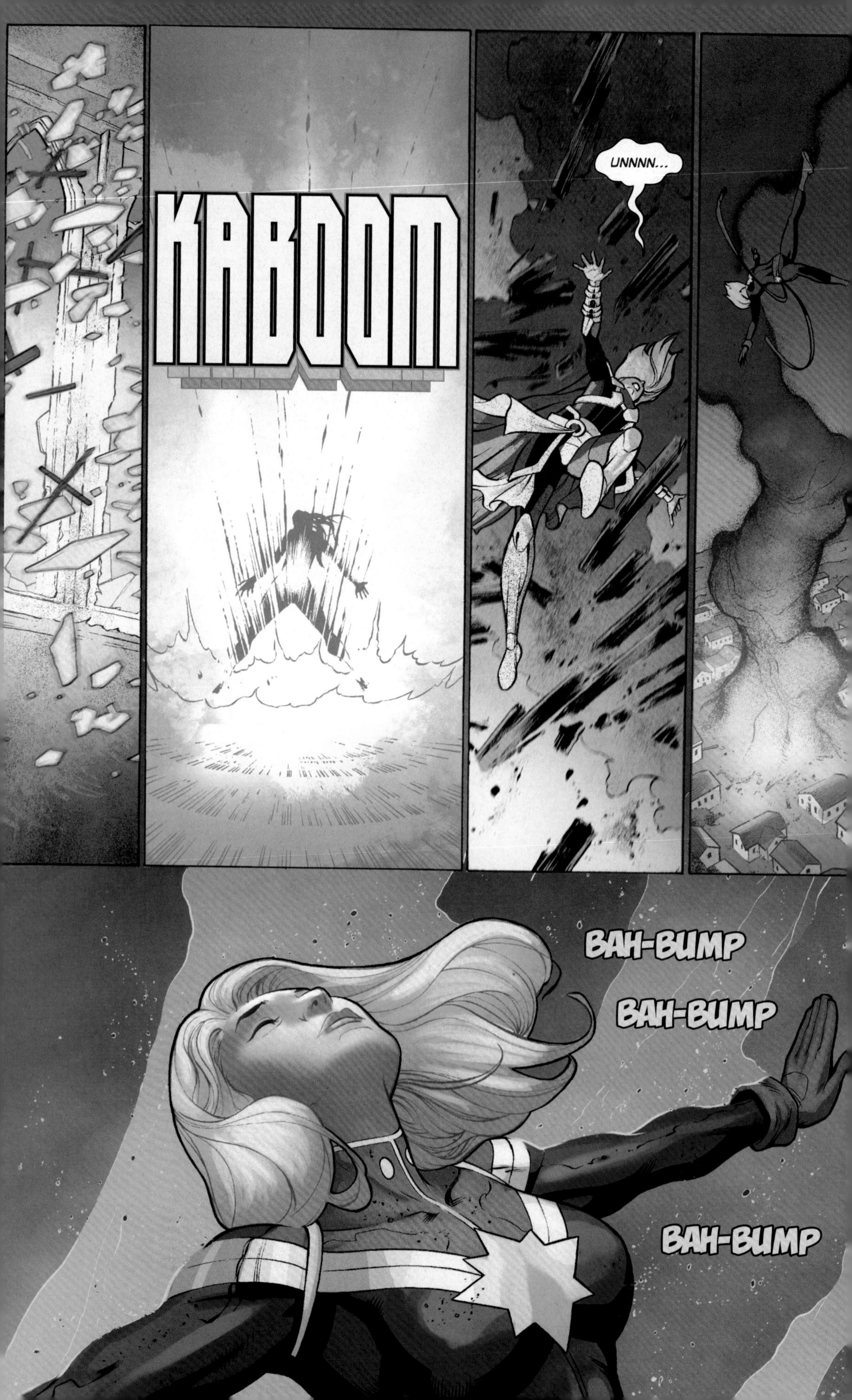
KABOOM
UNNNN...
BAH-BUMP
BAH-BUMP
BAH-BUMP

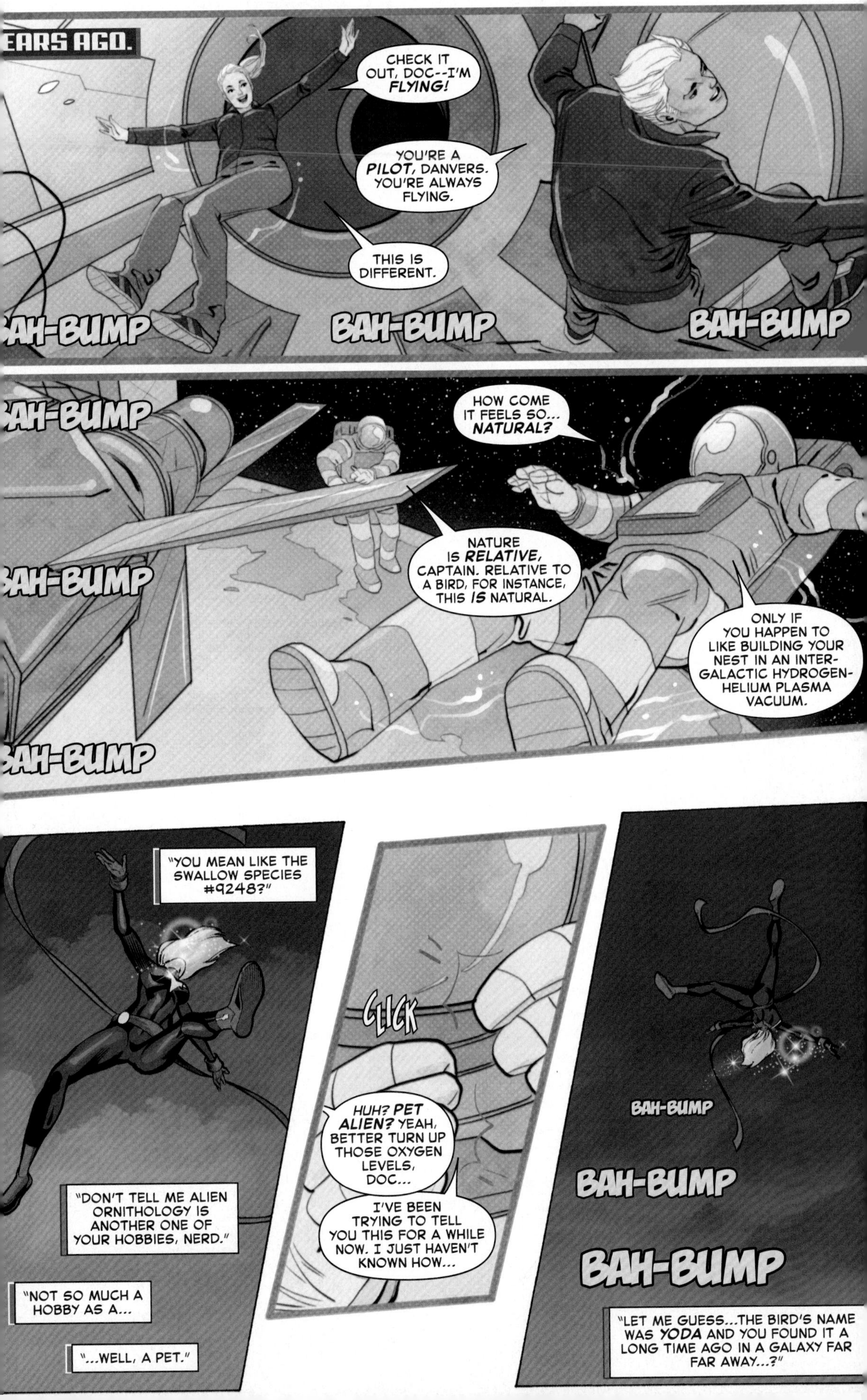
EARS AGO.
CHECK IT OUT, DOC--I'M FLYING!
YOU'RE A PILOT, DANVERS. YOU'RE ALWAYS FLYING.
THIS IS DIFFERENT.
AH-BUMP
BAH-BUMP
BAH-BUMP
AH-BUMP
HOW COME IT FEELS SO... NATURAL?
NATURE IS RELATIVE, CAPTAIN. RELATIVE TO A BIRD, FOR INSTANCE, THIS IS NATURAL.
ONLY IF YOU HAPPEN TO LIKE BUILDING YOUR NEST IN AN INTER-GALACTIC HYDROGEN-HELIUM PLASMA VACUUM.
AH-BUMP
AH-BUMP
"YOU MEAN LIKE THE SWALLOW SPECIES #9248?"
"DON'T TELL ME ALIEN ORNITHOLOGY IS ANOTHER ONE OF YOUR HOBBIES, NERD."
"NOT SO MUCH A HOBBY AS A...
"...WELL, A PET."
CLICK
HUH? PET ALIEN? YEAH, BETTER TURN UP THOSE OXYGEN LEVELS, DOC...
I'VE BEEN TRYING TO TELL YOU THIS FOR A WHILE NOW. I JUST HAVEN'T KNOWN HOW...
BAH-BUMP
BAH-BUMP
BAH-BUMP
"LET ME GUESS...THE BIRD'S NAME WAS YODA AND YOU FOUND IT A LONG TIME AGO IN A GALAXY FAR FAR AWAY...?"

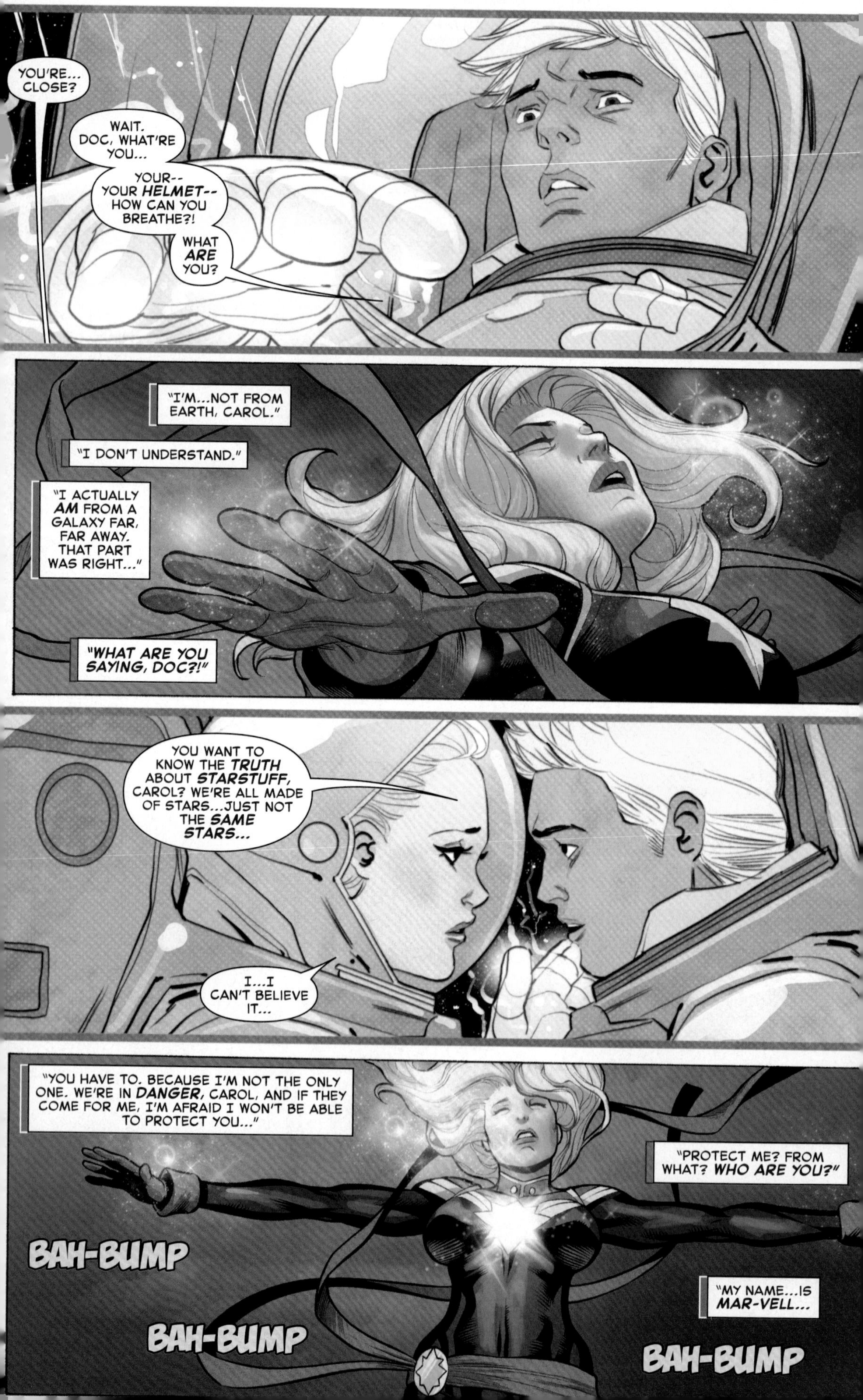
YOU'RE... CLOSE?
WAIT. DOC, WHAT'RE YOU...
YOUR-- YOUR HELMET-- HOW CAN YOU BREATHE?!
WHAT ARE YOU?
"I'M...NOT FROM EARTH, CAROL."
"I DON'T UNDERSTAND."
"I ACTUALLY AM FROM A GALAXY FAR, FAR AWAY. THAT PART WAS RIGHT..."
"WHAT ARE YOU SAYING, DOC?!"
YOU WANT TO KNOW THE TRUTH ABOUT STARSTUFF, CAROL? WE'RE ALL MADE OF STARS...JUST NOT THE SAME STARS...
I...I CAN'T BELIEVE IT...
"YOU HAVE TO. BECAUSE I'M NOT THE ONLY ONE. WE'RE IN DANGER, CAROL, AND IF THEY COME FOR ME, I'M AFRAID I WON'T BE ABLE TO PROTECT YOU..."
"PROTECT ME? FROM WHAT? WHO ARE YOU?"
BAH-BUMP
"MY NAME...IS MAR-VELL...
BAH-BUMP
BAH-BUMP

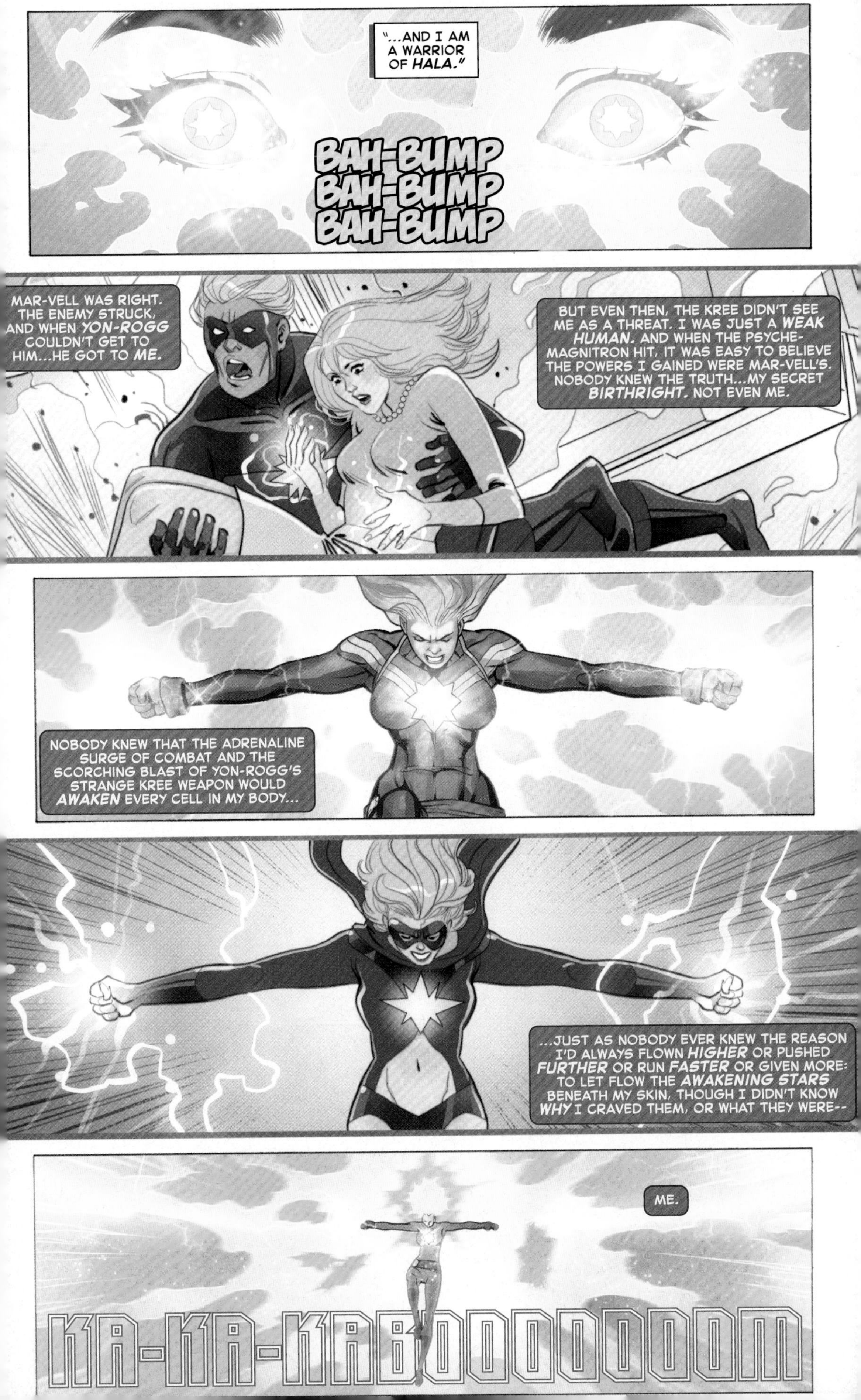
"...AND I AM A WARRIOR OF HALA."
BAH-BUMP
BAH-BUMP
BAH-BUMP
MAR-VELL WAS RIGHT. THE ENEMY STRUCK, AND WHEN YON-ROGG COULDN'T GET TO HIM...HE GOT TO ME.
BUT EVEN THEN, THE KREE DIDN'T SEE ME AS A THREAT. I WAS JUST A WEAK HUMAN. AND WHEN THE PSYCHE-MAGNITRON HIT, IT WAS EASY TO BELIEVE THE POWERS I GAINED WERE MAR-VELL'S. NOBODY KNEW THE TRUTH...MY SECRET BIRTHRIGHT. NOT EVEN ME.
NOBODY KNEW THAT THE ADRENALINE SURGE OF COMBAT AND THE SCORCHING BLAST OF YON-ROGG'S STRANGE KREE WEAPON WOULD AWAKEN EVERY CELL IN MY BODY...
...JUST AS NOBODY EVER KNEW THE REASON I'D ALWAYS FLOWN HIGHER OR PUSHED FURTHER OR RUN FASTER OR GIVEN MORE: TO LET FLOW THE AWAKENING STARS BENEATH MY SKIN, THOUGH I DIDN'T KNOW WHY I CRAVED THEM, OR WHAT THEY WERE--
ME.
KA-KA-KABOOOOOOOOM

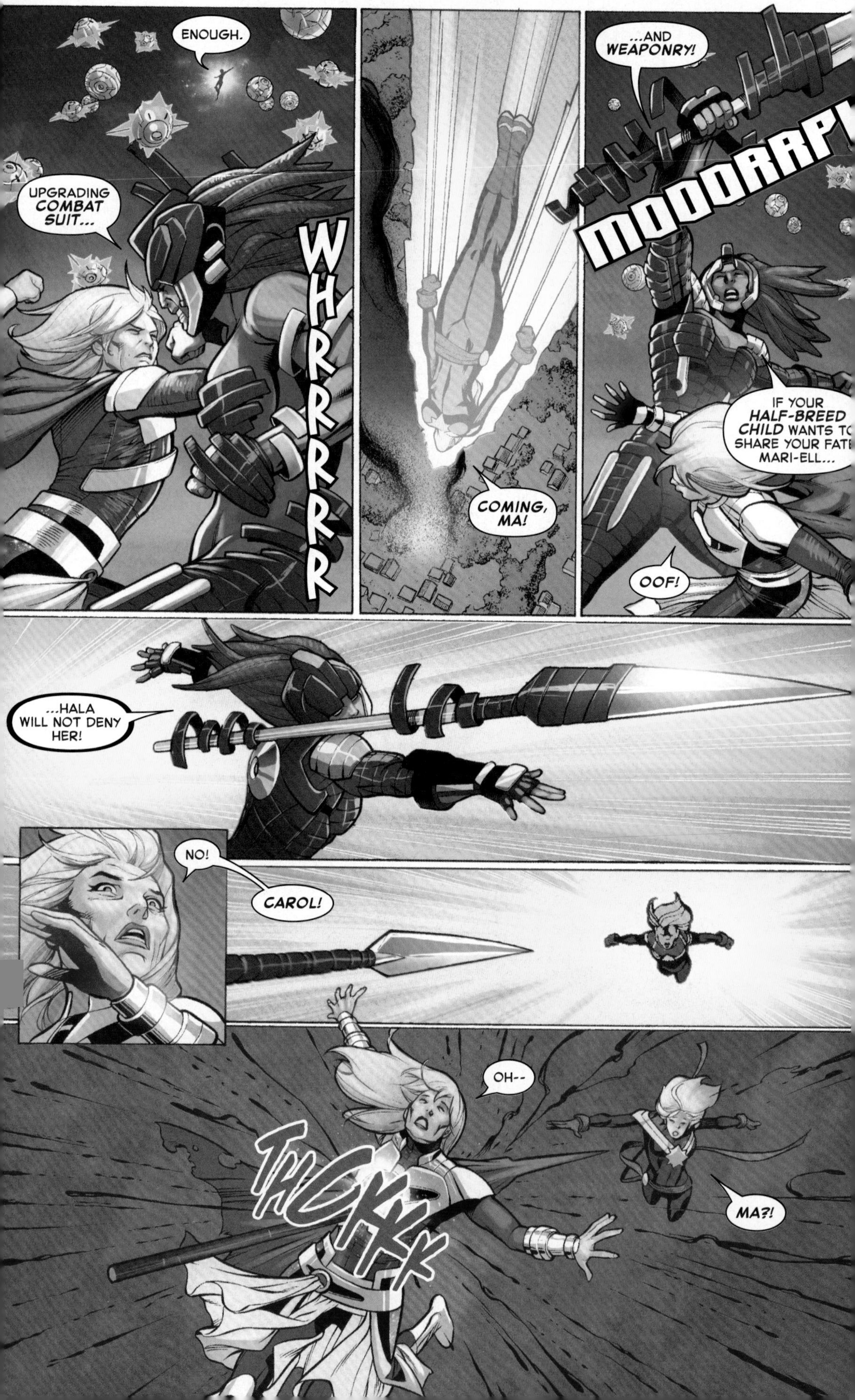

ENOUGH.
UPGRADING COMBAT SUIT...
WHRRRRR
COMING, MA!
...AND WEAPONRY!
MOOORRP
IF YOUR HALF-BREED CHILD WANTS TO SHARE YOUR FATE MARI-ELL...
OOF!
...HALA WILL NOT DENY HER!
NO!
CAROL!
OH--
THCKK
MA?!

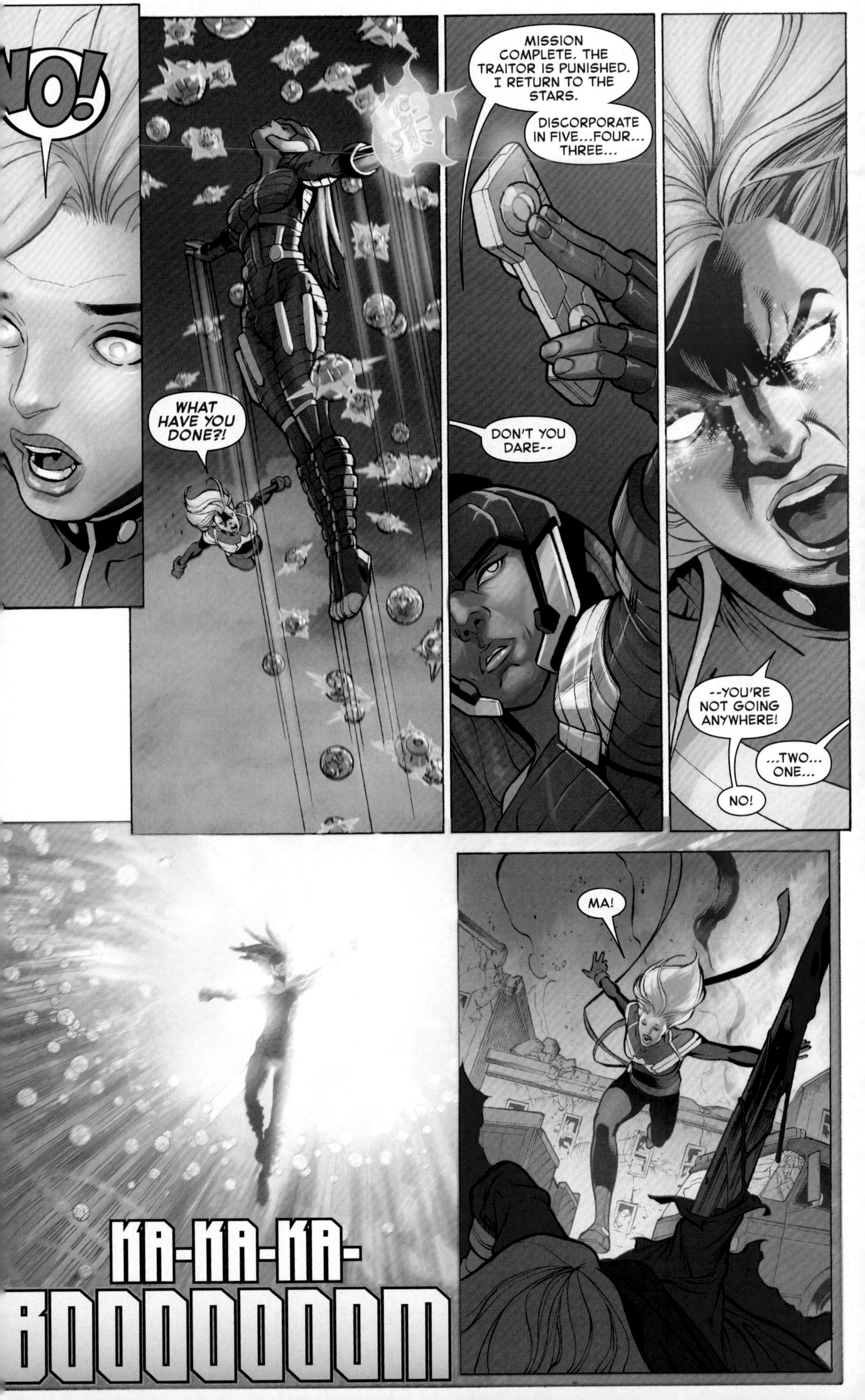
NO!
WHAT HAVE YOU DONE?!
MISSION COMPLETE. THE TRAITOR IS PUNISHED. I RETURN TO THE STARS.
DISCORPORATE IN FIVE...FOUR... THREE...
DON'T YOU DARE--
--YOU'RE NOT GOING ANYWHERE!
...TWO... ONE...
NO!
KA-KA-KA-BOOOOOOOM
MA!

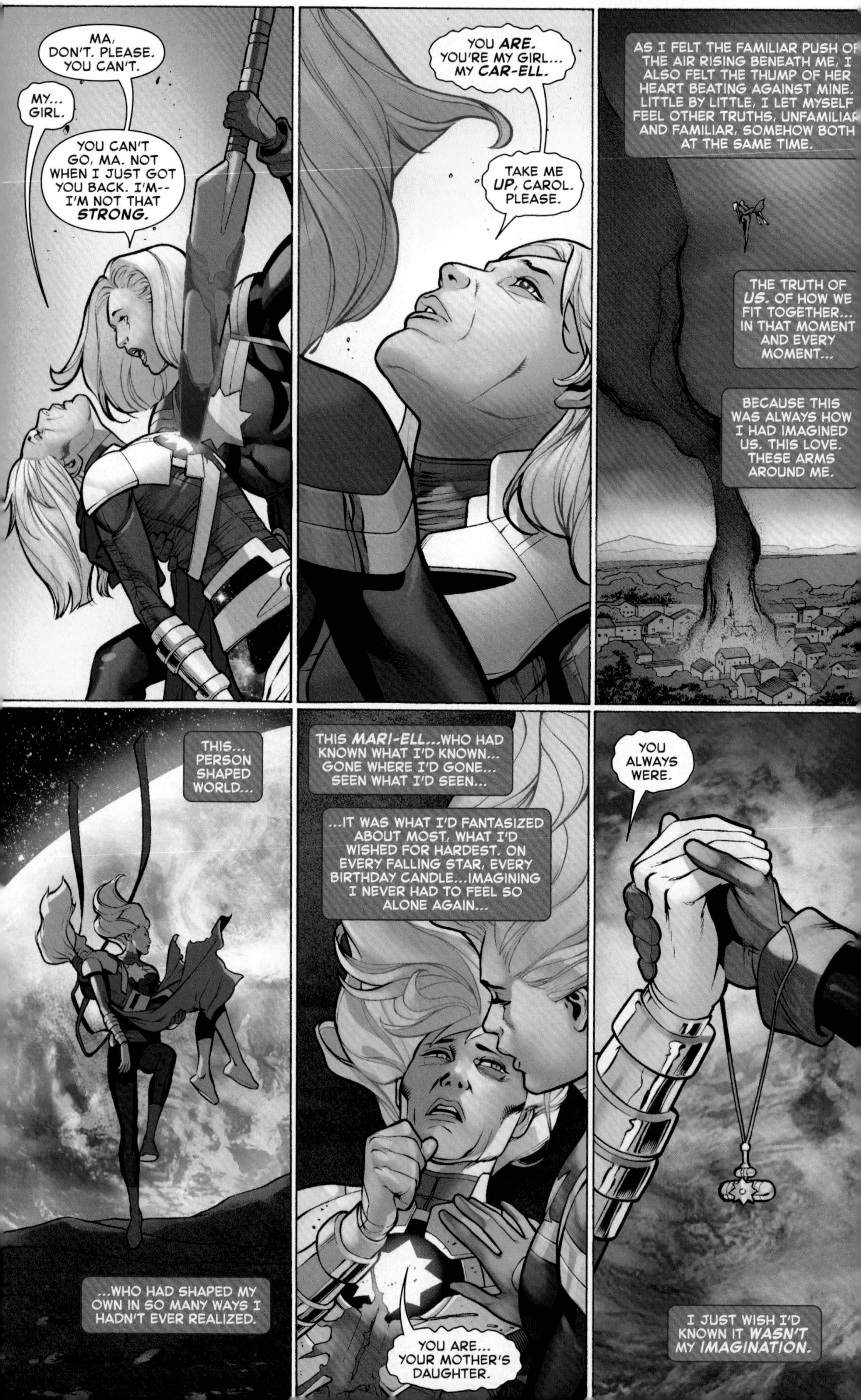
MA, DON'T. PLEASE. YOU CAN'T.
MY... GIRL.
YOU CAN'T GO, MA. NOT WHEN I JUST GOT YOU BACK. I'M-- I'M NOT THAT STRONG.
YOU ARE. YOU'RE MY GIRL... MY CAR-ELL.
TAKE ME UP, CAROL. PLEASE.
AS I FELT THE FAMILIAR PUSH OF THE AIR RISING BENEATH ME, I ALSO FELT THE THUMP OF HER HEART BEATING AGAINST MINE. LITTLE BY LITTLE, I LET MYSELF FEEL OTHER TRUTHS, UNFAMILIAR AND FAMILIAR, SOMEHOW BOTH AT THE SAME TIME.
THE TRUTH OF US. OF HOW WE FIT TOGETHER... IN THAT MOMENT AND EVERY MOMENT...
BECAUSE THIS WAS ALWAYS HOW I HAD IMAGINED US. THIS LOVE. THESE ARMS AROUND ME.
THIS... PERSON SHAPED WORLD...
...WHO HAD SHAPED MY OWN IN SO MANY WAYS I HADN'T EVER REALIZED.
THIS MARI-ELL...WHO HAD KNOWN WHAT I'D KNOWN... GONE WHERE I'D GONE... SEEN WHAT I'D SEEN...
...IT WAS WHAT I'D FANTASIZED ABOUT MOST, WHAT I'D WISHED FOR HARDEST. ON EVERY FALLING STAR, EVERY BIRTHDAY CANDLE...IMAGINING I NEVER HAD TO FEEL SO ALONE AGAIN...
YOU ARE... YOUR MOTHER'S DAUGHTER.
YOU ALWAYS WERE.
I JUST WISH I'D KNOWN IT WASN'T MY IMAGINATION.

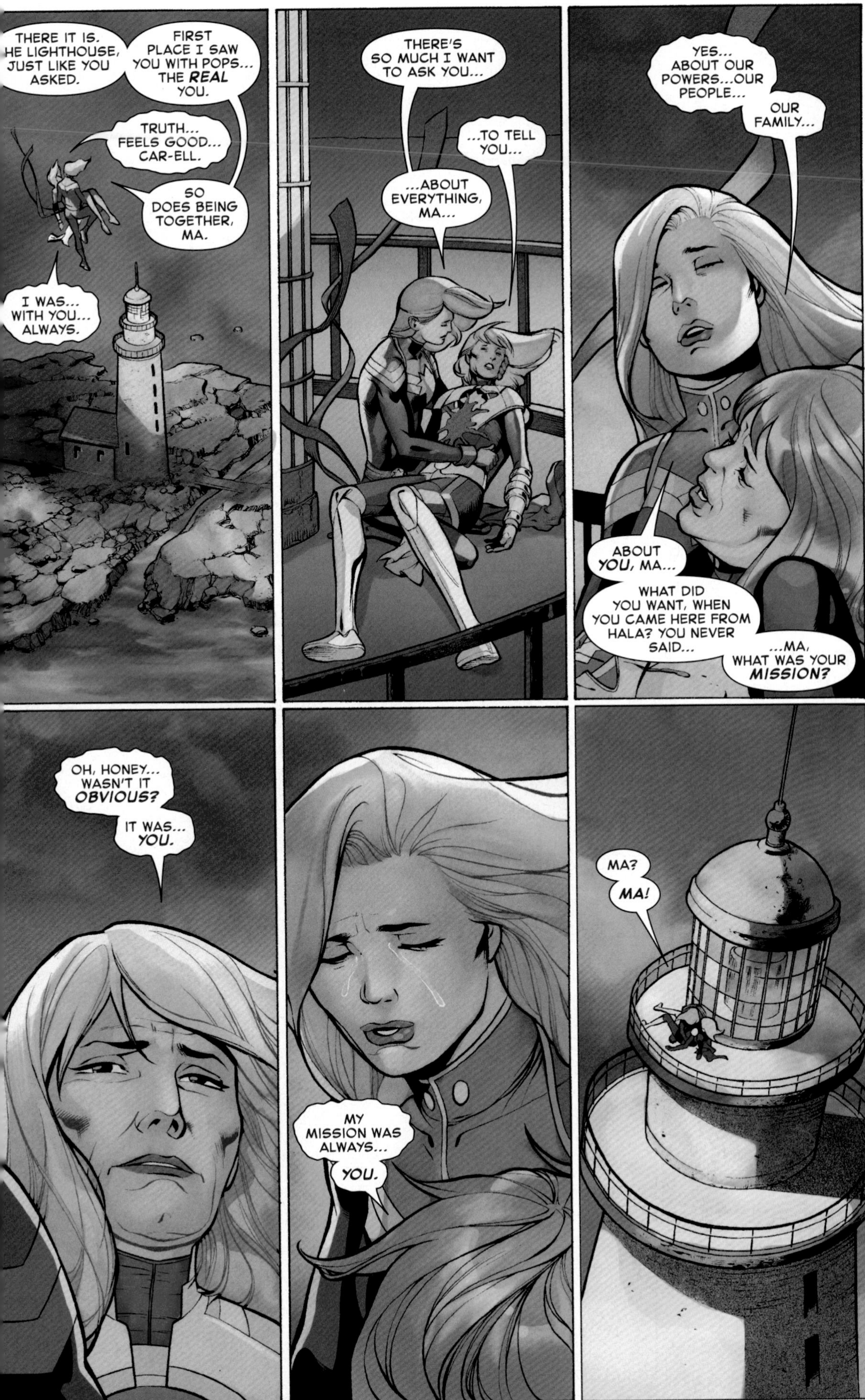

THERE IT IS. HE LIGHTHOUSE, JUST LIKE YOU ASKED.
FIRST PLACE I SAW YOU WITH POPS... THE REAL YOU.
TRUTH... FEELS GOOD... CAR-ELL.
SO DOES BEING TOGETHER, MA.
I WAS... WITH YOU... ALWAYS.
THERE'S SO MUCH I WANT TO ASK YOU...
...ABOUT EVERYTHING, MA...
...TO TELL YOU...
YES... ABOUT OUR POWERS...OUR PEOPLE...
OUR FAMILY...
ABOUT YOU, MA...
WHAT DID YOU WANT, WHEN YOU CAME HERE FROM HALA? YOU NEVER SAID...
...MA, WHAT WAS YOUR MISSION?
OH, HONEY... WASN'T IT OBVIOUS?
IT WAS... YOU.
MY MISSION WAS ALWAYS...
YOU.
MA?
MA!

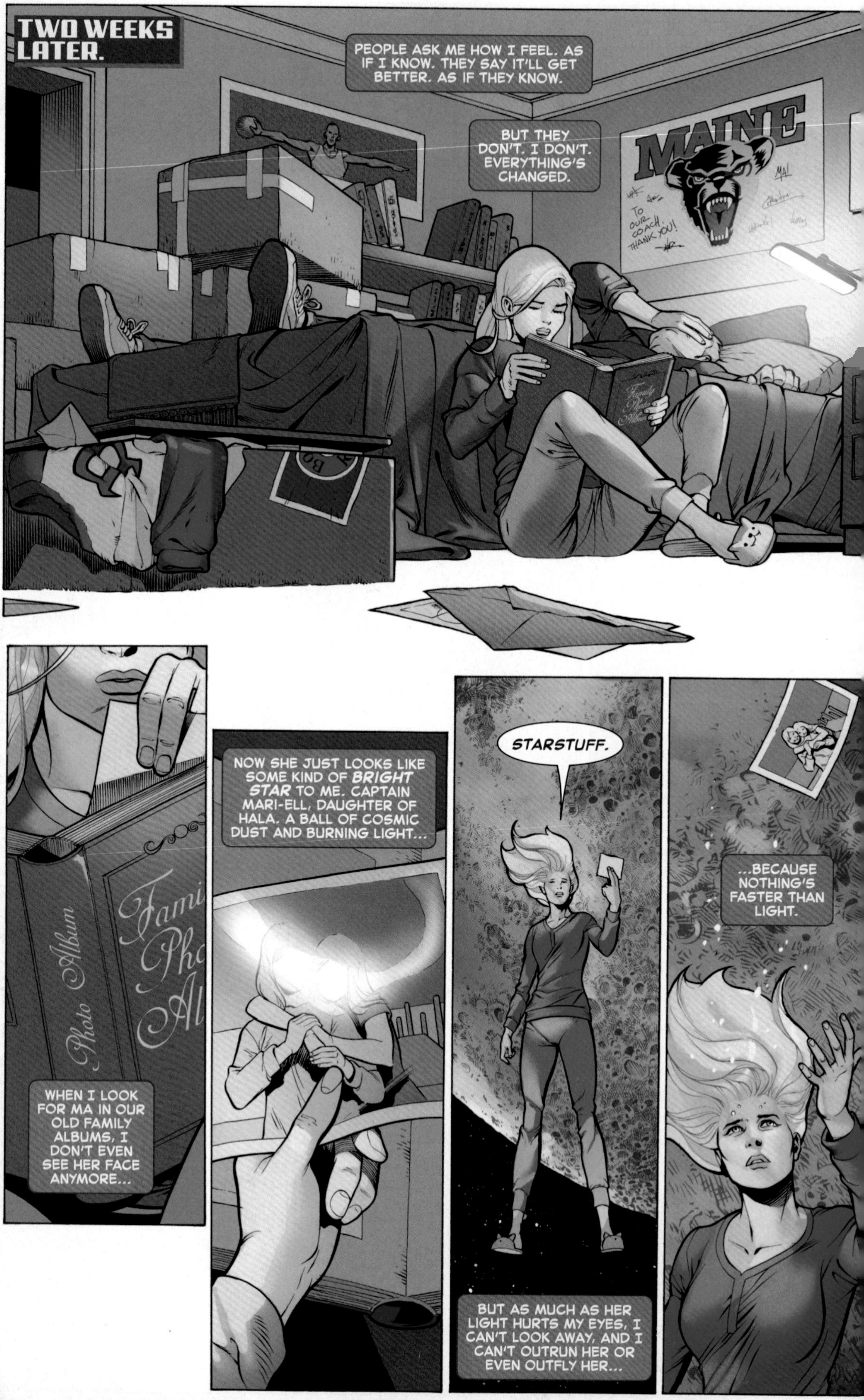
TWO WEEKS LATER.
PEOPLE ASK ME HOW I FEEL. AS IF I KNOW. THEY SAY IT'LL GET BETTER. AS IF THEY KNOW.
BUT THEY DON'T. I DON'T. EVERYTHING'S CHANGED.
MAINE
TO OUR COACH. THANK YOU!
Family Photo Album
Photo Album
WHEN I LOOK FOR MA IN OUR OLD FAMILY ALBUMS, I DON'T EVEN SEE HER FACE ANYMORE...
NOW SHE JUST LOOKS LIKE SOME KIND OF BRIGHT STAR TO ME. CAPTAIN MARI-ELL, DAUGHTER OF HALA. A BALL OF COSMIC DUST AND BURNING LIGHT...
STARSTUFF.
BUT AS MUCH AS HER LIGHT HURTS MY EYES, I CAN'T LOOK AWAY, AND I CAN'T OUTRUN HER OR EVEN OUTFLY HER...
...BECAUSE NOTHING'S FASTER THAN LIGHT.

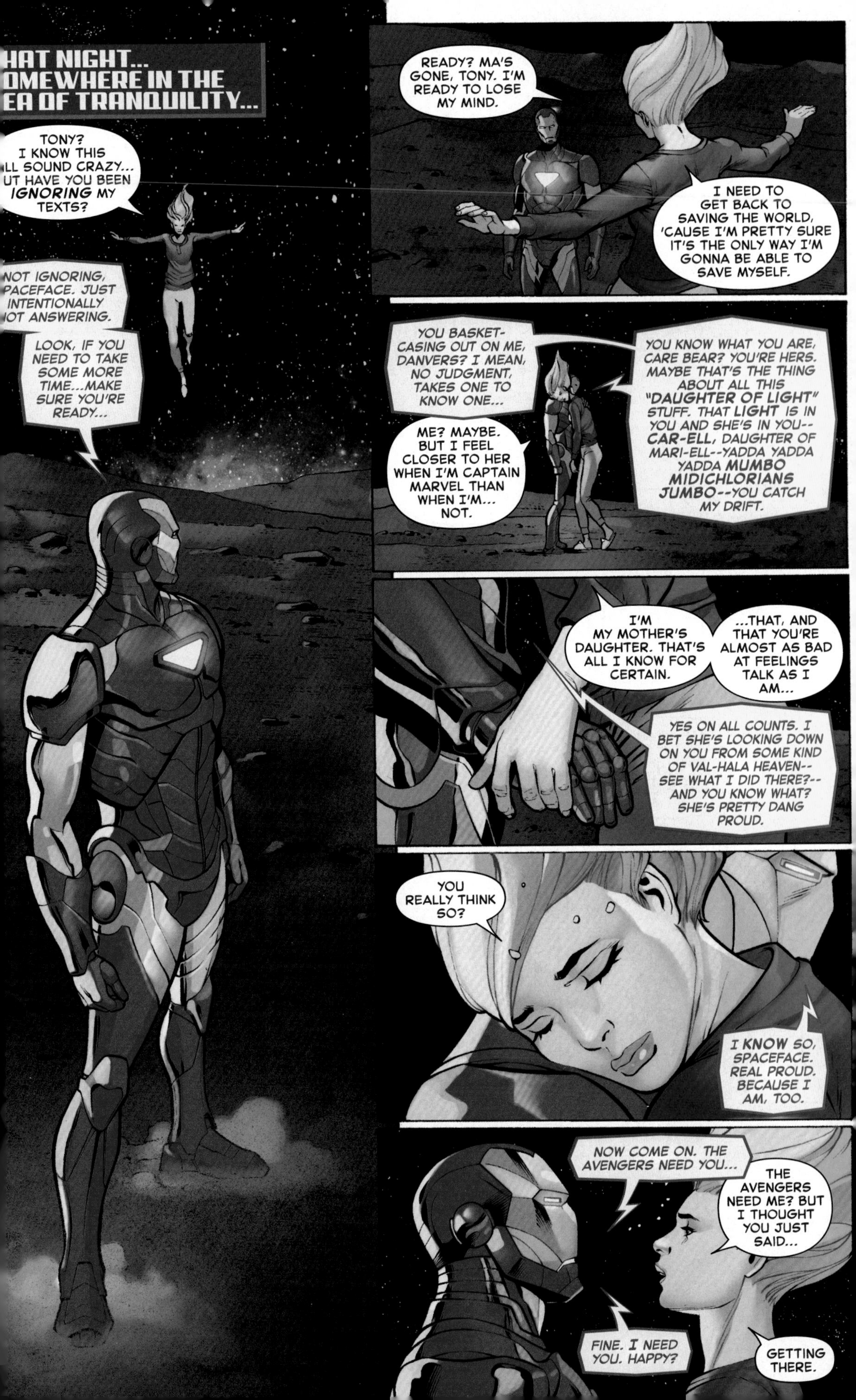
HAT NIGHT... OMEWHERE IN THE EA OF TRANQUILITY...
TONY? I KNOW THIS LL SOUND CRAZY... UT HAVE YOU BEEN IGNORING MY TEXTS?
NOT IGNORING, PACEFACE. JUST INTENTIONALLY OT ANSWERING.
LOOK, IF YOU NEED TO TAKE SOME MORE TIME...MAKE SURE YOU'RE READY...
READY? MA'S GONE, TONY. I'M READY TO LOSE MY MIND.
I NEED TO GET BACK TO SAVING THE WORLD, 'CAUSE I'M PRETTY SURE IT'S THE ONLY WAY I'M GONNA BE ABLE TO SAVE MYSELF.
YOU BASKET-CASING OUT ON ME, DANVERS? I MEAN, NO JUDGMENT, TAKES ONE TO KNOW ONE...
ME? MAYBE. BUT I FEEL CLOSER TO HER WHEN I'M CAPTAIN MARVEL THAN WHEN I'M... NOT.
YOU KNOW WHAT YOU ARE, CARE BEAR? YOU'RE HERS. MAYBE THAT'S THE THING ABOUT ALL THIS "DAUGHTER OF LIGHT" STUFF. THAT LIGHT IS IN YOU AND SHE'S IN YOU-- CAR-ELL, DAUGHTER OF MARI-ELL--YADDA YADDA YADDA MUMBO MIDICHLORIANS JUMBO--YOU CATCH MY DRIFT.
I'M MY MOTHER'S DAUGHTER. THAT'S ALL I KNOW FOR CERTAIN.
...THAT, AND THAT YOU'RE ALMOST AS BAD AT FEELINGS TALK AS I AM...
YES ON ALL COUNTS. I BET SHE'S LOOKING DOWN ON YOU FROM SOME KIND OF VAL-HALA HEAVEN-- SEE WHAT I DID THERE?-- AND YOU KNOW WHAT? SHE'S PRETTY DANG PROUD.
YOU REALLY THINK SO?
I KNOW SO, SPACEFACE. REAL PROUD. BECAUSE I AM, TOO.
NOW COME ON. THE AVENGERS NEED YOU...
THE AVENGERS NEED ME? BUT I THOUGHT YOU JUST SAID...
FINE. I NEED YOU. HAPPY?
GETTING THERE.

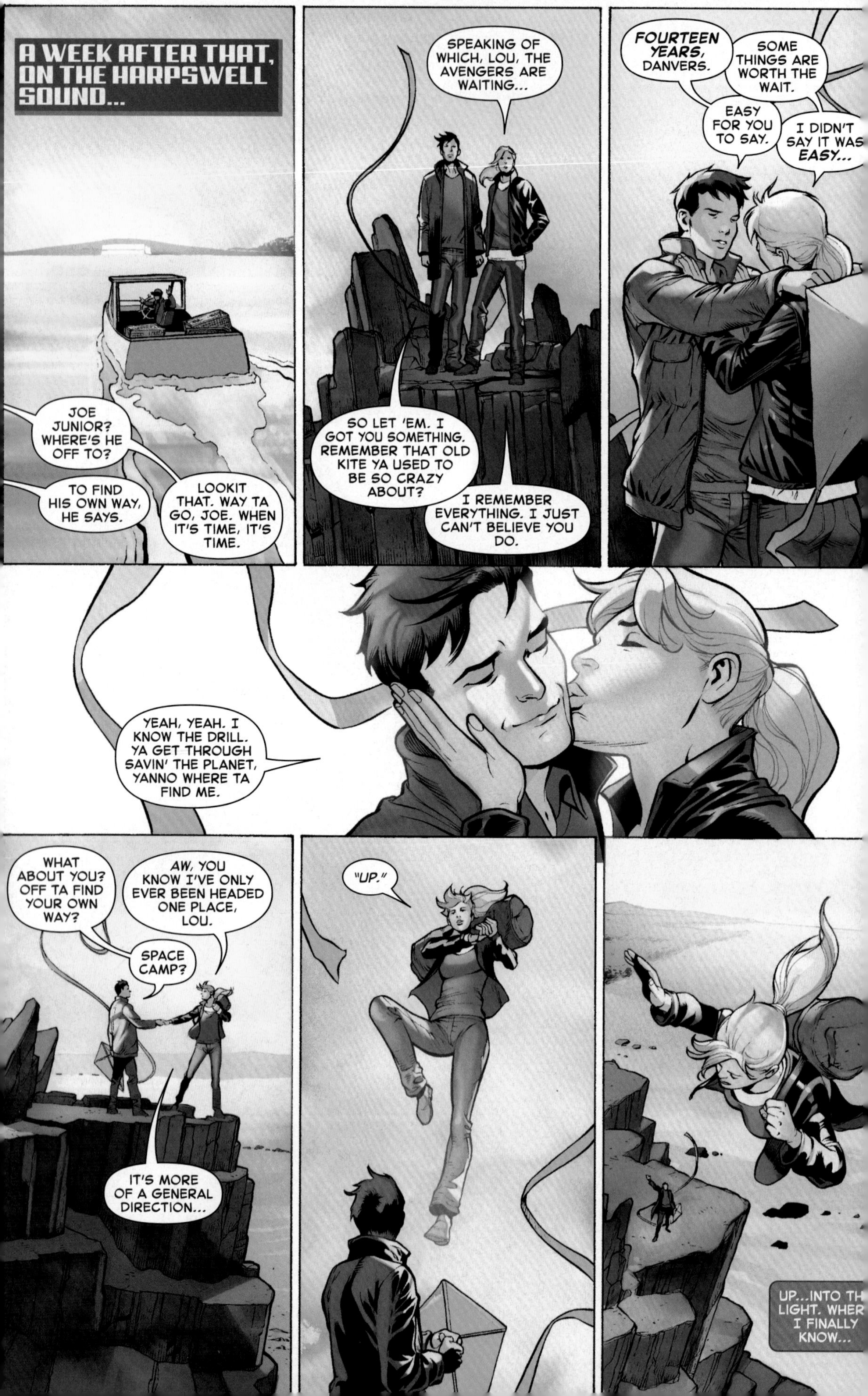
A WEEK AFTER THAT, ON THE HARPSWELL SOUND...
JOE JUNIOR? WHERE'S HE OFF TO?
TO FIND HIS OWN WAY, HE SAYS.
LOOKIT THAT. WAY TA GO, JOE. WHEN IT'S TIME, IT'S TIME.
SPEAKING OF WHICH, LOU, THE AVENGERS ARE WAITING...
SO LET 'EM. I GOT YOU SOMETHING. REMEMBER THAT OLD KITE YA USED TO BE SO CRAZY ABOUT?
I REMEMBER EVERYTHING. I JUST CAN'T BELIEVE YOU DO.
FOURTEEN YEARS, DANVERS.
SOME THINGS ARE WORTH THE WAIT.
EASY FOR YOU TO SAY.
I DIDN'T SAY IT WAS EASY...
YEAH, YEAH. I KNOW THE DRILL. YA GET THROUGH SAVIN' THE PLANET, YANNO WHERE TA FIND ME.
WHAT ABOUT YOU? OFF TA FIND YOUR OWN WAY?
AW, YOU KNOW I'VE ONLY EVER BEEN HEADED ONE PLACE, LOU.
SPACE CAMP?
IT'S MORE OF A GENERAL DIRECTION...
"UP."

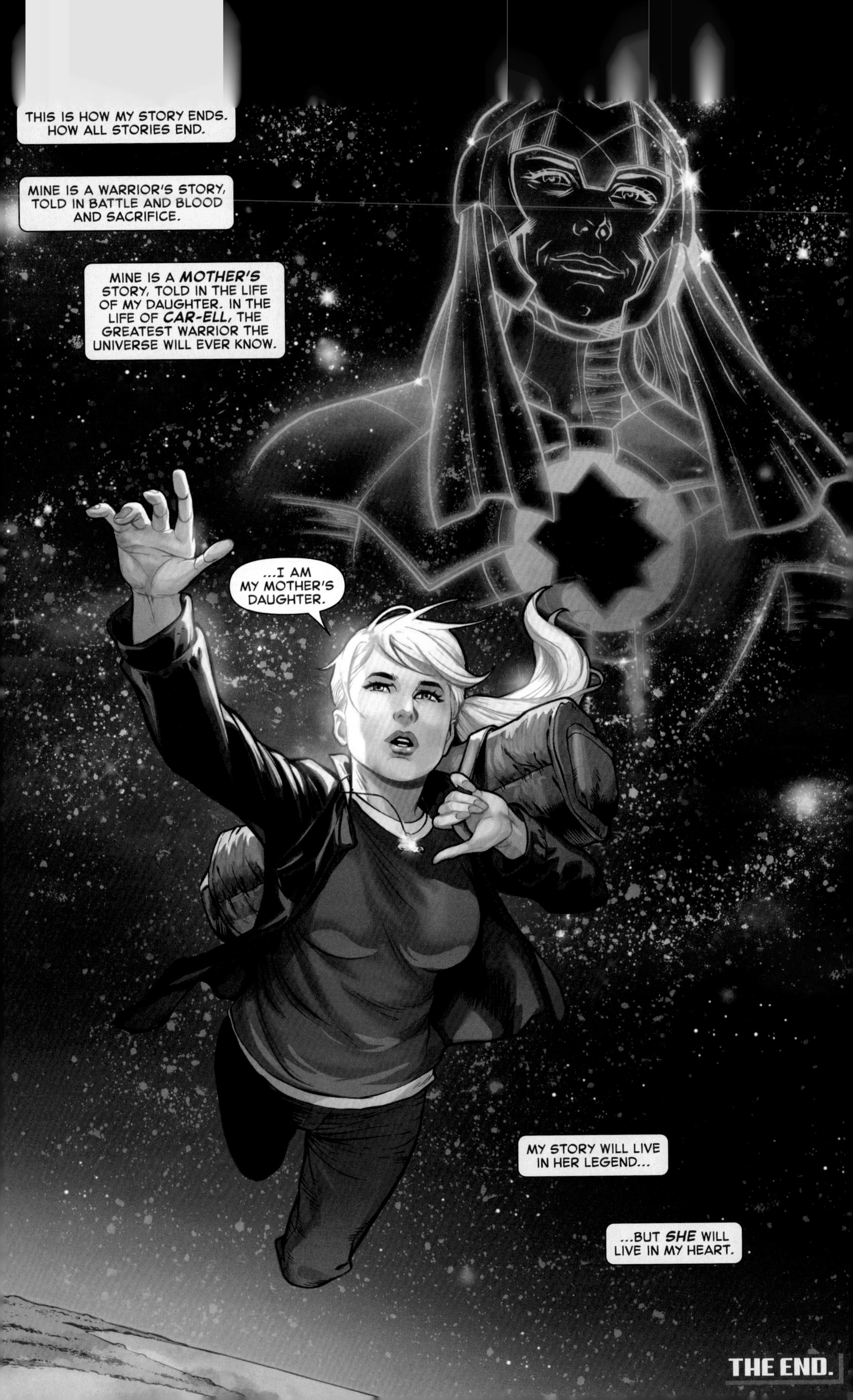
THIS IS HOW MY STORY ENDS. HOW ALL STORIES END.
MINE IS A WARRIOR'S STORY, TOLD IN BATTLE AND BLOOD AND SACRIFICE.
MINE IS A *MOTHER'S* STORY, TOLD IN THE LIFE OF MY DAUGHTER. IN THE LIFE OF *CAR-ELL*, THE GREATEST WARRIOR THE UNIVERSE WILL EVER KNOW.
...I AM MY MOTHER'S DAUGHTER.
MY STORY WILL LIVE IN HER LEGEND...
...BUT *SHE* WILL LIVE IN MY HEART.
THE END.

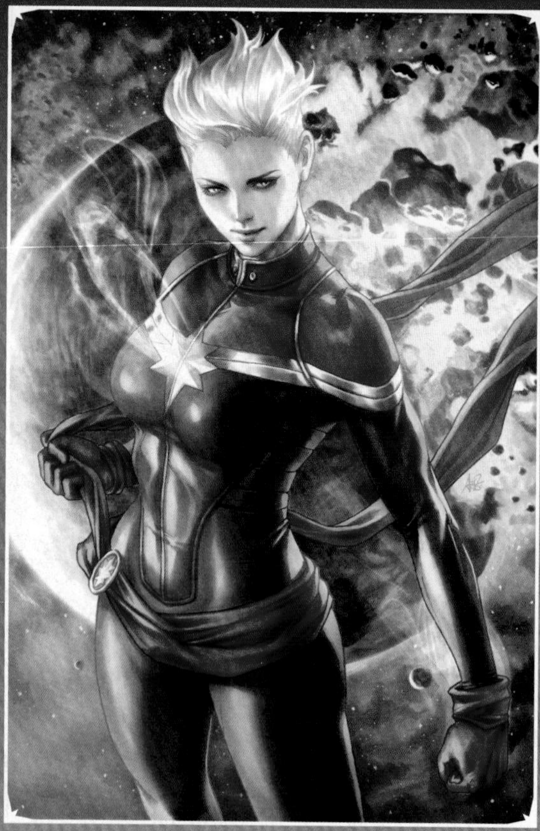

#1 VARIANT
BY **ARTGERM**

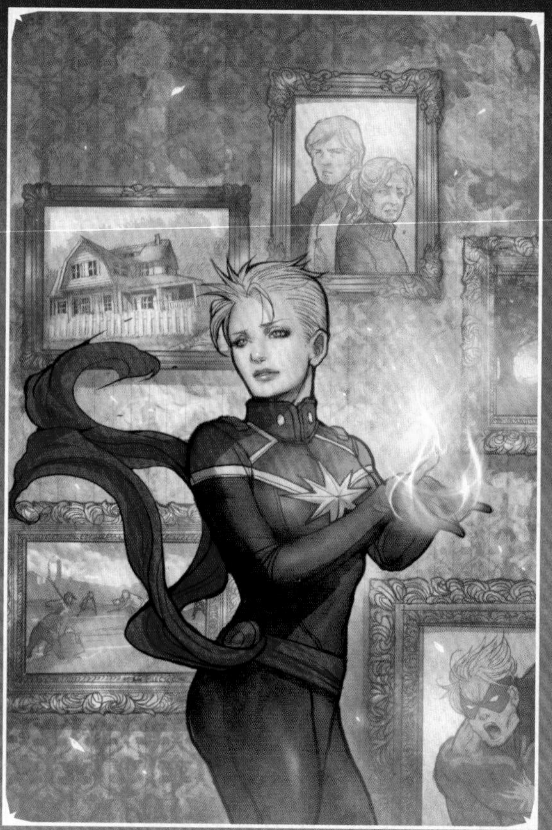

#1 VARIANT
BY **SANA TAKEDA**

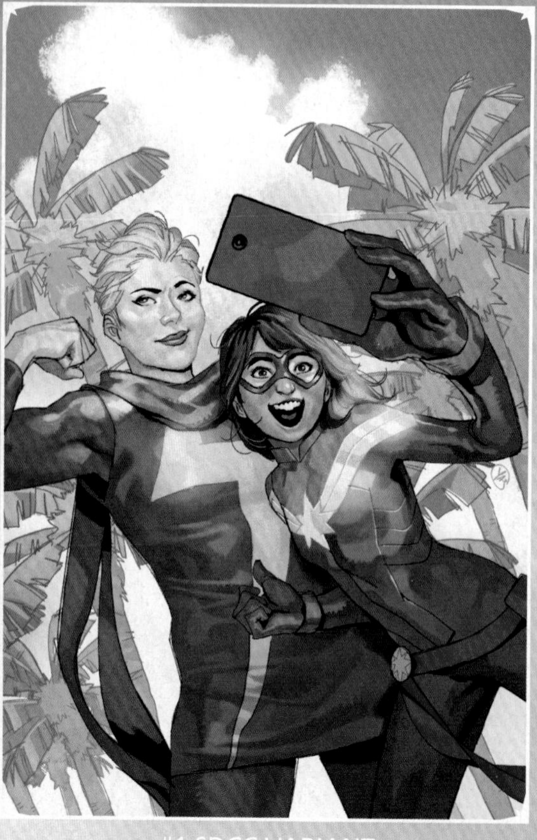

#1 SDCC VARIANT
BY **YASMINE PUTRI**

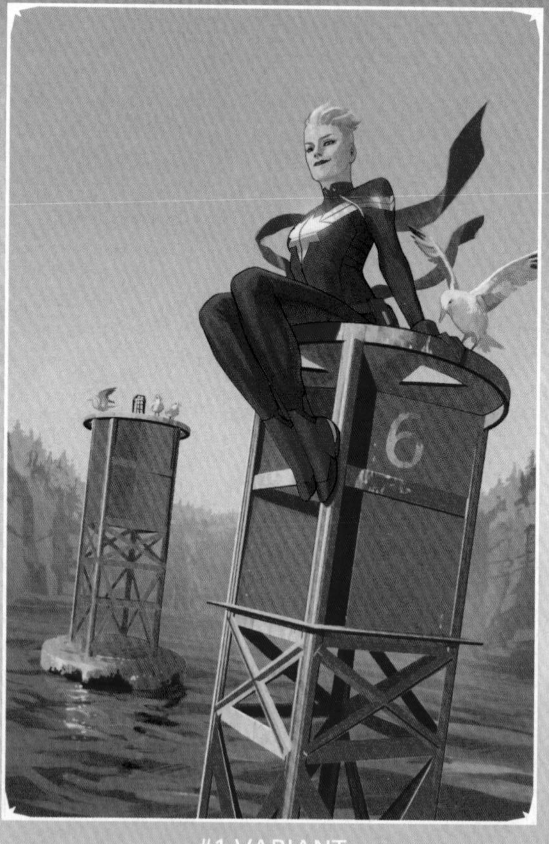
6

#1 VARIANT
BY **FIONA STAPLES**

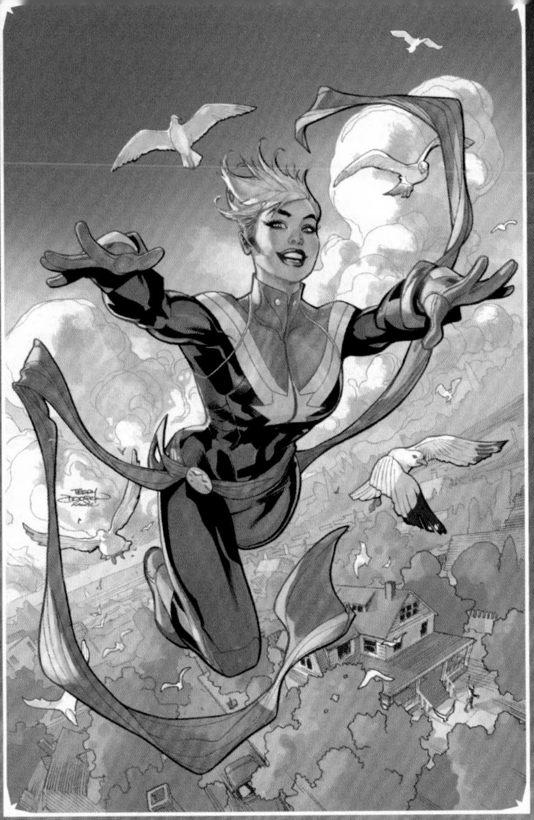

#2 VARIANT
BY **TERRY DODSON**
& **RACHEL DODSON**

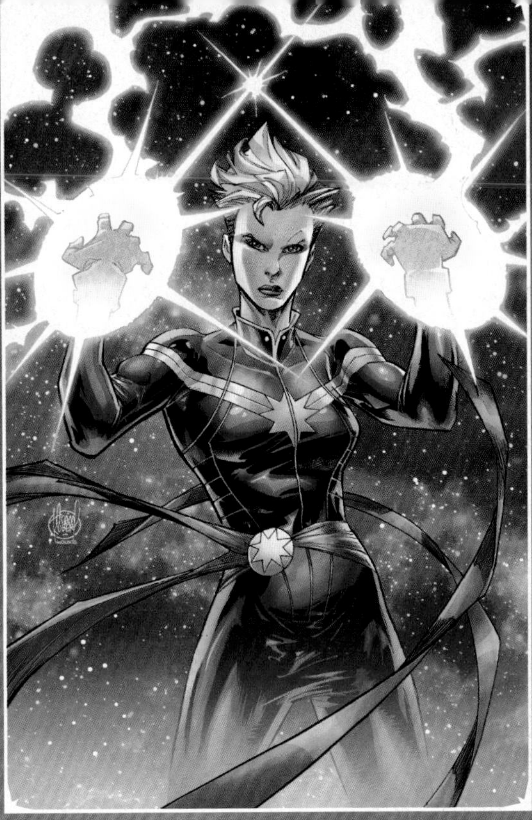

#2 VARIANT
BY **ADAM KUBERT**
& **PAUL MOUNTS**

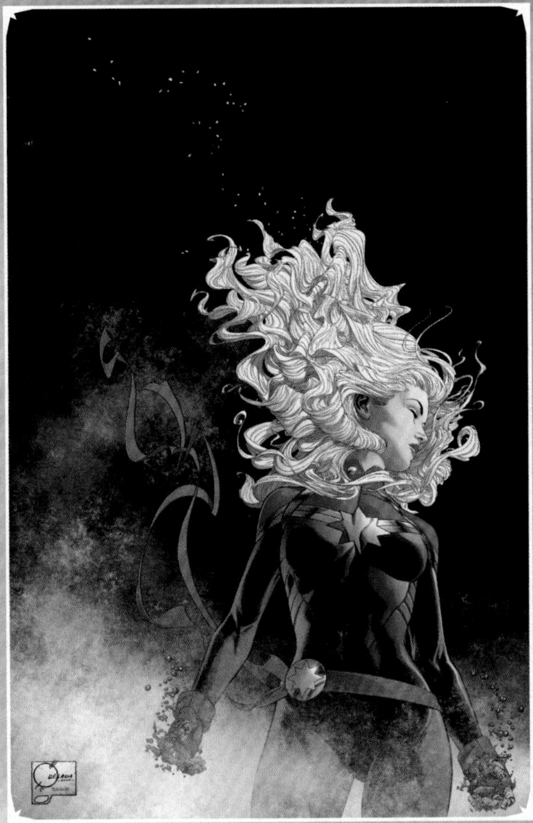

#3 VARIANT
BY **JOE QUESADA**
& **RICHARD ISANOVE**

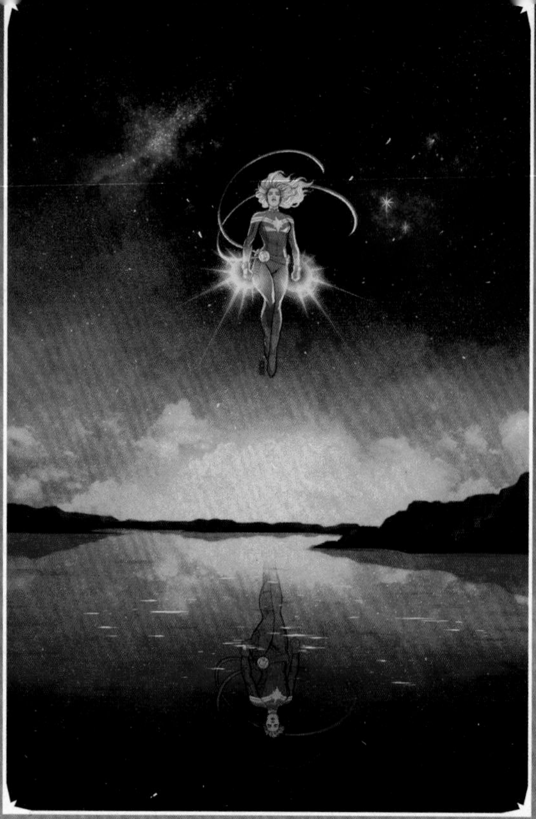

#4 VARIANT
BY **JEN BARTEL**

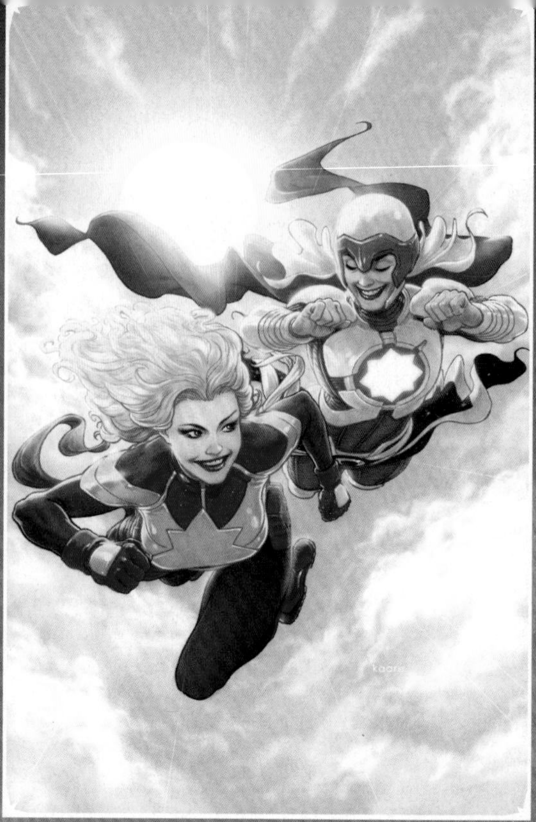

#5 VARIANT
BY **KAARE ANDREWS**

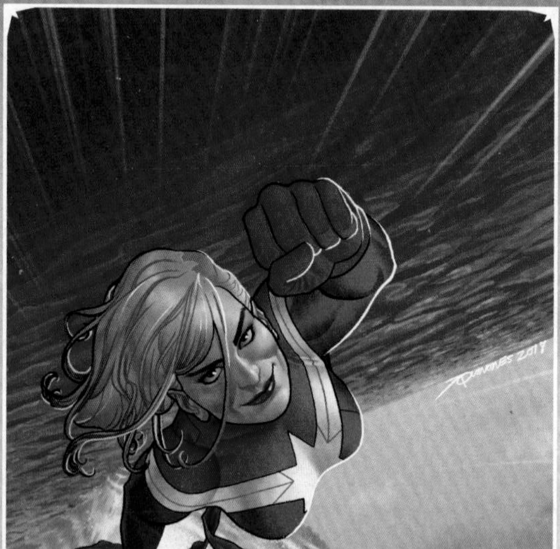

#5 VARIANT
BY **JOE QUINONES**